THE MISHNAH IN CONTEMPORARY PERSPECTIVE

HANDBOOK OF ORIENTAL STUDIES
HANDBUCH DER ORIENTALISTIK

SECTION ONE

THE NEAR AND MIDDLE EAST

EDITED BY

H. ALTENMÜLLER · B. HROUDA · B.A. LEVINE · R.S. O'FAHEY
K.R. VEENHOF · C.H.M. VERSTEEGH

VOLUME SIXTY-FIVE

THE MISHNAH
IN CONTEMPORARY PERSPECTIVE

EDITED BY

ALAN J. AVERY-PECK

AND

JACOB NEUSNER

BRILL
LEIDEN • BOSTON • KÖLN
2002

This book is printed on acid-free paper.

Library of Congress Cataloging-in-Publication Data

The Mishnah in contemporary perspective / edited by Alan J. Avery-Peck and Jacob Neusner.
      p. cm. — (Handbook of oriental studies. Section one, The Near and Middle East ; v. 65)
    Includes index.
    ISBN 9004125159 (alk. paper)
    1. Mishnah—Criticism, interpretation, etc.—History. I. Avery-Peck, Alan J. (Alan Jeffery), 1953- II. Neusner, Jacob, 1932- III. Handbuch der Orientalistik. Erste Abteilung, Nahe und der Mittlere Osten ; Bd. 65.
BM497.8 .M55   2002
296.1'2306—dc21   2002025415

Die Deutsche Bibliothek – CIP-Einheitsaufnahme

Handbuch der Orientalistik. – Leiden ; Boston ; Köln : Brill.
    Teilw. hrsg. von H. Altenmüller. – Teilw. hrsg. von B. Spuler.
    Literaturangaben
    Teilw. mit Parallelt.; Handbook of oriental studies
Abt. 1. Der Nahe und Mittlere Osten = The Near and Middle East / hrsg. von H. Altenmüller ...
    Teilw. hrsg. von B. Spuler
    Bd. 65. The Mishnah in contemporary perspective / ed. by Alan J. Avery-Peck and Jacob Neusner. 2002
    ISBN 90–04–12515 9

ISSN 0169-9423
ISBN 90 04 12515 9

© *Copyright 2002 by Koninklijke Brill NV, Leiden, The Netherlands*

All rights reserved. No part of this publication may be reproduced, translated, stored in a retrieval system, or transmitted in any form or by any means, electronic, mechanical, photocopying, recording or otherwise, without prior written permission from the publisher.

*Authorization to photocopy items for internal or personal use is granted by Brill provided that the appropriate fees are paid directly to The Copyright Clearance Center, 222 Rosewood Drive, Suite 910, Danvers MA 01923, USA.
Fees are subject to change.*

PRINTED IN THE NETHERLANDS

TABLE OF CONTENTS

Preface vii

INTRODUCTION

The Mishnah Viewed Whole
    Jacob Neusner 3

PART ONE

THE MISHNAH IN HISTORICAL AND RELIGIOUS CONTEXT

The Division of Agriculture and Second Century Judaism: The Holiness of the Devastated Land
    Alan J. Avery-Peck 41

The Mishnah in Rabbinic Context: Tosefta and Sifra
    Jacob Neusner 91

The Mishnah in Roman and Christian Contexts
    Jacob Neusner 121

Appendix: Roman Legal Codification in the Second Century
    Stephen A. Stertz 149

PART TWO

THE MISHNAH IN LITERARY AND AESTHETIC CONTEXT

The Mishnah and Ancient Book Production
    Catherine Hezser 167

The Mishnah in the Later Midrashim
    Rivka Ulmer 193

An Aesthetic Usage of Scriptures in the Ancient Rabbinic Legal Codes
    Herbert W. Basser 235

PART THREE

THE MISHNAH IN SOCIAL CONTEXT

MASTER AND PARENT: COMPARATIVE ASPECTS OF A DUAL
LOYALTY (MISHNAH BABA MEZIAH 2:11 AND MARK 3:31-35)
    GERALD J. BLIDSTEIN 255

General Index 267

PREFACE

In this and the succeeding volumes, the editors place on display a broad selection of approaches to the study of the Mishnah in the contemporary academy. The work derives in the main from North American and European centers of learning and shows the intellectual vitality of scholarship there. What we prove in diverse ways is that the Mishnah forms a critical focus of the study of Judaism.

Why from the beginning has Mishnah-study formed the center of the curriculum of Judaism? The reason is that the document has earned its place. In the entire history of civilization, only a few traditions of learning set forth in singular documents have for more than a brief time sustained the life of a society. But the Mishnah has defined the life of Israel, the Jewish people throughout the world, from the time it was promulgated, at the end of the second century, to the present day. To find parallels to the astonishing power of that book to define the meaning of the life of the society to which it speaks, we should have to point, in India, to the Vedas, in Iran and India, to the Zoroastrian Scriptures, in Islam, to the Quran, and, in the Christian West, to the Bible, that is, the Old and New Testaments as Christianity put them together. The Quran, the Vedas, the Zoroastrian Avesta, above all, the Bible—these few writings still enjoy a paramount place. But among all the many other writings that have told entire societies what it meant to live in community, we cannot count very many that still deliver the same message, with the same authority, to the same world that they originally addressed. And among the enduring, world-defining documents that humanity has known, the Mishnah is surely the one of which fewest people have heard.

The Vedas, Quran, and Bible form part of common culture. So too, everyone knows the Hebrew Scriptures, the Old Testament of Christianity. They are easy to enter. But, even if it is known as the first document of the Oral part of the Torah of Sinai, the Mishnah is hardly accessible. Falling into the hands of someone who has never seen it before, the Mishnah must cause puzzlement. It provides naked information—contents out of context. It presents disputes about facts scarcely explained, facts hardly urgent outside of a circle of faceless disputants. The opening lines (famous among the students of the document) suffice to make the point (M. Ber. 1:1):

A. From what time do they recite the Shema in the evening?
B. From the hour that the priests [who had immersed after uncleanness and awaited sunset to complete the process of purification] enter [a state of cleanness, the sun having set, so as] to eat their heave offering—
C. "until the end of the first watch," the words of R. Eliezer.
D. And sages say, "Until midnight."
E. Rabban Gamaliel says, "Until the rise of dawn."

It would require many paragraphs to explain the meaning of these seventy-five words, and it would take many more to place the whole into its theological and religious context. Here is a fine example of the Mishnah's opacity, how its radical assumption that its audience brings to the document a vast corpus of learning shapes its discourse. On its own, out of all context, that well-known passage is simply incomprehensible, taking for granted, as it does, a considerable body of information. The issues and the argument presuppose modes of thought and analysis in no way articulated; nor is what is at stake self-evident. Consequently, we start with the impression that we join a conversation already long under way about topics we can never grasp anyhow.

No one can take for granted that what is before us makes sense in any context but the Mishnah's own, inaccessible world. The Mishnah in many tractates does not discuss topics of common interest. For before us is a remarkable statement of concerns for matters not only wholly remote from our own world, but, in the main, alien to the world of the people who made the Mishnah itself. It is as if people set out to write letters about things they had never seen, to people they did not know—letters from an unknown city to an undefined and unimagined world: the Mishnah is a letter, written on blank paper, from no one special, located in utopia, to whom it may concern, at an indeterminate time and no where in particular. Perhaps its very power to speak from deep to deep is its lack of locative specificity. But internal evidence within the Mishnah certainly proves mute about all questions of authorship: where, when, why, for what purpose, to which audience? We have no answers to such basic questions as these.

Equally surprising, the Mishnah is a book without an author. No where in its pages does it identify its authorities or sponsorship. It permits only slight variations, if any, in its authorities' patterns of language and speech, so there is no place for individual characteristics of expression. It nowhere tells us when it speaks. It does not address a particular place or time and rarely speaks of events in its own day. It never identifies its prospective audience. In the entire mass of sayings and rules, there is scarcely an "I" or a "you." The Mishnah begins nowhere. It ends abruptly. There is no predicting where it will commence or explaining why it is done. Where, when, why the document is laid out and set forth are questions not deemed urgent and not answered.

While the Mishnah clearly addresses Israel, the Jewish people, it is remarkably indifferent to the Hebrew Scriptures. It makes no effort at imitating the Hebrew of the Hebrew Bible, as do the writers of the Dead Sea Scrolls. It does not attribute its sayings to biblical heroes, prophets, or holy men, as do the writings of the pseudepigraphs of the Hebrew Scriptures. It does not claim to emerge from a fresh encounter with God through revelation, as is not uncommon in Israelite writings of the preceding four hundred years; the Holy Spirit is not alleged to speak here. So all the devices by which other Israelite writers gain credence for their messages are ignored. Perhaps the authority of the Mishnah was self-evident to its authors. But, self-evident or not, they in no way take the trouble to explain to their audience why people should conform to the descriptive statements contained in their holy book.

If we turn to the contents of the document, we are helped not at all in determining the place of the Mishnah's origination, the purpose of its formation, the reasons for its anonymous and collective plane of discourse and monotonous tone of voice. For the Mishnah covers a carefully defined program of topics. But it never tells us why one topic is introduced and another is omitted or what the agglutination of these particular topics is meant to accomplish in the formation of a system or imaginative construction. Discourse on a theme begins and ends as if all things are self-evident—including, as we said, the reason for beginning at one point and ending at some other.

One might imagine upon first glance that the Mishnah is a simple rulebook. It appears on the surface to lack all traces of eloquence and style, revealing no evidence of system and reflection. First glance indicates that in hand is yet another shard from remote antiquity—no different from king-lists inscribed on ancient shards, the random catalogue of (to us) useless, meaningless facts: a cook-book, a placard of posted tariffs, detritus of random information, accidentally thrown up on the currents of historical time. Who would want to have made such a thing? Who would now want to refer to it?

The answer to that question is deceptively straight-forward. The Mishnah is important because it is a principal component of the canon of Judaism. Yet that answer begs the question: Why should some of the ancient Jews of the Holy Land have brought together these particular facts and rules into a book and set them forth for the Israelite people? Why should the Mishnah have been received, as much later on it certainly was received, as a half of the "whole Torah of Moses at Sinai" if it is already entirely obvious that little in the actual contents of the document evoked the character or the moral authority of the written Torah of Moses? This being the case, how can the Mishnah be deemed a book of religion, a program for consecration, a mode of sanctification? Why should Jews from the end of the second century to our own day have deemed the study of the Mishnah to be a holy act, a deed of service to God through the study of an important constituent of God's Torah, God's will for Israel, the Jewish people?

In fact, the Mishnah is precisely that, a principal holy book of Judaism. The Mishnah has been and now is memorized in the circle of all those who participate in the religion, Judaism. Of still greater weight, the three great documents formed around the Mishnah and so shaped as to serve, in part, as commentaries to the Mishnah, namely, the Tosefta (ca. 300 C.E.), the Talmud of the Land of Israel (ca. 400 C.E.) and, particularly, the Talmud of Babylonia (ca. 600 C.E.), mark the center of the curriculum of Judaism as a living religion. And all of this is present tense: the Mishnah, together with the Talmud and related writings, is studied and guides the life of Jews throughout the world.

When was the Mishnah made up, and who did the work? The world addressed by the Mishnah is hardly congruent to the worldview presented within the Mishnah. Let us now consider the time and context in which the document took shape. The Mishnah is made up of sayings bearing the names of authorities who lived, as we just said, in the later first and second centuries. (The book contains very little in the names of people who lived before the destruction of the Temple of Jerusalem in 70.) These authorities generally fall into two groups, namely, two distinct sets of names, each set of names randomly appearing together, but rarely, if ever, with names of the other set. The former set of names is generally supposed to represent authorities who lived between the destruction of the Temple in 70 and the advent of the second war against Rome, led by Simeon Bar Kokhba, in 132. The latter set of names belongs to authorities who flourished between the end of that war, ca. 135, and the end of the second century.

The Mishnah itself is generally supposed to have come to closure at the end of the second century, and its date, for conventional purposes only, is ca. 200. Now, of these two groups—sages from 70-130, and from 135-200—the latter is represented far more abundantly than the former. Approximately two thirds of the named sayings belong to mid-second century authorities. This is not surprising, since these are the named authorities whose (mainly unnamed) students collected, organized, and laid out the document as we now have it. So, in all, the Mishnah represents the thinking of Jewish sages who flourished in the middle of the second century. It is that group which took over whatever they had in hand from the preceding century—and from the whole legacy of Israelite literature even before that time—and revised and reshaped the whole into the Mishnah. Let us briefly consider their world, because the urgent question presented by that world precipitated the answer that, from then to now, Jews have found compelling as the reference-point of their lives as a holy people.

In the aftermath of the war against Rome in 132-135, the Temple was declared permanently prohibited to Jews, and Jerusalem was closed off to them as well. So there was no cult, no Temple, no holy city, to which, at this time, the description of the Mishnaic laws applied. We observe at the very outset, therefore, that a sizable proportion of the Mishnah deals with matters to which the sages had no material access or practical knowledge at the time of their work. For the Mishnah contains a division on the conduct of the cult, namely, the fifth, as well as one on the conduct of matters so as to preserve the cultic purity of the sacrificial system along the lines laid out in the book of Leviticus, the sixth division. In fact, a fair part of the second division, on appointed times, takes up the conduct of the cult on special days, e.g., the sacrifices offered on the Day of Atonement, Passover, and the like. Indeed, what the Mishnah wants to know about appointed seasons concerns the cult far more than it does the synagogue. The fourth division, on civil law, for its part, presents an elaborate account of a political structure and system of Israelite self-government, in tractates Sanhedrin and Makkot, not to mention Shebuot and Horayot. This system speaks of king, priest, Temple, and court. But it was not the Jews, their kings, priests, and judges, but the Romans, who conducted the government of Israel in the land of Israel in the time in which the second century authorities did their work.

So it would appear that well over half of the document before us speaks of cult, Temple, government, priesthood. The Mishnah takes up a profoundly priestly and Levitical conception of sanctification. When we consider that, in the very time in which the authorities before us did their work, the Temple lay in ruins, the city of Jerusalem was prohibited to all Israelites, and the Jewish government and administration that had centered on the Temple and based its authority on the holy life lived there were in ruins, the fantastic character of the Mishnah's address to its own catastrophic day becomes clear. Much of the Mishnah speaks of matters not in being in the time in which the Mishnah was created, because the Mishnah wishes to make its statement on what really matters.

If we now ask ourselves why people of general culture in our own age should take an interest in that long-ago time, the answer is not difficult to find. And it is not a claim for mere antiquarianism. The sages of the Mishnah addressed Israel at the very end of its thousand-year life of sanctification through God's service in the Temple, of anointed kings and holy priests organizing (at least in theory) time and space in accord with the model of the sacred Temple and along lines of structure emanating therefrom. The Mishnah is the work of men who survived the second war against Rome. When we realize that that war was fought roughly three generations after the destruction of the Temple, we notice yet another point of importance. When the Temple had been destroyed earlier, in 586 B.C., the prophetic promises of divine forgiveness had been kept. So the Temple was restored: Israel regained its homeland. Now, half a millennium later, the Temple had lain in ruins for another three generations. A great and noble war had been fought to regain Jerusalem, rebuild the Temple, and restore the cult. But what had happened was incomprehensible. The pattern established in the first destruction and restoration now proved no longer to hold. Indeed, nothing stood firm. This time around, not only was the Temple not rebuilt, the cult not restored. Jerusalem itself was declared off-limits to Israelites. The very center was made inaccessible.

In this context, it is not difficult to look for points of commonalty between one age of uncertainty and another, also cut loose from ancient moorings. What the second-century sages of the Mishnah have to teach the generations of the last decades of the twentieth century and the first of the twenty-first, is how to make use of imagination and fantasy to confront, defy, and overcome chaos and disorder. Behind the Mishnah lay the ruins of half a millennium of continuous, orderly, and systematic Israelite life, which had been centered on the regular and reliable offering of the produce of the field and flock upon the altar of the Temple in Jerusalem, the ordering of society around that Temple, the rhythmic division of time in response to that cult, and the placing of people and things into their proper station in relationship to that center. One disastrous war had ended in the destruction of the Temple. The second, three generations later, had made certain it would not be rebuilt in the foreseeable future—nor, as it now appears, ever. In the aftermath of these two terrible wars the Israelite nation entered upon an existence far more precarious in mind than in material reality. Within a century the social and agricultural effects of the wars had worn off. Galilean synagogues of the third and fourth century testify to an age of material surplus and good comfort. But it would be a very long time before the psychological effects of dislocation and disorientation would pass. In some ways, for the Jewish people, they never have. Our age, which looks back upon the destruction of enduring political and social arrangements in the aftermath of two terrible wars (with numerous skirmishes in-between and since), has the power to confront the second century's world of ancient Judaism, because, it seems, there is a measure of existential congruence between the two ages and their common problems. For both are the kind that challenge the imagination and the will.

So the Mishnah is a book deliberately formed for the very group, Israel, and purpose that, for nearly two millennia, it indeed has served. What can we say about the Judaism that the Mishnah founded, that is to say, about the meaning and purpose of the whole. The "Judaism" expressed by the Mishnah is concrete and not abstract; we are the ones who have to translate its details into a message we can make our own, and that enormous task for the mature student accounts for the power of the Mishnah to speak to age succeeding age.

The Mishnah's mode of speech—the way it speaks, not only what it says—is testimony to its highest and most enduring, distinctive value. Now let us take note. This language does not speak of sacred symbols but of pots and pans, of menstruation and dead creeping things, of ordinary water that, because of the circumstance of its collection and location, possesses extraordinary power; of the commonplace corpse and ubiquitous diseased person; of genitalia and excrement, toilet seats and the flux of penises, of stems of pomegranates and stalks of leeks; of rain and earth and wood, metal, glass, and hide. This language is filled with words for neutral things of humble existence. It does not speak of holy things and is not symbolic in its substance. This language speaks of ordinary things, of things that everyone must have known. But because of the peculiar and particular way in which it is formed and formalized, this same language not only adheres to an aesthetic theory but expresses a deeply-embedded ontology and methodology of the sacred, specifically of the sacred within the secular, and of the capacity for regulation, therefore for sanctification, within the ordinary: All things in order, all things then hallowed by God who orders all things, so said the priests' creation-tale. The Mishnah is the other side of creation: a picture of that well-ordered, stable world that God called good, blessed, and sanctified. And, in its odd and strange portrait of a utopian, never-never-land, the Mishnah told Israel, the Jewish people, about that basic structure of life in society that, wherever they made their home, the holy people of God would comprise. And that accounts for the amazing power of the Mishnah to speak from age to age, and even to our own.

In the context of the study of the formation of Judaism, none need apologize for devoting sustained and systematic study to the Mishnah, which, along with Scripture, is the foundation-document of Rabbinic Judaism. The authors of the studies on the Mishnah collected in the present volumes represent the best of contemporary scholarship on that document. The editors invited a wide range of schools and viewpoints to participate, and we are proud of the quality and representative character of the studies at hand. We do not believe a more representative selection of contemporary Mishnah-study is available in any other collection.

To place the present studies in context, we call attention to a comparable exercise in defining the state of the question of the Mishnah, brought to press thirty years ago. That was one of two companion-works, produced to afford perspective on the condition of scholarship devoted to the Mishnah and the Talmuds. This the senior editor did to inform himself, as his own enterprise was getting under way, of the state of critical questions pertaining to the Rabbinic corpus of late antiquity. These titles, now reprinted, which he edited in 1970 and 1973 in the context of his doctoral seminar at Brown University (1968-1989), are as follows:

- *The Formation of the Babylonian Talmud. Studies on the Achievements of Late Nineteenth and Twentieth Century Historical and Literary-Critical Research.* Leiden, 1970: Brill. Reprint: Binghamton, 2002: Global Publications Classics in Judaic Studies Series.
- *The Modern Study of the Mishnah.* Leiden, 1973: Brill. Reprint: Binghamton, 2002: Global Publications Classics in Judaic Studies Series.

In addition, ten years later he returned to the state of scholarship in the following work, which remains in print today:

- *The Study of Ancient Judaism.* N.Y., 1981: Ktav. Second printing: Atlanta, 1992: Scholars Press for South Florida Studies in the History of Judaism. Now: Lanham, 2001: University Press of America.
  I. *The Study of Ancient Judaism: Mishnah, Midrash, Siddur.*
  II. *The Study of Ancient Judaism: The Palestinian and Babylonian Talmuds.*

Those state-of-the-question-volumes helped delineate where scholarship then situated itself, identifying the problems that people found urgent and the methods used in solving those problems. Since that time much has changed. Many, both older and younger, both Americans, Europeans, and Israelis, both Jews and gentiles, including all those who have contributed to these pages, have brought about or participated in the contemporary revolution in the description, analysis, and interpretation of the Mishnah. In the contrast between the results portrayed thirty years ago and those set forth in these pages, we see what has happened in the present generation of learning. Nearly all the active, publishing scholars of the academy (as distinct from the yeshiva) who are now at work are represented here.

Jacob Neusner
Research Professor of Religion and Theology
Bard College

Alan J. Avery-Peck
Kraft-Hiatt Professor of Judaic Studies
College of the Holy Cross

INTRODUCTION

THE MISHNAH VIEWED WHOLE

JACOB NEUSNER

Bard College

Falling into the hands of someone who has never seen this document before, the Mishnah must cause puzzlement. From the first line to the last, discourse takes up questions internal to a system that is never introduced. The Mishnah provides information without establishing context. It presents disputes about facts hardly urgent outside of a circle of faceless disputants. Consequently, we start with the impression that we join a conversation already long under way about topics we can never grasp anyhow. Even though the language is our own, the substance is not. We feel as if we are in a transit lounge at a distant airport. We understand the words people say but are baffled by their meanings and concerns, above all, by the urgency in their voices: What are you telling me? Why must I know it? Who cares if I do not?

No one can take for granted that what is before us makes sense in any context but the Mishnah's own, inaccessible world. Each step in the inquiry into the meaning and importance of the document must be laid forth with ample preparation, taken with adequate care. For before us is a remarkable statement of concerns for matters not only wholly remote from our own world, but, in the main, alien to the world of the people who made the Mishnah itself. It is as if people set down to write letters about things they had never seen, to people they did not know—letters from an unknown city to an undefined and unimagined world: the Mishnah is from no one special in utopia, to whom it may concern.

To state matters more directly: the Mishnah does not identify its authors. It permits only slight variations, if any, in its authorities' patterns of language and speech, so there is no place for individual characteristics of expression. It nowhere tells us when it speaks. It does not address a particular place or time and rarely speaks of events in its own day. It never identifies its prospective audience. There is scarcely a "you" in the entire mass of sayings and rules. The Mishnah begins nowhere. It ends abruptly. There is no predicting where it will commence or explaining why it is done. Where, when, why the document is laid out and set forth are questions not deemed urgent and not answered.

Indeed, the Mishnah contains not a hint about what its authors conceive their work to be. Is it a law-code? Is it a school-book? Since it makes statements describing what people should and should not do, or rather, do and do not do, we might suppose it is a law-code. Since, as we shall see in a moment, it covers topics of both practical and theoretical interest, we might suppose it is a school-book. But the Mishnah never expresses a hint about its authors' intent. The reason is that the authors do what they must to efface all traces not only of individuality but even of their own participation in the formation of the document. So it is not only a letter from utopia to whom it may concern. It also is a letter written by no one person—but not by a committee, either. Nor should we fail to notice, even at the outset, that while the Mishnah clearly addresses Israel, the Jewish people, it is remarkably indifferent to the Hebrew Scriptures. The Mishnah makes no effort at imitating the Hebrew of the Hebrew Bible, as do the writers of the Dead Sea Scrolls. The Mishnah does not attribute its sayings to biblical heroes, prophets or holy men, as do the writings of the pseudepigraphs of the Hebrew Scriptures. The Mishnah does not claim to emerge from a fresh encounter with God through revelation, as is not uncommon in Israelite writings of the preceding four hundred years; the Holy Spirit is not alleged to speak here. So all the devices by which other Israelite writers gain credence for their messages are ignored. Perhaps the authority of the Mishnah was self-evident to its authors. But, self-evident or not, they in no way take the trouble to explain to their document's audience why people should conform to the descriptive statements contained in their holy book.

If we turn to the contents of the document, we are helped not at all in determining the place of the Mishnah's origination, the purpose of its formation, the reasons for its anonymous and collective plane of discourse and monotonous tone of voice. For the Mishnah covers a carefully defined program of topics, as I shall explain presently. But the Mishnah never tells us why one topic is introduced and another is omitted, or what the agglutination of these particular topics is meant to accomplish in the formation of a system or imaginative construction. Nor is there any predicting how a given topic will be treated, why a given set of issues will be explored in close detail, and another set of possible issues ignored. Discourse on a theme begins and ends as if all things are self-evident—including, as I said, the reason for beginning at one point and ending at some other.

In all one might readily imagine, upon first glance at this strange and curious book, that what we have is a rulebook. It appears on the surface to be a book lacking all traces of eloquence and style, revealing no evidence of system and reflection, serving no important purpose. First glance indicates in hand is yet another sherd from remote antiquity—no different from the king-lists inscribed on the ancient sherds, the random catalogue of (to us) useless, meaningless facts: a cook-book, a placard of posted tariffs, detritus of random information, accidentally thrown up on the currents of historical time. Who would want to have made such a thing? Who would now want to refer to it?

The answer to that question is deceptively straight-forward: the Mishnah is important because it is a principal component of the canon of Judaism. Indeed, that answer begs the question: Why should some of the ancient Jews of the Holy Land have brought together these particular facts and rules into a book and set them forth for the Israelite people? Why should the Mishnah have been received, as much later on it certainly was received, as a half of the "whole Torah of Moses at Sinai"? The Mishnah was represented, after it was compiled, as the part of the "whole Torah of Moses, our rabbi," which had been formulated and transmitted orally, so it bore the status of divine revelation right alongside the Pentateuch. Yet it is already entirely obvious that little in the actual contents of the document evoked the character or the moral authority of the written Torah of Moses. Indeed, since most of the authorities named in the Mishnah lived in the century and a half prior to the promulgation of the document, the claim that things said by men known to the very framers of the document in fact derived from Moses at Sinai through a long chain of oral tradition contradicted the well-known facts of the matter. So this claim presents a paradox even on the surface: How can the Mishnah be deemed a book of religion, a program for consecration, a mode of sanctification? Why should Jews from the end of the second century to our own day have deemed the study of the Mishnah to be a holy act, a deed of service to God through the study of an important constituent of God's Torah, God's will for Israel, the Jewish people?

In fact, the Mishnah is precisely that, a principal holy book of

Judaism. The Mishnah has been and now is memorized in the circle of all those who participate in the religion, Judaism. Of still greater weight, the two great documents formed around the Mishnah and so shaped as to serve, in part, as commentaries to the Mishnah, namely, the Babylonian Talmud and the Palestinian Talmud, form the center of the curriculum of Judaism as a living religion. Consequently, the Mishnah is necessary to the understanding of Judaism. It hardly needs saying that people interested in the study of religions surely will have to reflect upon the same questions I have formulated within the context of Judaism, namely, how such a curious compilation of materials may be deemed a holy book. And, self-evidently, scholars of the formative centuries of Christianity, down to the recognition of Christianity as a legal religion in the fourth century, will be glad to have access to a central document of the kind of Judaism taking shape at precisely the same time as the Christianity studied by them was coming into being. In all, we need not apologize for our interest in this sizable monument to the search for a holy way of life for Israel represented, full and whole, in this massive thing, the Mishnah.

THE MISHNAH IN CONTEXT: ISRAELITE HISTORY IN THE LATER FIRST AND SECOND CENTURIES

The world addressed by the Mishnah is hardly congruent to the world-view presented within the Mishnah. Let us consider the time and context in which the document took shape. The Mishnah is made up of sayings bearing the names of authorities who lived in the later first and second centuries. (The book contains very little in the names of people who lived before the destruction of the Temple of Jersalem in A.D. 70.) These authorities generally fall into two groups, those authorities who lived between the destruction of the Temple in 70 and the advent of the second war against Rome, led by Simeon Bar Kokhba, in 132, and the authorities who flourished between the end of that war, ca. 135, and the end of the second century. The Mishnah itself is generally supposed to have come to closure at the end of the second century, and its date, for conventional purposes only, is ca. 200 C.E. Now, of the two groups—sages from 70-130, and from 135-200—the latter is represented far more abundantly than the former. Approximately two thirds of the named sayings belong to mid-second century authorities. This is not surprising, since these are the named authorities whose (mainly unnamed) students collected, organized, and laid out the document as we now have it. So, in all, the Mishnah represents the thinking of Jewish sages who flourished in the middle of the second century. It is that group which took over whatever they had in hand from the preceding century—and from the whole legacy of Israelite literature even before that time—and revised and reshaped the whole into the Mishnah. Let us briefly consider their world.

In the aftermath of the war against Rome in 132-135, the Temple was declared permanently prohibited to Jews, and Jerusalem was closed off to them as well. So there was no cult, no Temple, no holy city, meaning that a sizable proportion of the Mishnah deals with matters to which the sages had no material access or practical knowledge at the time of their work. For beyond the fifth division, on the conduct of the cult, and the sixth, on the preservation of the cultic purity of the sacrificial system, a fair part of the second division, on appointed times, takes up the conduct of the cult on special days, e.g., the sacrifices offered on the Day of Atonement, Passover, and the like. Indeed, what the Mishnah wants to know about appointed seasons concerns the cult far more than it does the synagogue. The fourth division, on civil law, for its part, presents an elaborate account of a political structure and system of Israelite self-government, in tractates Sanhedrin and Makkot, not to mention Shebuot and Horayot. This system speaks of king, priest, Temple, and court. But it was not the Jews, their kings, priests, and judges, but the Romans, who conducted the government of Israel in the land of Israel in the time in which the second century authorities did their work. So it would appear that well over half of the document before us speaks of cult, Temple, government, priesthood. As we shall see, moreover, the Mishnah takes up a profoundly priestly and Levitical conception of sanctification. When we consider that, in the very time in which the authorities before us did their work, the Temple lay in ruins, the city of Jersalem was prohibited to all Israelites, and the Jewish government and administration that had centered on the Temple and based its authority on the holy life lived there were in ruins, the fantastic character of the Mishnah's address to its own catastrophic day becomes clear. Much of the Mishnah speaks of matters not in being in the time in which the Mishnah was created, because the Mishnah wishes to make its statement on what really matters.

In the age beyond catastrophe, the problem is to reorder a world off course and adrift, to gain reorientation for an age in which the sun has come out after the night and the fog. The Mishnah is a document of imagination and fantasy, describing how things "are" out of the sherds and remnants of reality, but, in larger measure, building social being out of beams of hope. The Mishnah tells us something about how things were, but everything about how a small group of men wanted things to be. The document is orderly, repetitious, careful in both language and message. It is small-minded, picayune, obvious, dull, routine—everything its age was not. The Mishnah stands in contrast with the world to which it speaks. Its message is one of small achievements and modest hope. It means to defy a world of large disorders and immodest demands. The heirs of heroes build an unheroic folk in the new and ordinary age. The Mishnah's message is that what a person wants matters in important ways. It states that message to an Israelite world that can shape affairs in no important ways and speaks to people who by no means will the way things now are. The Mishnah therefore lays down a practical judgment upon, and in favor of, the imagination and will to reshape reality, regain a system, reestablish that order upon which trustworthy existence is to be built.

It is one thing to describe, in general, the world we encounter in the pages of the Mishnah. It is quite another to explain what we should look for and actually seek in reading what these people say. For those questions I asked at the outset, about why people then should have talked about an imaginary world have to be answered in all the specificity of the hundreds of chapters, set forth in the dozens of tractates, of which the Mishnah is composed. This brings me to the three concrete matters worth protracted attention (as mere history is not): (1) the specific modes of discourse attained by the Mishnah; (2) the system of world-building laid forth in the Mishnah; and (3) the interplay between that system and the massive heritage of Scripture that lay behind the Mishnah. These three things—language, system, heritage—have now to be explained.

1. *Language: The Mishnah's Patterned Language and Its Forms*

Let us start our study of the language of the Mishnah with the simple question of how the document is organized. The answer is that the preferred mode of lay-out is through themes, spelled out along the lines of the logic imbedded in those themes. The Mishnah is divided into its six principal divisions. The tractates of each division take up sub-topics of the principal theme. The chapters then unfold along the lines of the (to the framers) logic of the necessary dissection of the division. While that mode of organization may appear to be necessary or "self-evident" (it is how we should have written a law code, is it not?), we should notice that there are three others found within the document, but not utilized extensively or systematically. These therefore represent rejected options. One way is to collect diverse sayings around the name of a given authority. (The whole of tractate Eduyyot is organized in that way.) A second way is to express a given basic principle through diverse topics, e.g., a fundamental rule cutting across many areas of law, stated in one place through all of the diverse types of law through which the rule or principle may be expressed. A third way is to take a striking language-pattern and collect sayings on diverse topics that comform to the given language-pattern. (There also is the possibility of joining the second and the third ways.) But faced with these possible ways of organizing materials, the framers of the Mishnah chose to adhere to a highly disciplined thematic-logical principle of organization.

In antiquity paragraphing and punctuation were not commonly used. Long columns of words would contain a text—as in the Torah today—and the student of the text had the task of breaking up those columns into tractates, chapters, sentences, large and small sense-units. Now if we had the entire Mishnah in a single immense scroll and spread the scroll out on the ground we should have no difficulty at all discovering the point at which the first tractate ends and the second begins, and so on. For from Berakhot at the beginning to Uqsin at the end, the breaking points practically jump out at us: change of principal topic. So, the criterion of division, internal to the document and not merely imposed by copyists and printers, is thematic. That is, the tractates are readily distinguishable from one another since each treats a distinct topic.

The same is so within the tractates. Intermediate divisions of these same principal divisions are to be discerned on the basis of internal evidence, through the confluence of theme and form. That is to say, a given intermediate division of a principal one (a chapter of a tractate) will be marked by a particular, recurrent, formal pattern in accord with which sentences are constructed and also by a particular and distinct theme, to which these sentences are addressed. When a new theme commences, a fresh formal pattern will be used. Within the intermediate divisions, we are able to recognize the components, or smallest whole units of thought (hereinafter, cognitive units), because there will be a recurrent pattern of sentence-structure repeated time and again within the unit and a shifting at the commencement of the next theme. Each point at which the recurrent pattern commences marks the beginning of a new cognitive unit. In general, an intermediate division will contain a carefully enumerated sequence of exempla of cognitive units, in the established formal pattern, commonly in groups of three or five or multiples of three or five (pairs for the first division).

The cognitive units resort to a remarkably limited repertoire of formulary patterns. The Mishnah manages to say whatever it wants in one of the following ways:

1. the simple declarative sentence, in which the subject, verb, and predicate are syntactically tightly joined to one another, e.g., he who does so and so is such and such;
2. the duplicated subject, in which the subject of the sentence is stated twice, e.g., He who does so and so, lo, he is such and such;
3. mild apocopation, in which the subject of the sentence is cut off from the verb, which refers to its own subject, and not the one with which the sentence commences, e.g., He who does so and so..., it [the thing he has done] is such and such;
4. extreme apocopation, in which a series of clauses is presented, none of them tightly joined to what precedes or follows, and all of them cut off from the predicate of the sentence, e.g., He who does so and so..., it [the thing he has done] is such and such..., it is a matter of doubt whether... or whether...lo, it [referring to nothing in the antecedent, apocopated clauses of the subject of the sentence] is so and so...
5. In addition to these formulary patterns, in which the distinctive formulary traits are effected through variations in the relationship between the subject and the predicate of the sentence, or in which the subject itself is given a distinctive development, there is yet a fifth. In this last one we have a contrastive complex predicate, in which case we may have two sentences, independent of one another, yet clearly formulated so as to stand in acute balance with one another in the predicate, thus, He who does...is unclean, and he who does not...is clean.

It naturally will be objected: Is it possible that a simple declarative sentence may be asked to serve as a formulary pattern, alongside the rather distinctive and unusual constructions that follow? True, by itself, a tightly constructed sentence consisting of subject, verb, and complement, in which the verb refers to the subject, and the complement to the verb, hardly exhibits traits of particular formal interest. Yet a sequence of such sentences, built along the same gross grammatical lines, may well exhibit a clearcut and distinctive pattern. When we see that three or five "simple declarative sentences" take up one principle or problem, and then, when the principle or problem shifts, a quite distinctive formal pattern will be utilized, we realize that the "simple declarative sentence" has served the formulator of the unit of thought as aptly as did apocopation, a dispute, or another more obviously distinctive form or formal pattern. The contrastive predicate is one example: the Mishnah contains many more.

The important point of differentiation, particularly for the simple declarative sentence, therefore appears in the intermediate unit, as I just said, thus in the interplay between theme and form. It is there that we see a single pattern recurring in a long sequence of sentences, e.g., the X that has lost its Y is unclean because of its Z. The Z that has lost its Y is unclean because of its X. Another example will be a long sequence of highly developed sentences, laden with relative clauses and other explanatory matter, in which a single syntactical pattern will govern the articulation of three or six or nine exempla. That sequence will be followed by one repeated terse sentence pattern, e.g., X is so and so, Y is such and such, Z is thus and so. The former group will treat one principle or theme, the latter some other. There can be no doubt, therefore, that the declarative sentence in recurrent patterns is, in its way, just as carefully formalized as a sequence of severely apocopated sentences or of contrastive predicates or duplicated subjects.

In order to appreciate the highly formal character of the Mishnah, we rapidly turn to its correlative document, the Tosefta, brought to redaction between ca. 200 C.E. and 400. The Tosefta's tractates follow those of the Mishnah. This is hardly surprising, since the Tosefta is a supplement to the Mishnah. When, however, we examine the ways in which the Tosefta's tractates are subdivided, we do not see the slightest effort to group materials in accord with a confluence of common theme and form, or to redact intermediate divisions in accord with a single fixed number of exempla, e.g., three's or five's. Furthermore, the Tosefta's units of thought are not highly patterned and exhibit none of the traits of carefully stylized formulation that we find in the Mishnah—except in those pericopae in which the Mishnah itself is cited and glossed (and they are very many). Accordingly, the Tosefta, a document dependent on the Mishnah, in no way exhibits careful traits of structured redaction, formal correspondence between formulary patterns and distinctive themes, for the internal demarcation of an intermediate division, or highly formalized formulation of individual units of thought. The Mishnah's traits emerge most clearly in the contrast established by its supplementary document. The mode of grouping cognitive units in the Tosefta is in accord with one of three fixed relationships to the Mishnah. Pericopae which cite the Mishnah verbatim will stand together. There commonly will follow units which do not cite the Mishnah but which clearly complement the principal document, augmenting its materials in some obvious ways. And, at the end will be grouped together still other groups which supplement the Mishnah but which in no clear way depend upon the Mishnah for full and exhaustive exegesis. Accordingly, The Toseftta's arrangement of its materials clearly relates to the Mishnah; and the contrast in the ways in which the Mishnah's own groups of cognitive units are set forth could not be more blatant.

This brief survey of the literary traits of the Mishnah permits us to turn to the question: What is to be learned about the authorities who bear responsibility for the peculiar way in which the Mishnah is formulated and redacted from the way in which they express their ideas? We speak, in particular, of the final generation represented in the Mishnah itself, the authorities of the period ca. 200 C.E. who gave the document its present literary character.

The dominant stylistic trait of the Mishnah as they formulated it is the acute formalization of its syntactical structure and its carefully framed sequences of formalized language, specifically, its intermediate divisions, so organized that the limits of a theme correspond to those of a formulary pattern. The balance and order of the Mishnah are particular to the Mishnah. So the document itself now must be asked to testify to the intentions of the people who made it so. About whom does it speak? And why, in particular, have its authorities distinctively shaped language in rhymes and balanced, matched, declarative sentences, imposing upon the conceptual, factual prose of the law a peculiar kind of poetry? Why do they create rhythmic order, grammatically balanced sentences containing discrete law, laid out in what seem to be carefully enumerated sequences, and the like? Language not only contains culture, which could not exist without it. Language, in our case, linguistic and syntactical style and stylization, expresses a world-view and ethos. Whose world-view is contained and expressed in the Mishnah's formalized rhetoric?

There is no reason to doubt that if we asked the authorities behind the Mishnah the immediate purpose of their systematic use of formalized language, their answer would be to facilitate memorization. For that is the proximate effect of the acute formalization of their document. Much in its character can be seen as mnemonic.

So the Mishnah's is language for an occasion. The occasion is particular: formation and transmission of special sorts of conceptions in a special way. The predominant, referential function of language, giving verbal structure to the message itself, is secondary in our document. The expressive function, conveying the speaker's attitude toward what he is talking about, the conative function, focusing upon who is being addressed, and other ritualized functions of language come to the fore. The Mishnah's language, therefore, as I said, is special, meant as an expression of a non-referential function. So far as the Mishnah was meant to be memorized by a distinctive group of people for an extraordinary purpose, it is language that includes few and excludes many, unites those who use it, and sets them apart from others who do not.

The formal aspects of Mishnaic rhetoric are empty of content. This is proved by the fact that pretty much all themes and conceptions can be reduced to the same few formal patterns. These patterns are established by syntactical recurrences, as distinct from recurrence of sounds. The same words do not recur. Long sequences of patterned and disciplined sentences fail to repeat the same words—that is, syllabic balance, rhythm, or sound—yet they do establish a powerful claim to order and formulary sophistication and perfection. That is why we could name a pattern, he who...it is...-apocopation: the arrangement of the words as a grammatical pattern, not their substance, is indicative of pattern. Accordingly, while we have a document composed along what clearly are mnemonic lines, the Mishnah's susceptibility to memorization rests principally upon the utter abstraction of recurrent syntactical patterns, rather than on the concrete repetition of particular words, rhythms, syllabic counts, or sounds.

A sense for the deep, inner logic of word-patterns, of grammar and syntax, rather than for their external similarities, governs the Mishnaic mnemonic. And that yields the fundamental point of this analysis: Even though the Mishnah is to be memorized and handed on orally, it expresses a mode of thought attuned to abstract relationships, rather than concrete and substantive forms. The formulaic, not the formal, character of the Mishnaic rhetoric yields a picture of a subculture—the sages who made up the book—which speaks of immaterial, and not material, things. In this subculture the relationship, rather than the thing or person which is related, is primary, constitutes the principle of reality. The thing in itself is less than the thing in cathexis with other things, so too the person. It is self-evident that the repetition of form creates form. But what is repeated, as I have explained, is not external or superficial form. Rather we find formulary patterns of deep syntax, patterns effected through persistent grammatical or syntactical relationships and affecting an infinite range of diverse objects and topics. Form and structure emerge not from concrete, formal things but from abstract and unstated, but ubiquitous and powerful relationships.

This fact—the creation of pattern through grammatical relationship of syntactical elements, more than through concrete sounds—tells us that the people who memorized conceptions reduced to these particular forms were capable of extraordinarily abstract cognition and perception. Hearing peculiarities of word-order in diverse cognitive contexts, their ears and minds perceived regularities of grammatical arrangement, repeated functional variations of utilization of diverse words. They grasped from such subleties syntactical patterns not expressed by recurrent external phenomena such as sounds, rhythms, or key-words, and autonomous of particular meanings. What they heard, it is clear, were not only abstract relationships but also principles conveyed along with and through these relationships. For, I repeat, what was memorized was a recurrent and fundamental notion, expressed in diverse examples but in recurrent rhetorical-syntactical patterns. Accordingly, what the memorizing student of a sage could and did hear was what lay far beneath the surface of the rule: the unstated principle, the unsounded pattern. This means that the prevalent mode of thought was attuned to what lay beneath the surface; minds and ears perceived what was not said behind what was said and how it was said. They besought that ineffable and metaphysical reality concealed within, but conveyed through, spoken and palpable, material reality.

Social interrelationships within the community of Israel are left behind in the ritual speech of the Mishnah, just as, within the laws, natural realities are made to give form and expression to supernatural or metaphysical regularities. The Mishnah speaks of Israel, but the speakers are a group apart. The Mishnah talks of this-worldly things, but the things stand for and speak of another world entirely. The language of the Mishnah and its formalized grammatical rhetoric create a world of discourse quite separate from the concrete realities of a given time, place, or society. The exceedingly limited repertoire of grammatical patterns by which all things on all matters are said gives symbolic expression to the notion that beneath the accidents of life are a few comprehensive relationships. Unchanging and enduring patterns lie deep in the inner structure of reality and impose structure upon the accidents of the world. This means, as I have implied, that reality for Mishnaic rhetoric consists in the grammar and syntax of language: consistent and enduring patterns of relationship among diverse and changing concrete things or persons. What lasts is not the concrete thing but the abstract interplay governing any and all sorts of concrete things.

There is, therefore, a congruence between rhetorical patterns of speech and the substantive framework of discourse established by these same patterns. Just as we accomplish memorization by perceiving not what is said but how it is said and is persistently arranged, so we undertake to address and describe a world in which what is concrete and material is secondary. How things are said about what is concrete and material in diverse ways and contexts is principal. The Mishnah is silent about the context of its speech—place and time and circumstance—because context is trivial. Principle, beginning in syntactical principles by which all words are arranged in a severely limited repertoire of grammatical sentences ubiquitously pertinent but rarely made explicit, is at the center.

The skill of the formulators of the Mishnah is to manipulate the raw materials of everyday speech. What they have done is so to structure language as to make it strange, to impose a fresh perception upon what to others (and what in The Toseftta) are merely unpatterned and ordinary ways of saying things. What is said in the Mishnah is simple. How it is said is arcane. Ordinary folk cannot have had much difficulty understanding the words which refer to routine actions and objects. How long it must have taken to grasp the meaning of the patterns into which the words are arranged! How hard it was and is to do so is suggested (at the very least) by the necessity for the creation of the Tosefta, the Talmuds, and the commentaries in the long centuries since the Mishnah came into being. In this sense the Mishnah speaks openly about public matters, yet its deep structure of syntax and grammatical forms shapes what is said into an essentially secret and private language. It takes many years to master the difficult argot, though only a few minutes to memorize the simple patterns. That constitutes a paradox reflective of the situation of the creators of the Mishnah.

Up to now I have said only a little about tense structure. The reason is that the Mishnah exhibits remarkably indifference to the potentialities of meaning inherent therein. Its persistent preference for the plural participle, thus the descriptive present tense,—"they do...," "one does...,"—is matched by its capacity to accept the mixture of past, present, and future tenses. These can be found jumbled together in a single sentence and, even more commonly, in a single pericope. It follows that the Mishnah is remarkably uninterested in differentiation of time-sequences. This fact is most clearly shown by the Gemisch of the extreme-apocopated sentence with its capacity to support something like the following: "He who does so and so...the rain came and wet it down...if he was happy...it [is] under the law, If water be put." Clearly, the matter of tense, past, present, future, is conventional. Highly patterned syntax is meant to preserve what is said without change (even though we know changes in the wording of traditions were effected for many centuries thereafter). The language is meant to be unshakeable. Its strict rules of rhetoric are meant not only to convey, but also to preserve, equally strict rules of logic, equally permanent patterns of relationship. What was at stake in this formation of language in the service of permanence? Clearly, how things were said was intended to secure eternal preservation of what was said. Change affects the accidents and details. It cannot reshape enduring principles. Language will be used to effect and protect their endurance. What is said, moreover, is not to be subjected to pragmatic experimentation. Unstated, but carefully considered, principles shape reality. They are not shaped and tested by and against reality. Use of pat phrases and syntactical cliches, divorced from different thoughts to be said and different ways of thinking, testifies to the prevailing notion of unstated, but secure and unchanging, reality behind and beneath the accidents of context and circumstance: God is one, God's world is in order, each line carefuly drawn, all structures fully coherent.

Two facts have been established.

First, the formalization of the Mishnaic thought-units is separate from the utilization of sound, rhythm, and extrinsic characteristics of word-choice. It depends, rather, upon recurrent grammatical patterns independent of the choices of words set forth in strings. The listener or reader has to grasp relations of words in a given sequence of sentences quite separate from the substantive character of the words themselves.

Accordingly, second, the natural language of Middle Hebrew is not apt to be represented by the highly formal language of Mishnah. Mishnaic language constitutes something more than a random sequence of words used routinely to say things. It is meant as a highly formulaic way of expressing a particular set of distinctive conceptions. It is, therefore, erroneous to refer to Mishnaic language. Rather, we deal with the Mishnaic revision of the natural language of Middle Hebrew. And, it is clear, what the Mishnah does to revise that natural language is ultimately settled in the character of the grammar, inclusive of syntax, of the language. Middle Hebrew has a great many more grammatical sequences than does Mishnaic Hebrew. It follows, Mishnaic Hebrew declares ungrammatical—that is, refuses to make use of—constructions that Middle Hebrew will regard as wholly grammatical and entirely acceptable. The single striking trait of the formalization of Mishnaic language, therefore, is that it depends upon grammar. And just as Chomsky says, "Grammar is autonomous and independent of meaning," so in the Mishnah, the formalization of thought into recurrent patterns is beneath the surface and independent of discrete meanings. Yet the Mishnah imposes its own discipline, therefore its own deeper level of unitary meaning, upon everything and anything which actually is said.

There are these two striking traits of mind reflected within Mishnaic rhetoric; first, the perception of order and balance; second, the perception of the mind's centrality in the construction of order and balance. I refer to the imposition of wholeness upon discrete cases in the case of the routine declarative sentence and upon discrete phrases in the case of the apocopated one. Both order and balance are contained from within and are imposed from without. The relationships revealed by grammatical consistencies internal to a sentence and the implicit regularities revealed by the congruence and cogency of cases rarely are stated. But they always are to be discerned. Accordingly, the one thing the Mishnah invariably does not make explicit but which always is necessary to know is, I stress, the presence of the active intellect, the participant who is the hearer. It is the hearer who ultimately makes sense of, perceives the sense in, the Mishnah. Once more we are impressed by the Mishnah's expectation of high sophistication and profound sensitivity to order and to form on the part of its impalpable audience. Again we note that, to the Mishnah, the human mind imposes meaning and sense upon the world of sense-perceptions.

In this sense the Mishnah serves both as a book of laws and as a book for learners, a law-code and a schoolbook. But it is in this sense alone.

If the Mishnah is a law-code, it is remarkably reticent about punishments for infractions of its rules. It rarely says what one must do or must not do, if he or she becomes unclean. The Mishnah hardly even alludes to punishments or rewards consequent upon disobedience or obedience to its laws. Clean and unclean rhetorically are the end of the story and generate little beyond themselves.

If the Mishnah serves as a schoolbook, it never informs us about its institutional setting, speaks of its teachers, sets clear-cut, perceptible, educational goals for its students, nor, above all, attempts to stand in relationship to some larger curriculum or educational and social structure. Its lack of context and unself-conscious framework of discourse hardly support the view that, in a this-worldly and ordinary sense, we have in our hands of a law-code or a schoolbook.

Nor is the Mishnah a corpus of "traditions," that is, true teachings that lay claim to authority or to meaning by virtue of the authorities cited therein. That is why the name of an authority rarely serves as a redactional fulcrum. It is also why the tense-structure is ahistorical and anti-historical. Sequences of actions generally are stated other than in the descriptive present tense. Rules attain authority not because of who says them but because (it would seem) no specific party, at a specific time, stands behind them. The Mishnah, as I have emphasized, is descriptive of how things are. It is indifferent to who has said so, uninterested in the cumulative past behind what it has to say. These are not the traits of a corpus of "traditions." I am inclined to think that law-code, schoolbook, and corpus of traditions all are not quite to the point of the accurate characterization of the Mishnah.

Yet, if not quite to the point, all nonetheless preserve a measure of proximate relevance to the definition of the Mishnah. The Mishnah does contain descriptive laws. These laws require the active participation of the mind of the hearer, thus are meant to be learned through reason, not merely obeyed as ritual, and self-evidently are so shaped as to impart lessons, not merely rules to be kept. The task of the hearer is not solely or primarily to obey, though I think obedience is taken for granted. The Mishnah calls one to participate in the process of discovering principles and uncovering patterns of meaning. The very form of the Mishnaic rhetoric, its formalization and function of that form—all testify to the role of the learner and hearer, that is, the student, in the process of definitive and indicative description (not communication) of what is, and of what is real.

Self-evidently, the Mishnah's persistent citation of authorities makes explicit the claim that some men, now dead, have made their contribution and, therefore, have given shape and substance to tradition, that tradition which is shaped by one and handed onward by another. Choices were made: authorities made them. So the Mishnah indeed is, and therefore is meant as, a law-code, a schoolbook, and a corpus of tradition. It follows that the purpose for which the Mishnah was edited into final form was to create such a multipurpose document, a tripartite goal attained in a single corpus of formed and formal sayings. And yet it is obvious that the Mishnah is something other than these three things in one. It transcends the three and accomplishes more than the triple goals which on the surface form the constitutive components of its purpose.

To describe that transcendent purpose and conclude this part of the discussion, we turn to Wittgenstein's saying, "The limits of my language mean the limits of my world."

On the one side, the Mishnah's formulaic rhetoric imposes limits, boundaries, upon the world. What fits into that rhetoric and can be said by it constitutes world, world given shape and boundary by the Mishnah. The Mishnah implicitly maintains, therefore, that a wide range of things fall within the territory mapped out by a limited number of linguistic conventions, grammatical sentences. What is grammatical can be said and, therefore, constitutes part of the reality created by the Mishnaic word. What cannot be contained within the grammar of the sentence cannot be said and therefore falls outside the realm of the Mishnaic reality. The Mishnaic reality consists in those things which can attain order, balance, and principle. Chaos lies without.

On the other side, if we may extrapolate from the capacity of the impoverished repertoire of grammar before us to serve for all sorts of things, then we must concede that all things can be said by formal revision. Everything can be reformed, reduced to the order and balance and exquisite sense for the just match, characteristic of the Mishnaic pericope. Anything of which we wish to speak is susceptible to the ordering and patterning of the Mishnaic grammar and syntax. That fact is implicit throughout the Mishnah. Accordingly, the territory mapped out by the Mishnaic language encompasses the whole of the pertinent world under discussion. There are no thematic limitations of the Mishnaic formalized speech.

Clearly, the Mishnah is formulated in a disciplined and systematic way. We therefore must now ask how the language of the Mishnah adumbrates the character and concerns of the Mishnah's substantive ideas, its religious world-view and the way of life formulated to express that world view. For I maintain that the document before us constitutes much more than an ancient rule-book, of no special interest or humanistic value, which happens to have survived. The Mishnah is, rather, a book deliberately formed for the very group, Israel, and purpose which, for nearly nineteen centuries, it indeed has served. So the language just now described, as much as the system awaiting description, has to be asked to testify to the meaning and purpose of the whole.

The "Judaism" expressed by the Mishnah not only speaks about values. Its mode of speech—the way it speaks, not only what it says—is testimony to its highest and most enduring, distinctive value. Now let us take note. This language does not speak of sacred symbols but of pots and pans, of menstruation and dead creeping things, of ordinary water which, because of the circumstance of its collection and location, possesses extraordinary power; of the commonplace corpse and ubiquitous diseased person; of genitalia and excrement, toilet seats and the flux of penises, of stems of pomegranates and stalks of leeks; of rain and earth and wood, metal, glass and hide. This language is filled with words for neutral things of humble existence. It does not speak of holy things and is not symbolic in its substance. This language speaks of ordinary things, of things which everyone must have known. But because of the peculiar and particular way in which it is formed and formalized, this same language not only adheres to an aesthetic theory but expresses a deeply-embedded ontology and methodology of the sacred, specifically of the sacred within the secular, and of the capacity for regulation, therefore for sanctification, within the ordinary: All things in order, all things then hallowed by God who orders all things, so said the priests' creation-tale.

World-view and ethos are synthesized in language. The synthesis is expressed in grammatical and syntactical regularities. What is woven into some sort of ordered whole is not a cluster of sacred symbols. The religious system is not discerned with such symbols at all. Knowledge of the conditions of life is imparted principally through description of the commonplace facts of life, which symbolize, stand for, nothing beyond themselves and their consequences, e.g., for the clean and the unclean or liability and exemption from liability. That description is effected through the construction of units of meaning, intermediate divisions composed of cognitive elements. All is balanced, explicit in detail, but reticent about the whole; balanced in detail but dumb about the character of the balance. What is not said is what is eloquent and compelling, as much as what is said. Accordingly, that simple and fundamental congruence between ethos and world-view is to begin with, for the Mishnah, the very language by which the one is given cognitive expression in the other. The medium of patterned speech conveys the meaning of what is said.

2. *System: The Mishnah as a Statement of a World-View*

By "Judaism" I mean a world-view and way of life formed by a group of people who regard themselves, and are properly regarded by others, as Israelites, in which the life of the group is both defined and explained within the framework of Israel's holiness. By this definition, there have been diverse forms or kinds of Judaism. But from the time of the Mishnah onward, most of these kinds have referred not only to Scripture but also to the Mishnah and its companions, the two Talmuds and cognate writings. So these diverse kinds have formed exemplifications of a single, fundamental kind of Judaism. If, therefore, we wish to make sense of nearly all religious expressions of "being Jewish" and nearly all types of Judaism from the second century to the twentieth, we must begin with the Mishnah (though, obviously, we must not end there.)

The Judaism shaped by the Mishnah consists of a coherent worldview and comprehensive way of living. It is a world-view that speaks of transcendent things, a way of life in response to the supernatural meaning of what is done, a heightened and deepened perception of the sanctification of Israel in deed and in deliberation. Sanctification means two things, first, distinguishing Israel in all its dimensions from the world in all its ways; second, establishing the stability, order, regularity, predictability, and reliability of Israel at moments and in contexts of danger. Danger means instability, disorder, irregularity, uncertainty, and betrayal. Each topic of the system as a whole takes up a critical and indispensable moment or context of social being. Each orders what is disorderly and dangerous. Through what is said in regard to each of the Mishnah's principal topics, what the system as a whole wishes to declare is fully expressed. Yet if the parts severally and jointly give the message of the whole, the whole cannot exist without all of the parts, so well-joined and carefully crafted are they all.

Let me now describe and briefly interpret the six components of the Mishnah's system. The critical issue in the economic life, which means, in farming, is in two parts, revealed in the first division. First, Israel, as tenant on God's holy Land, maintains the property in the ways God requires, keeping the rules which mark the Land and its crops as holy. Next, the hour at which the sanctification of the Land comes to form a critical mass, namely, in the ripened crops, is the moment ponderous with danger and heightened holiness. Israel's will so affects the crops as to mark a part of them as holy, the rest of them as available for common use. The human will is determinative in the process of sanctification.

Second, in the second division, what happens in the Land at certain times, at Appointed Times, marks off spaces of the Land as holy in yet another way. The center of the Land and the focus of its sanctification is the Temple. There the produce of the Land is received and given back to God, the one who created and sanctified the Land. At these unusual moments of sanctification, the inhabitants of the Land in their social being in villages enter a state of spatial sanctification. That is to say, the village boundaries mark off holy space, within which one must remain during the holy time. This is expressed in two ways. First, the Temple itself observes and expresses the special, recurring holy time. Second, the villages of the Land are brought into alignment with the Temple, forming a complement and completion to the Temple's sacred being. The advent of the appointed times precipitates a spatial reordering of the Land, so that the boundaries of the sacred are matched and mirrored in village and in Temple. At the heightened holiness marked by these moments of Appointed Times, therefore, the occasion for an affective sanctification is worked out. Like the harvest, the advent of an appointed time, a pilgrim festival, also a sacred season, is made to express that regular, orderly, and predictable sort of sanctification for Israel which the system as a whole seeks.

If for a moment we now leap over the next two divisions, the third and fourth, we come to the counterpart of the divisions of Agriculture and Appointed Times. These are the fifth and sixth divisions, namely Holy Things and Purities, which deal with the everyday and the ordinary, as against the special moments of harvest, on the one side, and special time or season, on the other.

The fifth division is about the Temple on ordinary days. The Temple, the locus of sanctification, is conducted in a wholly routine and trustworthy, punctilious manner. The one thing that may unsettle matters is the intention and will of the human actor. This is subjected to carefully prescribed limitations and remedies. The division of Holy Things generates its companion, the Sixth division, the one on cultic cleanness, Purities. The relationship between the two is like that between Agriculture and Appointed Times, the former locative, the latter utopian, the former dealing with the fields, the latter with the interplay between fields and altar.

Here too, in the sixth division, once we speak of the one place of the Temple, we address, too, the cleanness which pertains to every place. A system of cleanness, taking into account what imparts uncleanness and how this is done, what is subject to uncleanness, and how that state is overcome—that system is fully expressed, once more, in response to the participation of the human will. Without the wish and act of a human being, the system does not function. It is inert. Sources of uncleanness, which come naturally and not by volition, and modes of purification, which work naturally, and not by human intervention, remain inert until human will has imparted susceptibility to uncleanness, that is, introduced into the system, that food and drink, bed, pot, chair, and pan, which to begin with form the focus of the system. The movement from sanctification to uncleanness takes place when human will and work precipitate it.

This now brings us back to the middle divisions, the third and fourth, on Women and Damages. They take their place in the structure of the whole by showing the congruence, within the larger framework of regularity and order, of human concerns of family and farm, politics and workaday transactions among ordinary people. For without attending to these matters, the Mishnah's system does not encompass what, at its foundations, it is meant to comprehend and order. So what is at issue is fully cogent with the rest.

In the case of Women, the third division, attention focuses upon the point of disorder marked by the transfer of that disordering anomaly, woman, from the regular status provided by one man, to the equally trustworthy status provided by another. That is the point at which the Mishnah's interests are aroused: once more, predictably, the moment of disorder.

In the case of Damages, the fourth division, there are two important concerns. First, there is the paramount interest in preventing, so far as possible, the disorderly rise of one person and fall of another and in sustaining the status quo of the economy, the house and household, of Israel, the holy society in eternal stasis. Second, there is the necessary concommitant in the provision of a system of political institutions to carry out the laws which preserve the balance and steady state of persons.

The two divisions that take up topics of concrete and material concern, the formation and dissolution of families and the transfer of property in that connection, the transactions, both through torts and through commerce, that lead to exchanges of property and the potential dislocation of the state of families in society, are both locative and utopian. They deal with the concrete locations in which people make their lives, household and street and field, the sexual and commercial exchanges of a given village. But they pertain to the life of all Israel, both in the Land and otherwise. These two divisions, together with the household ones of Appointed Times, constitute the sole opening outward toward the life of utopian Israel, that diaspora in the far reaches of the ancient world, in the endless span of time. This community from the Mishnah's perspective is not only in exile but unaccounted for, outside the system, for the Mishnah declines to recognize and take it into account. Israelites who dwell in the land of (unclean) death instead of in the Holy Land simply fall outside of the range of (holy) life. Priests, who must remain cultically clean, may not leave the Land—and neither may most of the Mishnah.

Now if we ask ourselves about the sponsorship and source of special interest in the topics just now reviewed, we shall come up with obvious answers.

So far as the Mishnah is a document about the holiness of Israel in its Land, it expresses that conception of sanctification and theory of its modes which will have been shaped among those to whom the Temple and its technology of joining Heaven and holy Land through the sacred place defined the core of being, I mean, the caste of the priests.

So far as the Mishnah takes up the way in which transactions are conducted among ordinary folk and takes the position that it is through documents that transactions are embodied and expressed (surely the position of the relevant tractates on both Women and Damages), the Mishnah expresses what is self-evident to scribes. Just as, to the priest, there is a correspondence between the table of the Lord in the Temple and the locus of the divinity in the heavens, so, to the scribe, there is a correspondence between the documentary expression of the human will on earth, in writs of all sorts, in the orderly provision of courts for the predictable and just disposition of exchanges of persons and property, and Heaven's judgment of these same matters. When a woman becomes sanctified to a particular man on earth, through the appropriate document governing the transfer of her person and property, in heaven as well, the woman is deemed truly sanctified to that man. A violation of the writ therefore is not merely a crime. It is a sin. That is why the Temple rite involving the wife accused of adultery is integral to the system of the division of Women. So there are scribal divisions, the third and fourth, and priestly divisions, the first, fifth, and sixth; the second is then shared between the two groups.

These two social groups are not categorically symmetrical with one another, the priestly caste and the scribal profession. But for both groups the Mishnah makes self-evident statements. We know, moreover, that in time to come, the scribal profession would become a focus of sanctification. The scribe would be transformed into the "rabbi," honored man par excellence, locus of the holy through what he knew, just as the priest had been and would remain locus of the holy through what he could claim for genealogy. The divisions of special interest to scribes-become-rabbis and to their governance of Israelite society, those of Women and Damages, together with certain others particularly relevant to utopian Israel beyond the system of the Land—those tractates would grow and grow. Many, though not all, of the others would remain essentially as they were with the closure of the Mishnah. So we must notice that the Mishnah, for its part, speaks for the program of topics important to the priests. It takes up the persona of the scribes, speaking through their voice and in their manner.

What about the lay person pretending to be a priest, namely, the Pharisee. Two matters require some attention. First, we want to ask what we learn about the Pharisees from the Mishnah. Second, we inquire about the relationship of the Pharisees to the Mishnah. So far as the Mishnah takes for granted that Jews must strictly observe the Sabbath in a certain way, carefully tithe the agricultural produce they eat, and preserve a state of cultic or Levitical cleanness, it certainly accords with views attributed to Pharisees. Yet the Mishnah rarely refers to the Pharisees, and when it does, it does not represent them as its definitive authorities, who are sages, not Pharisees at all. A few of the Mishnah's authorities, particularly Gamaliel and Simeon b. Gamaliel, are known from independent sources to have been Pharisees. But that is the sum and substance of it. Consequently, to assign the whole of the Mishnah to the Pharisees who flourished before 70 and who are known to us from diverse sources, all of them composed in the form in which we know them after 70, is hardly justified. We learn little about the Pharisees from the Mishnah, except in the handful of sayings referring to them (M. Hag. 2:4-7; M. Sot. 3:4; M. Toh. 4:12; and M. Yad. 4:6-8), or assigned to people who we have good reason to believe were Pharisees.

As to the relationship of the Pharisees to the Mishnah, we learn somewhat more. For the Mishnah contains a great many principles and propositions that can be shown to go back to the period before 70. Some of the most striking and important of these principles, those in the divisions on Agriculture and Purities in particular, but also a few in the divisions on Appointed Times and Women, may be shown to serve sectarian, and not general or societal, interests. It would carry us far afield to specify what these propositions are and why they evidently speak out of a sectarian context. The main point should not be missed. When we speak about the Pharisees, we speak about Jews who thought that when they ate their meals at home, they should do so in the way, in general, in which the priests eat their meals of meat, meal, and wine, supplied from the leftovers of God's meal on the altar of the Temple in Jerusalem. So some of them were priests who pretended that their homes were little Temples. And, it seems reasonable to suppose, others of them were lay people pretending to be priests and engaged in the same fantasy.

But this too requires qualification. First, Pharisees were not the only Jews who had a special interest in the cultic cleanness of their food. The Essene community at Qumran also maintained that its food was in a state of cultic cleanness, as if it were prepared on the altar of God in the holy Temple. Consequently, we cannot take for granted that when a saying indicates the conviction that ordinary food must be kept pure as if it were the Lord's food in the Temple, that saying must derive from a Pharisee and from no other sect, group, or source. That simply is not so.

Second, there are many other parts of the document in which interests of all priests are at hand. For instance, there is the whole of the fifth division, Holy Things. In vast stretches of the first division, Agriculture, in which the separation of tithes and heave-offering as the priestly ration is described, all priests are equally represented. No one had to be a Pharisee in particular to take up these matters. Any priest who cared about his income (either at the present time or in the time in which the Mishnah's law would everywhere prevail) would take these same matters to heart. So the Mishnah is very much a priestly document. It may also be a document reflecting in some measure the partisan interests of a certain kind of priests (and associated lay people). But it cannot be called a document only or mainly of this second group. Its social constituency, as I said, included a large cohort of priests interested in their income and emoluments. Some of these may have regarded as important those special matters stressed in parts of the sixth division, but all of them will have cared about the laws of the first, second, fifth, and the bulk of the sixth divisions as well.

We now turn to the third and last of our main topics, to another side of context, not the one of synchronic history, nor the one of language and culture, but the Mishnah's diachronic setting in Israelite revelation: the Mishnah and God's word in the revelation of the Torah to Moses at Mount Sinai.

3. *Heritage: Mishnah and Scripture. The Open Canon of Judaism*

To this point in the discussion, one might imagine that the Mishnah falls into the category of documents found in a desert cave, produced by a nascent group with no past at all, a document like the Pentateuch, addressed to a mixed multitude of a no-people. For up to now I have introduced the Mishnah as if it stood only at the head of a long line of Israelite religion and law but not at the end of one. That, of course, is not so. Every significant creation in ancient Israel from the formation of the Hebrew Scriptures and conclusion of the canon onward necessarily forms a response to the Torah. This Torah is the revelation of God to Moses at Mount Sinai, contained in the Pentateuch as well as the other biblical books,. For each such fresh creation is inevitably a reworking of available materials of revelation. Each therefore either claims for itself a place within the canon defined by the Israelite Scriptures. Or it deliberately excludes itself and seeks a place outside of, but in relationship to, that same canon. Consequently, at the end of this account of the Mishnah, we have to ask about the relationship between the Mishnah and the Holy Scriptures that define and frame the Israelite world—world view, way of life—to which the framers of the Mishnah addressed themselves and within which they too took shape.

On the surface, Scripture plays little role in the Mishnaic system. The Mishnah rarely cites a verse of Scripture, refers to Scripture as an entity, links its own ideas to those of Scripture, or lays claim to originate in what Scripture has said, even by indirect or remote allusion to a Scriptural verse of teaching. So, superficially, the Mishnah is totally indifferent to Scripture. That impression, moreover, is reinforced by the traits of the language of the Mishnah. The framers of Mishnaic discourse, amazingly, never attempt to imitate the language of Scripture, as do those of the Essene writings at Qumran. The very redactional structure of Scripture, found so serviceable to the writer of the Temple scroll, remarkably, is of no interest whatever to the organizers of the Mishnah and its tractates, except in a very few cases (Leviticus 16, Yoma; Exodus 12, Pesahim).

I wish now to dwell on these facts. Formally, redactionally, and linguistically the Mishnah stands in splendid isolation from Scripture. It is not possible to point to many parallels, that is, cases of anonymous books, received as holy, in which the forms and formulations (specific verses) of Scripture play so slight a role. People who wrote holy books commonly imitated the Scripture's language. They cited concrete verses. They claimed at the very least that direct revelation had come to them, as in the angelic discourses of 4 Erza and Baruch, so that what they say stands on an equal plane with Scripture. The internal evidence of the Mishnah's sixty-two usable tractates (excluding Abot), by contrast, in no way suggests that anyone pretended to talk like Moses and write like Moses, claimed to cite and correctly interpret things that Moses had said, or even alleged to have had a revelation like that of Moses and so to stand on the mountain with Moses. There is none of this. So the claim of Scriptural authority for the Mishnah's doctrines and institutions is difficult to locate within the internal evidence of the Mishnah itself.

We cannot be surprised that, in consequence of this amazing position of autonomous, autocephalic authority implicit in the character of Mishnaic discourse, the Mishnah should forthwith have demanded in its own behalf some sort of apologetic. Nor are we surprised that the Mishnah attracted its share of quite hostile criticism. The issue, in the third century, would be this: Why should we listen to this mostly anonymous document, which makes statements on the nature of institutions and social conduct, statements we obviously are expected to keep? Who are Meir, Yose, Judah, Simeon, and Eleazar—people who from the perspective of the third-century recipients of the document, lived fifty or a hundred years ago—that we should listen to what they have to say? God revealed the Torah. Is this Mishnah too part of the Torah? If so, how? What, in other words, is the relationship of the Mishnah to Scripture, and how does the Mishnah claim authority over us such as we accord to the revelation to Moses by God at Mount Sinai?

There are two important responses to the question of the place of Scripture in the Mishnaic tradition.

First and the more radical: the Mishnah constitutes torah. It too is a statement of revelation "Torah revealed to Moses at Sinai." But this part of revelation has come down in a form different from the well-known, written part, the Scripture. This tradition truly deserves the name "tradition," because for a long time it was handed down orally, not in writing, until given the written formulation now before us in the Mishnah. This sort of apologetic for the Mishnah appears, to begin with, in Abot, with its stunning opening chapter, linking Moses on Sinai through the ages to the earliest-named authorities of the Mishnah itself, the five pairs, on down to Shammai and Hillel. Since some of the named authorities in the chain of tradition appear throughout the materials of the Mishnah, the claim is that what these people say comes to them from Sinai through the processes of *qabbalah* and *massoret*—handing down, "traditioning."

So the reason (from the perspective of the Torah-myth of the Mishnah) that the Mishnah does not cite Scripture is that it does not have to. It stands on the same plane as Scripture. It enjoys the same authority as Scripture. This radical position is still more extreme than that taken by pseudepigraphic writers, who imitate the style of Scripture, or who claim to speak within that same gift of revelation as Moses. It is one thing to say one's holy book is Scripture because it is like Scripture, or to claim that the author of the holy book has a revelation independent of that of Moses. These two positions concede to the Torah of Moses priority over their own holy books. The Mishnah's apologists make no such concession, when they allege that the Mishnah is part of the Torah of Moses. They appeal to the highest possible authority to the Israelite framework, claiming the most one can claim in behalf of the book which, in fact, bears the names of men who lived fifty years before the apologists themselves. That seems to me remarkable courage.

Then there is this matter of the Mishnah's not citing Scripture. When we consider the rich corpus of allusions to Scripture in other holy books, both those bearing the names of authors and those presented anonymously, we realize that the Mishnah claims its authority to be co-equal with that of Scripture. Many other holy books are made to lay claim to authority only because they depend upon the authority of Scripture and state the true meaning of Scripture. That fact brings us to the other answer to the question of the place of Scripture in the Mishnaic tradition.

Second, the earliest exegetical strata of the two Talmuds and the legal-exegetical writings produced in the two hundred years after the closure of the Mishnah take the position that the Mishnah is wholly dependent upon Scripture. Whatever is of worth in the Mishnah can be shown to derive directly from Scripture. So the Mishnah—"tradition"—is deemed distinct from, and subordinate to, Scripture. This position is expressed in an obvious way. Once the Talmuds cite a Mishnah-pericope, they commonly ask, "What is the source of these words?" And the answer invariably is, "As it is said in Scripture." This constitutes not only a powerful defense for the revealed truth of the Mishnah. For when the exegetes find themselves constrained to add proof-texts, they admit the need to improve and correct an existing flaw.

That the search for the Scriptural bases for the Mishnah's laws constitutes both an apologetic and a criticism is shown in the character of a correlative response to the Mishnah, namely, the Sifra and its exegesis of Leviticus, as we shall see in detail in Chapter 3. But the fundamental structure of the Sifra derives from the period after the Mishnah had taken shape, since the Sifra is a polemical document. The polemic is against the failure of the Mishnah to cite Scripture very much or systematically to link its ideas to Scripture through the medium of formal demonstration by exegesis. This polemic is expressed over and over again. The Sifra's rhetorical exegesis follows a standard redactional form. Scripture will be cited. Then a statement will be made about its meaning, or a statement of law correlative to that Scripture will be given. That statement sometimes cites the Mishnah, often verbatim. Finally, the author of Sifra invariably states, "Now is that not (merely) logical?" And the point of that statement will be, Can this position not be gained through the working of mere logic, based upon facts supplied (to be sure) by Scripture? The polemical power of Sifra lies in its repetitive demonstration that the stated position, citation of a Mishnah-pericope, is not only not the product of logic, but is, and only can be, the product of exegesis of Scripture.

What is still more to the point, exegesis in Sifra's and the Talmud's view is formal in character. That is, it is based upon some established mode of exegesis of the formal traits of Scriptural grammar and syntax, assigned to the remote antiquity represented by the names of Ishmael or Aqiba. So the polemic of Sifra and the Talmuds is against the positions that, first, what the Mishnah says (in the Mishnah's own words) is merely logical; and that, second, the position taken by the Mishnah can have been reached in any way other than through grammatical-syntactical exegesis of Scripture. That other way, the way of reading the Scripture through philosophical logic or practical reason, is explicitly rejected time and again. Philosophical logic and applied reason are inadequate. Formal exegesis is shown to be not only adequate, but necessary, indeed inexorable. It follows that Sifra undertakes to demonstrate precisely what the framers of the opening pericopes of the Talmud's treatment of the Mishnah's successive units of thought also wish to show.

The Mishnah is not autonomous. It is not independent. It is not correlative, that is, separate but equal. It is contingent, secondary, derivative, resting wholly on the foundations of the (written) revelation of God to Moses at Mount Sinai. Therein, too, lies the authority of the Mishnah as tradition.

So, there are two positions that would rapidly take shape when the Mishnah was published.

First, tradition in the form of the Mishnah is deemed autonomous of Scripture and enjoys the same authority as that of Scripture. The reason is that Scripture and ("oral") tradition are merely two media for conveying a single corpus of revealed law and doctrine.

Second, tradition in the form of the Mishnah is true because it is not autonomous of Scripture. Tradition is secondary and dependent upon Scripture.

The authority of the Mishnah is the authority of Moses. That authority comes to the Mishnah directly and in an unmediated way, because the Mishnah's words were said by God to Moses at Mount Sinai and faithfully transmitted through a process of oral formulation and oral transmission from that time until those words were written down by Judah the Patriarch at the end of the second century.

Or, that authority comes to the Mishnah indirectly, in a way mediated through the written Scriptures.

What the Mishnah says is what the Scripture says, rightly interpreted. The authority of tradition lies in its correct interpretation of the Scripture. Tradition bears no autonomous authority, is not an independent entity, correlative with Scripture. A very elaborate (and insufferably dull) technology of exegesis of grammar and syntax is needed to build the bridge between tradition as contained in the Mishnah and Scripture, the original utensil shaped by God and revealed to Moses to convey the truth of revelation to the community of Israel.

Or matters are otherwise. I hardly need to make them explicit.

Let me now state the facts of the relationship of the Mishnah to Scripture, beyond the picture of the third-century apologist-critics of the Mishnah.

First, there are tractates that simply repeat in their own words precisely what Scripture has to say, and at best serve to amplify and complete the basic ideas of Scripture. For example, all of the cultic tractates in the second division, on Appointed Times, which tell what one is supposed to do in the Temple on the various special days of the year, and the bulk of the cultic tractates of the fifth division, which deals with Holy Things, simply restate facts of Scripture. For another example, all of those tractates of the sixth division, on Purities, which specify sources of uncleanness, depend completely on information supplied by Scripture. I have demonstrated in detail that every important statement in Niddah, on menstrual uncleanness, and the most fundamental notions of Zabim, on the uncleanness of the person with flux referred to in Leviticus Chapter Fifteen, as well as every detail in Negaim, on the uncleanness of the person or house suffering the uncleanness described at Leviticus Chapters Thirteen and Fourteen—all of these tractates serve only to restate the basic facts of Scripture and to complement those facts with other important ones.

There are, second, tractates that take up facts of Scripture but work them out in a way in those Scriptural facts cannot have led us to predict. A supposition concerning what is important about the facts, utterly remote from the supposition of Scripture, will explain why the Mishnah-tractates under discussion say the original things they say in confronting those Scripturally-provided facts. For one example, Scripture takes for granted that the red cow will be burned in a state of uncleanness, because it is burned outside the camp—Temple. The priestly writers cannot have imagined that a state of cultic cleanness was to be attained outside of the cult. The absolute datum of tractate Parah, by contrast, is that cultic cleanness not only can be attained outside of the "tent of meeting." The red cow was to be burned in a state of cleanness even exceeding that cultic cleanness required in the Temple itself. The problematic which generates the intellectual agendum of Parah, therefore, is how to work out the conduct of the rite of burning the cow in relationship to the Temple: Is it to be done in exactly the same way, or in exactly the opposite way? This mode of contrastive and analogical thinking helps us to understand the generative problematic of such tractates as Erubin and Besah, to mention only two.

Third, there are, predictably, many tractates that either take up problems in no way suggested by Scripture or begin from facts at best merely relevant to facts of Scripture. In the former category are Tohorot, on the cleanness of foods, with its companion, Uqsin; Demai, on doubtfully tithed produce; Tamid, on the conduct of the daily whole-offering; Baba Batra, on rules of real estate transactions and certain other commercial and property relationships, and so on. In the latter category are Ohalot, which spins out its strange problems within the theory that a tent and a utensil are to be compared to one another (!); Kelim, on the susceptibility to uncleanness of various sorts of utensils; Miqvaot, on the sorts of water which effect purification from uncleanness; Ketubot and Gittin, on the documents of marriage and divorce; and many others. These tractates draw on facts of Scripture. But the problem confronted in these tractates in no way responds to problems important to Scripture. What we have here is a prior program of inquiry, which will make ample provision for facts of Scripture in an inquiry to begin with generated essentially outside of the framework of Scripture. First comes the problem or topic, then —if possible—comes attention to Scripture.

So there we have it: some tractates merely repeat what we find in Scripture. Some are totally independent of Scripture. And some fall in between. Clearly, we are no closer to a definitive answer to the question of the relationship of Scripture to the Mishnah than we were when we described the state of thought on the very same questions in the third and fourth centuries. We find everything and its opposite. But to offer a final answer to the question of Scripture-Mishnah relationships, we have to take that fact seriously. The Mishnah in no way is so remote from Scripture as its formal omission of citations of verses of Scripture suggests. In no way can it be described as contingent upon, and secondary to Scripture, as many of its third century apologists claimed. But the right answer is not that it is somewhere in-between. Scripture confronts the framers of the Mishnah as revelation, not merely as a source of facts. But the framers of the Mishnah had their own world with which to deal. They made statements in the framework and fellowship of their own age and generation. They were bound, therefore, to come to Scripture with a set of questions generated other than in Scripture. They brought their own ideas about what was going to be important in Scripture. This is perfectly natural.

The philosophers of the Mishnah conceded to Scripture the highest authority. At the same time what they chose to hear, within the authoritative statements of Scripture, will in the end form a statement of its own. To state matters simply: all of Scripture is authoritative. But only some of Scripture is relevant. And what happened is that the framers and philosophers of the tradition of the Mishnah came to Scripture when they had reason to. That is to say, they brought to Scripture a program of questions and inquiries framed essentially among themselves. So they were highly selective. That is why their program itself constituted a statement upon the meaning of Scripture. They and their apologists of one sort hastened to add, their program consisted of a statement of the meaning of Scripture.

In part, we must affirm the truth of that claim. When the framers of the Mishnah speak about the priestly passages of the Mosaic law codes, with deep insight they perceive profound layers of meaning embedded ("to begin with") in those codes. What they have done with the Priestly Code, moreover, they also have done, though I think less coherently, with the bulk of the Deuteronomic laws and with some of those of the Covenant Code. But their exegetical triumph—exegetical, not merely eisegetical—lies in their handling of the complex corpus of materials of the Priestly Code.

True, others will have selected totally different passages of Scripture, not in the Mosaic codes to begin with. Prophecy makes its impact on the holy books of other Israelites of the same ancient times, as, for instance, Q, Matthew, and Mark. Surely we must concede that, in reading those passages, other writers, interested in history and salvation, displayed that same perspicacity as did the framers of the Mishnaic tradition who interpreted the priestly code as they did and so formed a theory of Israel's sanctification. It is in the nature of Scripture itself that such should be the case. The same Scripture which gives us the prophets gives us the Pentateuch as well—and gives priority to the Pentateuchal codes as the revelation of God to Moses.

5. *Why Is the Mishnah Important?*

What joins the ages is not only our interest in their world. First, it also is our interest in any encompassing and important statement of how humankind might in imagination create a world. The Mishnah is a specimen of Utopia. That is why what we find in the Mishnah is more than insight into the world created within one kind of Judaism in the formative centuries of Western civilization.

In the Mishnah contemporary humanists may gain a more ample account of a tiny part of the potentialities of humanity: that part expressed within the Judaic tradition in its rabbinical formulation. When we find out what it is that the Mishnaic system contains within itself, we discover yet another mode for the measure of humankind. The human potentialities and available choices within one ecological frame of humanity, the ancient Jewish one, are defined and explored by the sages. The same question—the possibilities contained within the culture of ancient Judaism—is to be addressed to the diverse formations and structures, at other times in its history besides that of late antiquity. But we have to learn how to do the work in some one place, and only then shall we have a call to attempt it elsewhere. What we must do is first describe, then interpret.

But what do we wish to describe? I am inclined to think the task is to encompass everything deemed important by some one group, to include within, and to exclude from, its holy book, its definitive text. We wish to make sense of a system and its exclusions, its stance in a taxonomy of systems. For, on the surface, what sages put in they think essential, and what they omit they do not think important. If that is self-evident, then the affirmative choices are the ones requiring description and then interpretation. But what standpoint will permit us to fasten onto the whole and where is the fulcrum on which to place our lever? For, given the size of the evidence, the work of description may leave us with an immense, and essentially pointless, task of repetition: saying in our own words what the sources say, perfectly clearly, in theirs.

So when I say that a large part of the work is to describe the world-view of the sages of the Mishnah, at best I acquire a license to hunt for insight. What defines the work as well as I am able, is what has run through this introduction to the Mishnah: the idea of a system. That is a whole set of interrelated concerns and conceptions that, all together, both express a world-view and define a way of living for a particular group of people in a particular economic and political setting. The Mishnah brings to the surface the integrated conception of the world and of the way in which the people should live in that world. All in all, that system both defines and forms reality for Jews responsive to the sages of the Mishnah.

Now, self-evidently all that is worth knowing about the sages and the Jews around them is not contained within their system, that is, the Mishnah as they lay it out. There is, after all, the hard fact that the Jews did not have power fully to shape the world within which they lived out their lives and formed their social group. No one else did either. There were, indeed, certain persistent and immutable facts which form the natural environment, the material ecology for their system. These facts do not change and do have to be confronted. There are, for instance, the twin-facts of Jewish powerlessness and minority-status. Any system produced by Judaism for nearly the whole of its history will have to take account of the fact that the group is of no account in the world, a pariah-people. Another definitive fact is the antecedent heritage of Scripture and associated tradition, which define for the Jews a considerably more important role in the supernatural world than the natural world affords them. Israel is God's first love, not Rome's last victim. These two facts, the Jews' numerical insignificance and political unimportance and the Jews' inherited pretensions and fantasies about their own centrality in the history and destiny of the human race, created (and still create) a certain dissonance between any given Jewish world-view, on the one side, and the world to be viewed by the Jews, on the other. And so is the case for the Mishnah.

But we cannot take for granted that what we think should define the central tension of a given system in fact is what concerned the people who created and expressed that system. If we have no way of showing that our surmise may be wrong, then we also have no basis on which to verify our thesis as to the core and meaning of the system before us. The result can be at best good guesses. A mode for interpreting the issues of a system has therefore to be proposed.

One route to the interpretation of a system is to specify the sorts of issues it chooses to regard as problems, the matters it chooses for its close and continuing exegesis, our exegesis of the canon of topics. When we know the things about which people worry, we have some insight into the way in which they see the world. So, when we approach the Mishnah, we ask about its critical tensions, the recurring issues which occupy its great minds. It is out of concern with this range of issues, and not some other, that the Mishnah defines its principal areas for discussion. Here is the point at which the great exercises of law and theology will be generated—here and not somewhere else. This is a way in which we specify the choices people have made, the selections a system has effected. When we know what people have chosen, we also may speculate about the things they have rejected, the issues they regard as uninteresting or as closed. We then may describe the realm of thought and everyday life which they do not deem subject to tension and speculation.

It is these two sides to this vast document—the things people conceive to be dangerous and important, the things they set into the background as unimportant and uninteresting—which provide us with a key to the culture of community or, as I prefer to put it, to the system constructed and expressed by a given social group.

PART ONE

THE MISHNAH IN HISTORICAL AND RELIGIOUS
CONTEXT

THE DIVISION OF AGRICULTURE AND SECOND CENTURY JUDAISM: THE HOLINESS OF THE DEVASTATED LAND

ALAN J. AVERY-PECK

College of the Holy Cross

As the rabbis of the Mishnah formulated a system of law to control Israelite ritual and social life, more was at stake than simply implementing the rules first stated in Scripture. Scripture, indeed, would serve as a foundation for all that the Mishnah's authors would do and create. But it could be no more than a foundation. For, in developing their response to Scripture's ideas and practices, the rabbis needed to face the distinctive theological questions that faced their own day, in particular the questions raised by Roman control of the land of Israel after the destruction of the Jerusalem Temple and, then, after the failed Bar Kokhba revolt. In this setting, through their reading of Scripture, the Mishnaic masters would respond to pressing questions concerning the status of the covenant and the appropriate mode of observing a set of laws understood by Scripture to assure exactly the divine protection that, in the two failed wars against Rome, had not been forthcoming. In the face of Scripture's insistence upon the centrality of the land of Israel in God's plans for the people Israel, the devastation of that land would have to be explained. What did it mean to be a Jew living in the land of Israel after the Temple, the visible sign of God's presence and dominion, had been destroyed and in the face of clear evidence that neither the Temple's rebuilding nor Rome's removal from power could be expected in the foreseeable future? In what way was God's own presence in the land still to be felt?

Recognizing these questions as central in any thinking about Judaism in the first centuries, the particular importance of the Mishnaic Division of Agriculture is clear. Here the rabbis do more than regulate how Israelites are to plant, harvest, process, and eat the crops they grow for sustenance. Through these regulations, rather, they account for and describe the special character of the land of Israel even in its devastated state, identifying the ways in which the sanctity previously seen in Temple and recognized in the produce of the land still could be found. The Mishnah's authorities accomplish this through the quite distinctive approach they take in elaborating Scripture's agricultural law. If the question was the extent to which holiness still pertained to the devastated land, then the rabbis' response was that, despite all that had happened on the stage of human history, the land remained holy and its produce subject to sanctification, a sign of God's continuing presence and ownership of the land and all it produced.

The Mishnaic Division of Agriculture makes this point through its presentation of a theory familiar from Scripture, which details how Israelites are to maintain and use a land that is God's special possession. Following Scripture's theory, the Mishnah's rabbis do not understand the payment of tithes simply to be a method of supporting the Temple-cult or the needy of the Israelite community. Nor do they understand the other regulations that control use of the land to fulfill only general agricultural, social, or economic functions (e.g., the possible agricultural value of allowing all land to lie fallow once every seven years; the economic impact of legislating that certain produce, or its value, be brought to Jerusalem). The Mishnah's authorities, rather, see in these regulations descriptions of how Israelites are to use the land in accordance with the specific nature of God's creation of the universe and in keeping with God's special relationship with the people and land of Israel.

In creating the world, God rested on the seventh day. The land of Israel, God's special possession, therefore must rest each seventh year.[1] In creating the world, God distinguished discrete species of plants. In planting their fields, Israelites must not mix together different kinds.[2] Finally, since crops that grow upon the land of Israel partake of the bounty of God's property, they are bonded to God and may not be eaten until God's interest in them has been satisfied, through payment of agricultural offerings,[3] each of which the Mishnah's authorities describe in detail.

---

[1] See Louis Newman, *The Sanctity of the Seventh Year: A Study of Mishnah Tractate Shebiit* (Chico, 1983), p. 15.

[2] See Irving Mandelbaum, *A History of the Mishnaic Law of Agriculture: Kilayim* (Chico, 1982), p. 4.

[3] See Alan [Avery-]Peck, *The Priestly Gift in Mishnah: A Study of Tractate Terumot* (Chico, 1981), p. 3.

Since these themes, and much of what the rabbis have to say about them, are predictable on the basis of Scripture, what is significant for interpretation of the division as a product of the first centuries must be carefully defined. First is the very fact that the Mishnah's framers choose to take up systematically topics that Scripture refers to in a smattering of verses[4] and discusses with no consistent theological agendum.[5] Second, the Mishnah's framers become intensely concerned about agricultural offerings destined for priest, Levite, and Temple in a period in which the cult had been destroyed and priests and Levites had ceased to have a concrete function in the consecration of Israelite life. Third, and most important, in their discussions of these topics, the Mishnah's rabbis have a particular interest in the role of common Israelites, non-priests, in the processes of sanctification—that is, in how, by growing and processing food, Israelites cause holiness to come into being[6] and in how, before eating, they must dispose of that holiness, whether in the hands of the priests or through other of their own actions. These issues are absent from Scripture, which is concerned that the priest and Levite receive their designated share but which does not question how,

---

[4] A total of sixty-eight verses are scattered in nineteen passages, the majority of which contain only one or two lines. The overall number of verses is raised considerably by the long passage at Deut. 26:1-15, which discusses the liturgy for the presentation of the first fruits and for Scripture's "year of tithing."

[5] The unsystematic nature of Scripture's tithing laws has prevented scholars from reaching a consensus concerning their significance. The problem arises with the attempt to locate in Scripture a unitary system of agricultural offerings (see, e.g., Aharon Oppenheimer, "Terumot and Ma'aserot," in *Encyclopedia Judaica*, vol. 15, cols. 1025-1028). This approach leads to claims of a dual focus of the tithing system, upon piety, on the one hand, and taxation, on the other (see H. Guthrie, "Tithe," in *Interpreters Dictionary of the Bible*, vol. 3, pp. 654-655, and J. MacCulloch, "Tithes," in *Encyclopedia of Religion and Ethics*, vol. XII, pp. 346-350). As Richard Sarason, *A History of The Mishnaic Law of Agriculture: A Study of Tractate Demai* (Leiden, 1979), pp. 3-10, points out, in contrast to the unitary perspective of the Mishnah, the Deuteronomic and Priestly sources contain two distinct theories of tithing. The former holds that the separation of tithes acknowledges God's ownership and expresses gratitude for the fertility of the land of Israel. The latter holds that the tithes go to the Levites and Aaronide priests as compensation for serving in the Temple. Mishnaic authorities take Scripture's diverse statements and in part conflicting definitions and derive a unitary and focused set of laws concerned with the sanctification of Israelite life.

[6] This interest may account for the failure of the Mishnah's rabbis to speak systematically about first tithe, which is not consecrated. See Alan J. Avery-Peck, *Mishnah's Division of Agriculture: A History and Theology of Seder Zeraim* (Chico, 1985), p. 427, n. 5.

in the hands of non-priests, produce becomes sanctified as that share.⁷ The Mishnah's interest is the opposite.

In its reflections on the theme of sanctification, the Division of Agriculture reveals an ideology that emerged over the course of Rabbinic discussions of these topics, beginning while the Temple stood and then in the periods of Yavneh and Usha. The earliest generations of Rabbinic authorities, those living before 70 C.E. and in Yavnean times, are concerned primarily with matters of definition and with basic laws facilitating observance of rules that are only briefly sketched in Scripture. These rabbis, for instance, 1) give concrete measurements that define a field for purposes of the law of Diverse Kinds, 2) delineate what field labors may or may not be performed in the Sabbatical year, 3) outline the quantity of produce to be taken as each tithe and agricultural offering, and 4) indicate specifically how the offering is to be set aside. A single theory of law stands behind these materials. Yavneans consistently ignore the motivations or perceptions of the Israelite whose deeds are under scrutiny. The reasons or perceptions that lead an individual to act have no bearing upon the permissibility of that behavior. The status of a deed, rather, depends solely upon the nature of the actions through which it is carried out. It does not matter to Yavneans, for instance, why an Israelite collects stones from a field during the seventh year. In doing so, he makes possible the cultivation of the land, which is not allowed during the Sabbatical. Such actions therefore are forbidden. This is the case even if the individual simply desires to build a stone fence, a deed that itself is permitted.⁸

The later generation of authorities, those of the Ushan period, develop the Yavnean perspective in a consistent pattern. Ushans analyze actions in light of the intentions of the individual who performs them and on the basis of the perceptions of those who witness and interpret them. They thus understand the permissibility of

---
⁷ The Division of Agriculture has little to say about the actual transfer of agricultural offerings to priests and Levites. It thus ignores Scripture's central interest in favor of its own primary concern, the role of the non-priest in the processes of sanctification.

⁸ Along these same lines, Yavneans define physical entities in light of their shape and form, without regard to the use to which Israelites intend to put them. They deem a field, for instance, to be demarcated by geographical boundaries, by hills, streams, or trees that set off one area of land from adjacent lots. The farmer's own actions in choosing to treat one area as autonomous are immaterial.

field labor in the seventh year to depend upon the Israelite's intentions in carrying it out. An action is permitted so long as the individual does not intend to break the rules of the seventh year and so long as he works in a way that prevents others from assuming that he proposes to break the law.[9] Whereas Yavneans recognize the existence of an objective reality in the world, a preset order, that exists apart from any individual's perceptions of how things are or should be, Ushans thus recognize no order in the world other than that imposed by Israelites. While Yavneans deem correct acts to be those that conform completely to a preset ideal, such that behavior, not intention, counts, Ushans hold that Israelites own intentions and perceptions give meaning to their activities in planting, tilling and harvesting produce on the land of Israel.

The larger issues to be addressed concern the specific ways in which the Yavnean and Ushan perspectives respond to the circumstance of Judaism in the first centuries and include the question of how we might account for the shift in attitude that occurs over this period. To provide the detailed evidence that will allow us to answer these questions, we begin by examining each tractate in the Division of Agriculture so as more exactly to identify the central ideas and concerns of each period in the Mishnah's legal development.[10]

Tractate Peah

At issue in Tractate Peah is how portions of produce grown on the land of Israel come to have the status of an agricultural offering, such that they may be collected and eaten only by certain individuals, under specifically prescribed circumstances. While produce growing in the corners of the field does not have a status of consecration comparable to that of heave-offering, the Mishnah's authors see a close connection between the poor gifts discussed here and other

---

[9] In the same way, the efficacy of the individual's separation of agricultural offerings depends upon the intention with which the separation is carried out, not upon the physical actions by which the deed is accomplished. Similarly, in the Ushan view, Israelites' own perceptions define which crops are orderly and distinct or disorderly and mixed together, so as to be permitted or forbidden under the law of diverse kinds.

[10] On the following, see my *Mishnah's Division of Agriculture*, passim. Tractate Berakhot, which concerns liturgical practices rather than agricultural offerings, is not treated here.

tithes. Thus, the rabbis hold that produce becomes subject to poor gifts, like other agricultural offerings, only when the farmer determines to make personal use of it. His interest in the ripening crop awakens God's interest in the food and, with it, the obligation to tithe. This fact is stressed in the tractate's notion that even produce that is known early in its development to be destined for the poor, e.g., defective clusters, remains the property of the householder until the harvest begins. Until the farmer shows that he wants the produce, the poor have no right to it.

In light of its central concern for the designation of produce for the poor, Tractate Peah barely touches upon the social and economic problems associated with the administration of a poor tax. The questions of which poor may collect these offerings or of how much they should collect, let alone of how we assure that these gifts are paid at all, never are satisfactorily answered. Rather, the poor are important here only in light of the special role they play in the designation as an agricultural gift of the produce left by the farmer. What makes these agricultural gifts particularly interesting to the Mishnah's framers is that their achieving the status of an offering depends upon two individuals, the poor person alongside the farmer. The obligation of the farmer is fulfilled when, during the harvest, he either intentionally or unintentionally leaves certain produce behind in the field. Now the desires and actions of the poor come into play. By completing the harvest and thereby showing their own desire for the food, they validly acquire it as a poor offering. In this way, Tractate Peah illustrates the deep significance the Division of Agriculture in general accords the Israelites' desire for food. Food becomes subject to poor gifts only after the harvest begins. And it takes on the status of a poor offering only when the poor, by showing their own hunger for the food, invoke God's demand that the needy be fed.

A. *Tractate Peah before 70*

Deut. 24:19 states that a sheaf a farmer forgets in the field becomes the property of the poor. The Houses of Hillel and Shammai (M. Pe. 6:1-3, 6:5) dispute whether or not this law applies to a sheaf that might later be remembered. The question of how we judge what is "forgotten" has no implications for later developments in the tractate's law.

B. *Tractate Peah in the Time of Yavneh*

Yavneans establish the agenda of issues that concerns the tractate as a whole, revolving around the crucial question of how produce comes to have the status of an agricultural offering. In light of this basic issue, Yavnean's ideas here often parallel and depend upon ideas found as well in the Yavnean strata of Tractates Terumot and Maaserot, which deal with this same problem. Yavneans are clear (M. Pe. 4:10), for instance, that the rights of the poor to their share begin only when the farmer desires to take produce for his own personal use. Yavneans further note (M. Pe. 1:6) that produce designated to be a poor offering, like produce that is either heave-offering or tithes, is exempt from the separation of other agricultural gifts.

Certain details normative in Ushan times are disputed by Yavneans. Defective grape clusters are the property of the poor (Deut. 24:21). Yavneans argue the rule for a field all of which is defective clusters. Against Aqiba, Eliezer holds that all of the produce cannot have the status of an agricultural offering, for this would preclude the formal act of designation through which the farmer distinguishes his own share from the gift being made to the poor, Levite, or priest. While disputed here, Eliezer's view, that validly to set aside an agricultural offering the farmer must keep some produce for himself, is normative at Usha (M. Pe. 1:2-3C-E). Yavneans also argue whether or not the farmer may give poor tithes to any poor person he desires, just as he presents heave-offering and tithes to the priest or Levite of his choice (M. Pe. 4:9A-C). Ushans resolve that he may not, basing this view upon their notion that these offerings take on their special status only when the poor take them for themselves.

Yavneans develop the Shammaite view that distinctive sheaves do not fall under the law of the forgotten sheaf (M. Pe. 6:6), and they initiate discussion of what constitutes a field, a topic important because of the underlying assumption that Peah must be designated in each individual field. Yavneans argue whether a field is defined on geographical terms—an area distinguished by natural boundaries—or whether the farmer's own attitude, indicated in the way he plants and harvests a plot of land, controls the matter (M. Pe. 2:3-4, 3:2). In Ushan times, the latter view takes precedence, with the farmer's own intentions understood to override the natural boundaries that separate one plot of land from another (M. Pe. 3:3).

Finally, an issue introduced in the Yavnean periods remains moot in Usha. This concerns whether gleanings are comparable to consecrated offerings, such that the actual produce that is a gleaning must go to the poor. Alternatively, because gleanings are unconsecrated, so long as the poor receive the required quantity, they need not be given the same produce that was left behind in the field (M. Pe. 5:2G-K). While Ushans greatly expand discussion of this question, the issue remains unresolved.

C. *Tractate Peah in the Time of Usha*

Developing Yavnean concerns, Ushans conclude that, in most cases, the rules for setting aside poor gifts correspond to those for designating heave-offering and tithes. The farmer may not designate all of his field to be Peah (M. Pe. 1:2-3C-E), since, by not exercising his own right to the produce, he does not trigger the system of restrictions that, in the first place, requires payment of tithes. The same conception is revealed in the Ushan idea that no poor gifts—even defective clusters, identified at the beginning of their growth (M. Pe. 7:5, 8)—belong to the poor until the farmer begins harvesting and so lays claim to his own share. Gentiles may not set aside poor gifts (M. Pe. 4:9D-E), just as heave-offering they separate is not valid (M. Ter. 3:9). This is in line with the notion that agricultural offerings are paid to release God's lien upon the produce. Since God did not give the land to gentiles and does not sanction their growing of produce upon it, God has no share in the crops that result from their farm work.

Unlike Yavneans, Ushans are clear that, in one major respect, Peah and gleanings differ from heave-offering and tithes. While the latter are given by the householder to whichever priest or Levite he desires, poor gifts, Ushans state, must be left in the field for the poor themselves to collect (M. Pe. 4:1-3). On the one hand, Ushans appear simply to be stressing what is clear in Scripture: the poor are to go through the fields and take for themselves what is left behind after the harvest. At a deeper level, however, this Ushan development of an issue moot at Yavneh (M. Pe. 4:5, 9A-C) details a particularly Ushan conception. Ushans hold that produce becomes Peah or gleanings through the purposeful act of the farmer, who leaves incomplete the harvesting of his field. By leaving part of his produce unpicked, the farmer gives up his right to that food. The analogue to this conception is that the poor validly take possession of the produce only by completing the act of harvesting left incomplete by the farmer. Thus, in the designation and collection of poor gifts, nothing is left to chance or to intention not made concrete through specific behaviors. Rather, the transfer of produce from the farmer to the poor is formalized through the actions of the harvest that, in the system of tithes as a whole, indicate Israelites' purposeful use of the God-given land. This same Ushan attitude is found in the Ushan consensus that, should a farmer's notion of what constitutes a field be indicated in what crops he plants and harvests as a unit, his attitude, and not geographical boundaries, determines what constitutes a single field for purposes of the designation of Peah (M. Pe. 3:3-5).

Along with these theoretical issues, Ushans provide practical rules that make possible the implementation of the tithing laws. They indicate exactly where in each field Peah is to be set aside (M. Pe. 1:3A-B) and detail who is responsible for designating it (M. Peah 2:7-8, 3:5). They define what constitutes a defective cluster (M. Pe. 7:4) and clarify the conditions under which the law of the forgotten sheaf applies (M. Pe. 6:10, 7:1-2). Finally, Ushans indicate the quantity of poor tithe that the farmer is to distribute to each poor person (M. Pe. 8:5, 6, 7).

Conclusion

The distinctive agenda of issues of this tractate, like that of Tractate Terumot, was set in Yavnean times, when each of the tractate's major questions was first raised. Only in Ushan times, however, did the questions first posed at Yavneh receive answers that reveal an overriding legal theory. This theory holds that the Israelite farmer's desire for the produce of the land triggers the responsibility to pay agricultural tithes. Poor people's acquisition of their share likewise is bound up in the act of harvest, in the needy individual's completing what was left undone by the farmer. The Mishnah's contribution to Scripture's law thus is to look at Scripture's poor tax—paid according to Scripture to recognize that all Israel once was, and again might be, in need—as a tithe comparable to all other agricultural offerings and therefore susceptible to designation according to the same rules that apply in those other cases, in which God's claim upon the produce of the land is viewed as a response to the Israelite farmer's own claim to the food.

Tractate Demai

Tractate Demai describes how individuals who properly separate the required agricultural offerings are to assure that all of the food they eat outside of their homes or purchase to bring home has properly been tithed. To accomplish this, the tractate indicates how one determines whether or not someone else is trustworthy regarding tithing, legislates responsibility for tithing produce that leaves one's possession, and details the procedure for tithing produce about which there is a doubt whether or not it already was tithed.

The problem of the tractate arises when one group within a society imposes upon the act of eating mythic dimensions ignored by other members of their society. Tractate Demai, however, does not describe a self-contained sect living apart from, or even at the fringes of, the larger society. Rather, the very problem of how to deal with cases of doubt whether or not food is properly prepared for consumption arises only in the context of continuing interaction among people with different food preparation habits. While concerned with intra-group relations, Tractate Demai thus does not describe a self-contained sect. This is not entirely surprising, given the rabbis' clear intention to create of the people of Israel as a whole a nation living in holiness.

The specific problem of the tractate arises not with Pharisees, as we might expect, but late in the formation of the law, when Ushans determine that the responsibility to tithe extends to all produce one sells in the market, gives away, or even finds in the street and subsequently discards.[11] If, instead, one were responsible to tithe only that which he prepares to eat in his own meal (as Tractate Maaserot has it), the problem of doubtfully tithed produce would not arise at all. In light of this, the tractate as a conceptual whole comes into being only in Ushan times. Early authorities, including the Houses, know that certain Israelites fully tithe their produce and others do not. But Ushans alone legislate that one *must* tithe all produce that leaves his possession.

The general weight of Yavnean legislation, it bears noting, is to

---

[11] See Sarason, *Demai*, p. 4.

rule leniently and allow those who do and do not tithe to eat at the same table or otherwise to exchange produce. Ushans, by contrast, strictly limit interaction between those who are trusted to tithe and those who are not. In this way, Ushans define a society not envisioned by earlier Rabbinic authorities and certainly not foreseen by Scripture's agriculture law. In this society, strict lines demarcate one group of Israelites from another. Those who tithe as the rabbis require are set above the rest of the people of Israel. In light of the Ushan insistence that they do all in their power to prevent others from eating improperly tithed foods, indeed, they are made responsible for the salvation of the nation as a whole.

A. *Tractate Demai before 70*

One central idea goes back to the period before 70, the Shammaite notion (M. Dem. 3:1C-H) that people are responsible to prevent others from transgressing, for instance, by giving untithed produce as charity only to individuals known to tithe. While disputed by anonymous authorities, by Ushan times this idea leads to the pervasive idea that one must tithe all produce that leaves his possession. While the Shammaite position does not constitute the generative problematic of the tractate (it assumes that people may give away untithed food), it provides the tractate's underlying ethical proposition, that people are responsible to prevent each other from transgressing.

B. *Tractate Demai in the Time of Yavneh*

Yavneans provide only a smattering of comments, indicating their general lack of interest in the problems created by membership in a group that follows stringent dietary restrictions. Indeed, compared to the Ushan approach, Yavnean legislation is quite lax regarding produce that might not have been tithed. Contrary to Ushans (M. Dem. 5:1), for instance, Yavneans allow a householder to distribute doubtfully tithed produce to poor people who eat at his table (M. Dem. 3:lA-B). While certain problems considered in the Ushan stratum thus arise in Yavnean times, it appears that the focus and point of the tractate as a whole was determined only by the later authorities.

The Yavnean leniency regarding cases of doubt is highlighted in a discussion of individuals who claim to have tithed but are not known to be trustworthy. Yavneans rule that the testimony of such people may be accepted in any circumstance in which the questioner has no good alternative—for instance, if he otherwise will not be able to eat at all (M. Dem. 4:1). This view is rejected by Ushans, who instead develop a way of judging the likelihood that the testimony is true. Unlike Yavneans, Ushans would rather go hungry than eat possibly untithed food.

C. *Tractate Demai in the Time of Usha*

Ushans define membership in a group distinguished by observance of tithing and purity laws and delineate how group members are to follow these laws while living among individuals who cannot be trusted properly to tithe or even to respect the members' needs (M. Dem. 2:2, 3, 4, 3:3E-G, 4, 5, and 6). Description of the extent of permitted contact takes up the majority of the Ushan material. The ethical underpinning of these rules, that one must do whatever is possible to prevent others from transgressing, leads to the responsibility to tithe all produce that leaves one's possession and accounts for a range of practical issues that the Ushan materials take up, e.g., concerning the case of a sharecropper (M. Dem. 6:1, 7, 8-9, 10, 12). Ushans additionally develop a system for tithing produce about which there is a doubt whether or not it already was fully tithed (M. Dem. 5:1). The circumstances in which this tithing practice must be used also are detailed (M. Dem. 1:1, 1:3C-D, 5:3-4, 5:9, 5:6, 5:7, 5:8).

Conclusion

Distinguished by their dedication to tithing and cultic purity, the Pharisees from the period before 70 generally are regarded as the forbears of the Mishnah's rabbis. It therefore is surprising that Tractate Demai, which details exactly those matters believed to have concerned the Pharisees most, contains scarcely any materials from the period before 70. Only a single comment of any importance may be traced back to the House of Shammai, and this rule hardly can be said to account for the large corpus of law that, in the Ushan stratum, sets out the requirements for living a life dedicated to ideals assumed to have been upheld, in the period before 70, by the Pharisees.

The absence of rules from before 70 has important implications for our understanding of Rabbinic history. It implies that, whatever the claims of later Rabbinic authorities, the early Rabbinic movement did not inherit and make use of a substantial corpus of law and tradition deriving from the Pharisees. While the interests and concerns of the Pharisees and later rabbis may have been similar, as for specific laws, the Rabbinic movement began fresh. Later Rabbinic masters may have seen themselves as the Pharisees' heirs or have asserted a Pharisaic lineage to substantiate their claim to be authoritative teachers. In doing so, they adopted as their ancestors the group that non-Rabbinic and Rabbinic sources after 70 agree had the greatest power and esteem among the people. But in terms of an actual heritage of law deriving from the period before 70, exactly where we would most expect to find it, the rabbis' teachings are almost uniformly the product of the latest period in the development of Mishnaic law.

Tractate Kilaim

Reflecting upon Lev. 19:19 and Deut. 22:9-11's prohibitions against commingling different kinds of plants, animals, and fibers, Tractate Kilaim questions what constitutes a species and asks how different classes of things are to be kept separate. The point is that humans must maintain the world in the orderly—and hence holy—manner in which God created it. In Tractate Kilaim, the Mishnah's authorities thus describe in concrete terms how Israelite farmers are to raise their crops in conformity with the world's original order. By doing this, Israelites prepare the world for a resanctification by God comparable to the act of consecration that completed the earth's original creation.[12]

The most basic question left open by Scripture concerns how different species are to be kept separate. This issue attracts the attention of the Houses and continues to constitute the focus of concern throughout the formation of the tractate's law. This is not to say, however, that the tractate is the creation of the early period.

---

[12] See Mandelbaum, *Kilaim*, p. 3.

For while its generative question is asked by the time of the Houses, the proposed answer shifts dramatically with Ushan authorities. The Houses and Yavnean authorities define a species in light of botanical characteristics, holding that Scripture's law is transgressed whenever different classes are sown together within a single, geographically defined field. Ushans, by contrast, hold that, through intentions and perceptions, Israelites themselves ascertain whether or not different types of crops planted in the same vicinity are forbidden as Diverse Kinds. Their perception of the crops establishes whether the foods have been planted as a confused, and therefore forbidden, mixture or in an orderly, and hence permitted, pattern. According to Ushans, that is, the Israelite himself "both defines what constitutes a class and determines how to keep the different classes distinct from one another. Man thus imposes upon an otherwise disorderly world limits and boundaries which accord with human perception of order and regularity.... [W]hat appears to man as orderly becomes identified with the objective order of the world."[13] In this view, Israelites themselves bring the potential for sanctification into an otherwise disordered world.

A. *Tractate Kilaim before 70*

In the only material of the tractate from before 70, the Houses dispute the definition of a vineyard subject to Scripture's prohibition (M. Kil. 4:1-3, 5, 6:1). Their argument concerns the number and configuration of vines that comprise a vineyard and the area of tillage deemed integral to that vineyard, such that it may not be planted with a different kind.

B. *Tractate Kilaim in the Time of Yavneh*

Yavneans do little to develop the premise established before 70. They are concerned primarily with delineating the specific areas of land that may be deemed autonomous of adjacent ground (M. Kil. 2:10, 3.3, 4, 6). Like the Houses, Yavneans are not concerned with the overall appearance of the area but with its conformity to unvarying space requirements. This formalistic approach is best exemplified

---

[13] Ibid., p. 1.

by M. Kil. 4:8. Hananiah b. Hakinai holds that the original layout of a vineyard, not the way it appears at the present time, determines whether or not seed may be planted between the rows of vines.

A formalistic attitude also informs the Yavnean approach to produce already planted as Diverse Kinds. While Ushans will take into account the intentions of the farmer, Yavneans rule that even if Diverse Kinds are accidentally planted, the second kind immediately must be destroyed (M. Kil. 5:7). If it is not, all of the produce becomes forbidden. Yavneans touch briefly on two other matters, disputing whether or not plants that do not produce food are subject to the restrictions of Diverse Kinds (M. Kil. 5:8) and ruling that a vine growing upon part of a tree renders that part alone in the status of a trellis. Seed may not be planted there (M. Kil. 6:4). Ushans will develop this rule to take into account the intentions of the farmer who trains a vine upon his tree.

Yavneans hold that mingled fabrics (Lev. 19:19, Deut. 22:11), forbidden in a garment, may be used for other purposes (M. Kil. 9:3, 4).

C. *Tractate Kilaim in the Time of Usha*

Contrary to prior authorities, Ushans state that a field's status is determined by whether individuals who look at it will perceive a confused mixture of different types of plants or a logically mapped out grid of distinct crops. What concerns Ushans is not the specific size of any area of planting but the perceptions of the Israelites who look at it and who, on the basis of appearances, determine whether or not the farmer has properly planted his fields.

Ushans similarly define Diverse Kinds on the basis of appearance, not botanical divisions (M. Kil. 1:1-3). In this view, distinct kinds of plants that look alike may be planted together, for they do not give the appearance of being Diverse Kinds. This same approach appears in Ushan materials concerning forbidden and permitted layouts of diverse crops. So long as the onlooker is able to perceive a logical order in the way the farmer plants his field, Ushans deem the planting permitted (M. Kil. 2:7, 9, 3:1). Certain Ushans even allow Diverse Kinds of seeds actually to be mixed together and planted. Their only concern is that the secondary seed is of so minimal a quantity as not to give the field the outward appearance of a confused mixture (M. Kil. 2:1-2). Finally, along these same lines,

Ushans define a vineyard as any group of vines that people in general call a vineyard (M. Kil. 5:1). This is a quite different approach from that of the Houses, who gave specific requirements regarding numbers of vines and their configuration.

The Ushan approach appears as well in a case in which a farmer plants crops that are not Diverse Kinds but that appear to comprise a forbidden combination. Since onlookers will perceive the farmer to have transgressed, he should not plant in such a manner (M. Kil. 7:2D-F). While the farmer who does so anyway has not objectively transgressed and therefore cannot be held culpable, he should not in the first place cause even the appearance of a sin. Applied to the law of the Sabbatical year, this Ushan idea accounts for the majority of the materials in Tractate Shebiit.

According to Ushans, the perceptions and intentions of Israelites also determine whether crops planted as Diverse Kinds are forbidden for consumption. Ushans hold they are prohibited only if the farmer intended Diverse Kinds to grow in his field. If he did not, then even if he maintains the illegal mixture for some time, the produce remains permitted (M. Kil. 5:6). This is quite different from the Yavnean approach (M. Kil. 5:7), which requires the farmer immediately to destroy the offending crop. The Ushan view leads to the logical conclusion that an individual who plants a Diverse Kind in his neighbor's field does not render forbidden all of that field (M. Kil. 7:4-6). So long as the person who owns the field did not sanction the growth of the secondary crop, the presence of that crop has no impact. Upon discovering the offending plants, he need simply destroy them, indicating that he does not desire the food they produce.

This same Ushan perspective applies when a farmer trains vines upon a tree (M. Kil. 6:3, 5). If the tree is barren, the farmer clearly wishes to use the whole tree as a trellis. The area under it is an area of tillage and may not be sown. But if a vine is planted under part of a fruit bearing tree, only the affected branches are deemed a trellis. The rest of the tree, clearly desired by the farmer for its fruit, retains the status of a tree, such that no area of tillage need be left under it. Grains may be planted there, and if they should be grown over by the vine, the vine needs simply to be cut back. It does not render the properly planted seed forbidden. Again, the prohibitions against Diverse Kinds are nor automatic. They are, rather, a response to the specific intentions and desires of Israelites.

Taking up the prohibition against weaving a fabric of wool and linen, Ushans define forbidden cloth (M. Kil. 9:8-10) and, as before, make clear that no mixtures that appear forbidden should be worn (M. Kil. 9:2). The prominence for Ushans of appearances is indicated by their allowing the use of cloth that actually contains both wool and linen, so long as the presence of the mixture is not apparent (M. Kil. 9:1). Finally, in cases of ambiguity, the user's attitude determines whether or not a cloth object is deemed a garment (M. Kil. 9:5-6).

The mating or harnessing together of different kinds of animals (Lev. 19:19, Deut. 22:10), ignored in the earlier periods, receives some attention at Usha. Again concentrating upon appearances, Ushans rule that different kinds of animals may not be tied together in any way that looks as though they are harnessed to work as a team (M. Kil. 8:3, 4). This is the case even if the animals actually are not working together.

Conclusion

Tractate Kilaim describes how Israelites can maintain the distinctions established by God at the time of creation between different classes of plants, animals, and fibers. Its overall point emerges in the Ushan stratum. This material, comprising the majority of the tractates laws,[14] introduces the concept that appears throughout the tractates of the Division of Agriculture: the character of a field—ordered or disordered—or the culpability of an action—permitted or forbidden—is determined in light of the perceptions and intentions of the Israelites involved. These perceptions determine whether different plants growing together in a field have been planted in a logically ordered, and so permitted, or disordered, and so forbidden, manner. The farmer's culpability, and with it the question of whether or not he has maintained the distinctions established by God at creation, thus are judged only in light of what he intended and how others perceive his actions.

According to Ushans, order, and with it holiness, is not dependent upon a pre-ordained, transcendent model. It is, rather, a func-

---

[14] Thirty-one out of eighty-one units (39%) are Ushan, thirteen units (18%) are Yavnean. Only eight of the tractate's twenty-eight anonymous rules appear to derive from earlier than Ushan times.

tion of each Israelites' own desire to order, and thereby sanctify, the world. This notion of the role of common Israelites in establishing conditions of holiness is further developed in Tractate Shebiit, which follows. That tractate comprises the Mishnah's second essay on how Israelites are to grow produce under conditions of holiness.

Tractate Shebiit

Just as God ceased working on the seventh day and designated it a day of rest, so God established the seventh year as a Sabbath during which the land of Israel must be left untilled (Lev. 25:1-7). Each seventh year, Israelites may not sow their fields or in any way prepare them for planting; nor may farmers work orchards or vineyards so as to enhance the crop they will produce. The people must, rather, survive upon produce that grows on its own. This food is shared equally by all people, without regard for who owns the land upon which it is found. In a separate though perhaps related idea, Deut. 15:1-3 states that, in the seventh year, monetary demands of one Israelite upon another are cancelled.

Tractate Shebiit's concern, dictated by Scripture, is that Israelites use their land in accordance with God's plan of the time of creation. The tractate's function within the Division of Agriculture thus parallels that of Tractate Kilaim and, as we shall see, Orlah, which describe how Israelites are to grow food in conditions of sanctity. This parallel in function corresponds to a commonality of the basic points made by Tractates Shebiit and Kilaim. In Tractate Shebiit, as in Kilaim, Ushans rule that what is permitted and forbidden depends largely upon the intentions of the Israelite who carries out an action and upon the perceptions of people who see and judge what he has done. While describing a return to the perfect state in which God created the world, the compilers of both tractates judge the success of that return only in light of the desires and perceptions of Israelites: what they characterize as right and good is identified with the objective order and sanctity of the world.

This point, the one aspect of the laws before us absent from Scripture, is distinctive to the Ushan stratum of the Mishnah. Yavneans, by contrast, simply outline what Scripture itself makes relatively clear, forbidding all field work that has a concrete impact upon the growth of seventh year produce. In the Yavnean view, the appearance that the farmer is doing right or wrong has no role in determining the culpability of his actions. Like the Yavnean materials in Tractate Kilaim, those in this tractate depict an established and unvarying set of norms as defining proper conduct. These are applied without regard to extenuating circumstances or concern for the meaning an action has to those who carry it out or witness it. This approach leads only to a simple listing, predictable on the basis of Scripture, of field labors that promote the growth of produce or that have no impact upon the land. During the Sabbatical year the latter may be performed; the former may not.

A. *Tractate Shebiit before 70*

As at M. Dem. 3:1C-H, the Houses dispute whether or not a person is responsible to prevent another from transgressing (M. Sheb. 4:2A-K, 5:8). The Shammaites' position, that one is, is repeated as normative, M. Sheb. 5:6, 7. We recall that this same view is a basic datum of the Yavnean and Ushan strata of Tractate Demai.

Hillel instituted a legal fiction that circumvents the Sabbatical remission of debts (M. Sheb. 10:3-4). The prozbul-document assigns a private debt to a court, which may collect the debt even after the start of the seventh year. Developed in the periods of Yavneh and Usha, the basic notion of the prozbul appears original to the period before 70.

B. *Tractate Shebiit in the Time of Yavneh*

The ideas that, in the Ushan period, become the focus of this tractate are disputed at Yavneh. The most basic issue concerns whether or not the restrictions of the Sabbatical year extend back to the end of the sixth year of the Sabbatical cycle (M. Sheb. 1:4I-K). Anonymous authorities argue that they do, precluding farmers from doing in the sixth year field work that will aid the crop in the seventh. This notion, the foundation of the tractate's first two, otherwise wholly Ushan, chapters, was rejected by the Yavnean Ishmael, who held that the Sabbatical restrictions apply only in the Seventh year, so that a farmer could do any field work he desired through the whole of the sixth year, as the plain sense of Scripture suggests.

Yavneans argue whether or not a farmer may perform permitted field labors that might appear to be forbidden (e.g., gathering rocks for building, which looks like clearing a field for planting). The weight of the Yavnean material (e.g., M. Sheb. 3:10, 4:6) is clear that neither the intentions of the farmer nor the perceptions of onlookers are to be taken into account. We look, rather, only at the concrete fact of whether or not the farmer's actions promote the growth of a seventh-year crop. Dominance of this view would have precluded the Ushan discussions in the tractate's fifth, sixth, and eighth chapters. Behind that large block of Ushan material stands the Yavnean minority opinion of Yose the Galilean, M. Sheb. 4:6, who holds that a farmer may do nothing that appears to be forbidden, even if it is in fact a permitted activity.

C. *Tractate Shebiit in the Time of Usha*

Unlike Yavneans, Ushans agree upon a pointed ideology that presents an identifiable message: the intentions and perceptions of Israelites are primary in determining what is forbidden and permitted in the Sabbatical year. To understand how Ushans make this statement, let us first describe their larger theory of the restrictions of the Sabbatical year.

Ushans are concerned that the farmer not do field work that promotes the growth of produce in the seventh year. This means, on the one hand, that the farmer must be careful to avoid labors in the sixth year that prepare his field or trees for the crop of the Sabbatical year. On the other hand, since the Ushans are concerned only that the farmer not promote growth of the seventh year's crop, they do not entirely prohibit field activities during the Sabbatical year itself. The farmer may, that is, carry out work that maintains the land but does not directly promote the growth of the Sabbatical year's crop.

In light of this approach, the majority of the Ushan material addresses a narrow range of concerns. Ushans, first, define field labors that prepare the land for the following year's crop; these are prohibited in the sixth year. The second, most prominent element of the tractate concerns activities not intended to promote the growth of the Sabbatical year's crop, which therefore are permitted even in the seventh year itself. The problem is that, in carrying out such permitted activities, the farmer appears to transgress. Presumably building upon the Shammaites' notion that people are responsible to prevent others from breaking the law, Ushans insist that the permitted actions be carried out in a manner that assures that others will recognize that the individual is not transgressing. What matters is not the concrete character and purpose of an action but the perception of onlookers.

Much else in the tractate stands outside of the identifiable ideational structure just described. Yavneans and Ushans are clear that any growth of produce during the Sabbatical year is subject to the restrictions of that year (M. Sheb. 5:1, 3, 6:3, 4). This is the case even if the produce began to grow and ripen before the onset of the Sabbatical year or if it will not actually mature and be eaten until the seventh year has ended. Produce of the Sabbatical year must be used as food (M. Sheb. 7:3-4, 8:9-10), which assures that all of the people of Israel will be properly fed during the seventh year. The law of removal, which holds that, in the seventh year, food no longer found in the fields may not be stored in people's homes, receives attention in both periods (M. Sheb. 9:2-5, 8, 10:6, 7, 10:1, 2, 5, 8, 9). These discussions facilitate implementation of the Scriptural ordinances but do not present an identifiable ideology.

Conclusion

Certain ideas in this tractate derive from the period before 70. These include the concept of the prozbul and the idea of general importance, that people are responsible to prevent others from transgressing. The generative issue that accounts for the majority of these materials, however, is under dispute at Yavneh and is accepted as normative only in Usha. This idea, that the concrete effects of field labor are not the sole basis for determining its permissibility, parallels the generative idea of Tractate Kilaim. In both tractates, Israelites' perceptions and intentions serve as the standard by which conformity to God's law is determined. This point of view represents an important step beyond the Yavnean materials, which judge actions solely in light of their material consequences.

This shift in attitudes within the Mishnah is particularly important when we consider Scripture's priestly source, which holds that order is a precondition of holiness. This idea is developed in the priestly account at Gen. 1:1-2:4a, which depicts creation as "an act of ordering, the purpose of which is to make the world perfect and thus prepare it to be made holy."[15] The actual sanctity of the land

---

[15] Mandelbaum, *Kilaim*, p. 3.

of Israel depends upon God's designating it as holy. The Sabbath and, like it, the Sabbatical year are made holy by God's proclamation of the day of rest, which marks the completion of creation.

Compiled during and after the exile that followed the destruction of the first Temple, the priestly rules regarding Israelites' yearly planting of their fields and special use of the land during the seventh year demanded that Israelites "restore the world from its present condition of chaos to its original orderly state...so to make the world ready once again for sanctification."[16] This priestly view is parallel to that found in the Yavnean materials of Tractate Shebiit, which look for concrete indicators of what is right and wrong, holy and profane. Only in the Ushan period do we see an important step beyond the earlier picture: while Yavneans had Israelites adhere to a preordained order of creation, the later authorities regard Israelites, through their intentions and perceptions, as imposing order upon their world and so as actually participating in the processes of creation and sanctification. Thus, in the Ushan view, the sanctification of the Sabbatical year depends upon the Israelites themselves. They determine when in the sixth year the restrictions of the seventh begin to apply; through their intentions and perceptions they establish exactly what is permitted and forbidden during the holy time; and, in perhaps the tractate's most striking statement, an Ushan rule claims that the very sanctity of the land of Israel is in direct relation to the amount of time Israelites have dwelled upon it. In the view of Leviticus, the land is sanctified by God alone. In Tractate Shebiit, Israelites add to the holiness of the ground upon which they dwell—a striking idea given the physical devastation of that land in the period in which Ushans wrote.

Tractate Shebiit proclaims that the sanctity of the land of Israel and of the seventh year is activated and regulated by the intentions and actions of common Israelites. This same notion, we shall now see, is foremost in Tractate Terumot, which ascribes powers of sanctification to Israelites who set aside some of the produce of the land as the consecrated agricultural offerings ordained by Scripture.

---

[16] Ibid.

Tractate Terumot

A single fact about heave-offering interests the Mishnah's authorities and generates all of their discussions. This is that heave-offering is holy, as Num. 18:8, from which the concept of heave-offering is derived, makes clear. Heave-offering is the property of priests and may be eaten only by them and their families in a state of cultic purity, just as is the case for eating other holy offerings (Lev. 22:10-14).

With this much established, Tractate Terumot takes up a very specific line of questioning concerning how this gift to the priest comes to be holy. Most of the produce of the land may be eaten or otherwise used by anyone, without restriction. How does heave-offering come to be a consecrated offering? A related issue concerns the effect this holy produce has upon secular food with which it is mixed. Is the entire mixture now to be deemed holy? This issue is expanded to talk about other situations in which heave-offering is used as though it were secular, for instance, cases in which it is eaten by a non-priest. Finally, the tractate discusses the conditions under which heave-offering ceases to be holy, the end point of the process that began with its initial sanctification.

These issues are in place in Yavnean times. As we saw clearly in Tractates Kilaim and Shebiit, however, even as they continue along thematic lines established at Yavneh, Ushans incorporate their own, distinctive attitude. Thus the divergent legal perspectives held by Yavneans and Ushans, with which we have become familiar, inform as well the two major strata of Tractate Terumot. Yavneans again depict a pre-ordained order in the world. Through their actions, Israelites manipulate holiness in ways predictable on the model of a physical substance, with the Israelites' perceptions and intentions playing no role in determining what is or is not holy. Ushans, by contrast, see as central the people's desires and perceptions. These internal aspects of the Israelite's consciousness are envisioned to control holiness in ways that the Yavnean attention to physical transfer precludes.

In the Ushan understanding, the Israelite's will to consecrate food brings a status of sanctity upon that food, with physical actions being secondary. The attitude of the Israelite further determines the impact the consecrated offering has upon other produce with which it is mixed or cooked. This attitude, that is, not the physical character of the dish, takes precedence. Finally, the Israelite's own perception that food no longer is worthy of a status of consecration determines the point at which what was holy again is deemed secular. For Ushans, holiness thus is not transferred and maintained according to physical laws of exchange. Israelites, rather, bring a status of holiness upon certain produce and later remove that status according to their own will, without regard for the concrete acts of transfer deemed central to the preceding generation.

A. *Tractate Terumot before 70*

The Houses of Hillel and Shammai (M. Ter. 4:3) hold that the quantity of heave-offering to be separated from a batch of produce depends upon the temperament of the food's owner. As in the case of any charitable contribution, certain people are expected to be more generous than others. While this issue is basic to all consideration of the separation of agricultural gifts, it plays little role in the development of the law. Later authorities accept the quantity indicated by the Hillelites as average, one fiftieth of the crop. At the same time, later rabbis legislate that the actual separation must be carried out through an estimation, not an exact measurement, of the quantity of produce being taken as heave-offering. The Houses' discussion has little weight in later deliberations.

B. *Tractate Terumot in the Time of Yavneh*

Recognizing that heave-offering is a consecrated offering comparable to animal sacrifices offered and eaten in the Temple, Yavneans want to know how produce an Israelite sets aside becomes holy, and they further question what happens when that holy produce comes into contact with objects and foods within the secular world. Yavneans thereby develop a complete picture of the processes of sanctification and desanctification. Indeed, the Yavnean understanding of why produce comes to be holy underlies all of the Division of Agriculture. Since God provides the land upon which Israelites grow food, a share of the crops must be paid to God's representatives. For Yavneans, the physical act of separating heave-offering determines what produce will comprises this share. Like all that belongs to God, it henceforth is deemed holy and may be eaten, in the case of heave-offering, only by a priest. Since God's lien upon the batch has now been paid, the remainder of the produce now may be eaten by anybody.[17]

Particular to the Yavnean perspective is the notion that God's share of produce is separated from the crop and maintained in the Israelite's possession through physical actions. Yavneans view each separate batch of produce as a distinct entity from which God's share must be paid: the householder's actions in separating heave-offering from one batch have no physical effect upon another batch and so leave that other batch in an untithed state (M. Ter. 1:5). Only if all of the produce is the same may the Israelite place several batches together to create a single entity and separate heave-offering from all of the produce at once. The same notion presumably underlies the Yavnean idea (M. Ter. 4:5) that an entire batch cannot be designated heave-offering. Such a designation would not physically distinguish the offering from the Israelite's food. Leaving the batch physically unchanged, this approach is invalid.

If a large quantity of heave-offering is mixed with unconsecrated food, the whole mixture needs to be treated as heave-offering. But if a small amount of heave-offering is mixed with much unconsecrated food, the holy produce is understood to be so thinly distributed as to take on the character of the unconsecrated food with which it is mixed. All of this produce may be eaten by a non-priest. Notably, while Yavneans apply this rule only if there is a physical mixing of the priestly gift and other produce, Ushans will apply the law of neutralization in a much wider range of cases, including those in which heave-offering is not physically mixed with common food.

Heave-offering planted as seed yields a crop in the status of heave-offering (M. Ter. 9:4), since the crop is a physical extension of the original seed. But Yavneans are not concerned that heave-offering be cooked or otherwise prepared with secular food (M. Ter. 10:11E-H). If the heave-offering remains distinct and can be removed from

---

[17] Deeply concerned with the designation of produce as heave-offering, the Mishnah shows no comparable interest in the actual payment of the offering to a priest. This presumably is because the rules for turning the offering over to the priest would not provide an opportunity to discuss specific concerns regarding sanctification. This suggests the extent to which the Division of Agriculture is not simply or primarily intended to facilitate the actual observance of tithing regulations. Rather, it is a context in which the Mishnah's authorities explore their own particular interests and concerns.

the dish, it has no effect upon the produce with which it was cooked. We disregard the flavor it leaves as intangible.

In the one Yavnean discussion that will be developed in concrete ways at Usha, Eliezer and Joshua dispute the role played by the perceptions and intentions of common Israelites in determining culpability for wrong actions and the validity of right ones. Eliezer holds that the agricultural laws operate mechanically. Thus an individual's intention in performing a deed are of no concern. It is immaterial, for instance, that an individual who turns out not to be a priest ate heave-offering under the conception that he is a priest (M. Ter. 8:1-3). Objectively, what the individual did was prohibited, and so he is culpable. Joshua, by contrast, holds that an individual is culpable only if he could have known that his actions are prohibited. If he eats heave-offering under the life-long assumption that he is a priest and only afterwards turns not to be, he is not liable. This notion, that the privileges and restrictions of the agricultural system are activated by the intentions and perceptions of Israelites, forms the foundation of the Ushan stratum in this tractate and, as we have seen, of Tractates Kilaim and Shebiit. To that stratum we now turn.

C. *Tractate Terumot in the Time of Usha*

The Ushan contribution to this tractate is to read together the Yavnean picture of the processes of sanctification with Joshua's view concerning the primacy of the intentions and perceptions of Israelites. Ushans, that is to say, no longer view holiness in physical terms, claiming that it is manipulated only through physical acts of transfer. They understand holiness, rather, to be a function of the desires and perceptions of the Israelite householder who separates the priestly gift, protects it in his secular domain, and ultimately turns it over to a priest. Through these intentions and perceptions, Ushans hold, the Israelite controls what will be holy, determines the proper conditions under which sanctified produce must be maintained, and, finally, establishes the circumstances under which the produce ceases to be holy. In this Ushan approach, physical actions are secondary to the Israelite's will. Holiness for Ushans functions as a reflex of the desires and attitudes of common Israelites, not as a result of the physical processes and established procedures through which food is set aside for a priest.

The Ushan ideology is first expressed in the notion of how produce comes to have the status of heave-offering. This, Ushans say, depends upon more than the actions of an Israelite who sets apart some produce from the rest of the batch (M. Ter. 1:1). Validly to separate heave-offering, the Israelite must formulate the intention to render that which he separates holy (people not deemed to have powers of intention accordingly are excluded from separating this offering). In a common Ushan idea, the individual's intention becomes efficacious through an oral declaration expressing his plan (M. Ter. 3:5, 8). The net result of the Ushan picture is that, through thought, word, and, only at the end, deed, the Israelite determines which produce and how much of it is holy.

This primacy of intention is apparent in the Ushan approach to the separation of heave-offering from one batch on behalf of a different one, which Yavneans disallow. Ushans disregard the physical problem: if the householder designates and separates the heave-offering with proper intention, his actions are valid, even if they are objectively inappropriate (M. Ter. 2:1, 2, 4, 3:3-4). The same idea appears in the Ushan discussion of the laws for a non-priest who eats produce that might be heave-offering (M. Ter. 7:5-7). If one of two batches contains heave-offering, but it is not known which, an individual who eats one of them simply declares that the other batch contains the priestly gift. Someone who subsequently eats the other batch may make the same claim, and he too is not culpable. Ushans disregard the indisputable fact that someone has eaten heave-offering. The perception of each individual not to have done so determines his lack of culpability.

Yavneans hold that a farmer who sows heave-offering as seed must cultivate the crop and, when it ripens, sell it to a priest for the low value of heave-offering. Ushans, by contrast, are concerned with the farmer's intentions. The Yavnean approach applies only if he acted intentionally. But if he did not know he planted heave-offering, he is not culpable. He may plow up the field and avoid growing a crop that is heave-offering. He avoids making personal use of what he now knows is heave-offering but, at the same time, does not suffer any additional financial loss.

Ushans hold that heave-offering imparts its own status to unconsecrated food to which it imparts flavor. This is because, in such a case, even if the Israelite is able to remove the consecrated produce from the dish, he still benefits from its taste (M. Ter. 10:1, 3, 8, 11A-D; see also 11:4-8). Judah carries this idea to its logical conclusion. If the householder does not desire the flavor the heave-offering imparts, the unconsecrated food is unaffected. The impact of the heave-offering is determined by Israelites' likes and dislikes.

In all, the Yavnean picture of sanctification's being manipulated only through physical separation and exchange gives way in the Ushan period to a highly metaphysical understanding of holiness. In this understanding, sanctification revolves around Israelites. Their intentions determine what is to become heave-offering; their perceptions assure that the offering is not misplaced or destroyed through sacrilege; and common Israelites' attitudes towards heave-offering determine when the sanctified produce has become secular, such that it may be consumed by anyone. Through these ideas Ushans broadly reinterpret the Yavnean material and present the theory of sanctification that comprises the focus of this tractate as a whole.

Conclusion

The topics and organization of the tractate reveal the point that its framers wish to make. These topics are, first, the role of the Israelite in the designation and separation of heave-offering; second, his responsibility to maintain the priestly gift in conditions of sanctity; and, third, the part he plays in the determination of when heave-offering loses its status of consecration and may be consumed by non-priests. The tractate as a whole thus focuses upon common Israelites and their role in the processes of sanctification. While this concern is established by Yavneans, only in the Ushan period does the perspective distinctive to Mishnaic legislation emerge. Based upon the Yavnean minority opinion of Joshua, Ushans rule that in all aspects of the processes of sanctification, the intentions and desires of Israelites are central. At each point these determine the status of sanctification of produce set aside as the priest's share. The tractate as a whole thus comes to argue that common Israelites exercise powers of sanctification previously believed to be found solely in the hands of the priests. In the Division of Agriculture, common Israelites are described as bringing God's holiness into the world, assuring that it is properly maintained and, ultimately, determining the point at which it ceases to have a sanctified status.

Tractate Maaserot

Tractate Maaserot defines the class of produce subject to the separation of agricultural offerings and indicates when payment of those offerings must be made. It asks 1) when, in the course of a crop's growth and ripening, tithes *may* validly be separated and questions 2) when, in the subsequent harvesting and preparation of the produce, heave-offering and tithes *must be* paid.[18]

The Mishnah's answer to these questions reflects the understanding that Israelites owe agricultural offerings as payment for the use God grants them of the land of Israel. In light of this idea, the tractate points out that God is owed a share only once the produce actually has ripened and become useful as food. When the crop ripens, God's role in its production is complete, so that the obligation to pay the required tithes is incurred. While Israelites *may* now separate tithes, they need not do so, however, until they actually take the food for their own personal use, either to sell in the market or to prepare as a meal. God's absolute claim for a share of the crop, that is, is a reflex of the Israelites' exercising of their final claim to use the produce as their own.

The idea that the requirement to tithe depends upon the Israelites' desire for food is found primarily in the tractate's Ushan stratum, which comprises all but four of its rules. Ushans hold that, if an individual does not clearly intend food that he eats to constitute a meal, then no matter how much he actually consumes, he need not tithe. Conversely, whenever someone takes food for a meal, he must tithe, even if the food has not reached a state in its processing at which it normally is eaten. The individual's use of the food, rather than its physical condition, determine its status.

While Yavneans know that food must be tithed before it is used in a meal, they take no account of unusual or extenuating circumstances, instead stating simply that produce must be tithed when the individual brings it home, since that is where he normally eats his meals. This leads only to a minor ambiguity in the law, concerning whether or not courtyards are comparable to a home.

The distinctive attitude that underlies the Ushan approach to the law is familiar from the Ushan strata of the tractates already dis-

---

[18] See Martin Jaffee, *Mishnah's Theology of Tithing: A Study of Tractate Maaserot* (Chico, 1981), p. 1.

cussed. For the case of Tractate Maaserot, it is described by Jaffee:[19]

> What is striking in all of this is that the entire mechanism of restrictions and privileges, from the field to home or market, is set in motion solely by the intentions of the common farmer. Priests cannot claim their dues whenever they choose, and God himself plays no active role in establishing when the produce must be tithed. Indeed, the framers of Maaserot assume a profound passivity on the part of God. For them, it is human actions and intentions which move God to affect the world. God's claims against the Land's produce, that is to say, are only reflexes of those very claims on the part of Israelite farmers. God's interest in his share of the harvest, as I said, is first provoked by the desire of the farmer for the ripened fruit of his labor. His claim to that fruit, furthermore, becomes binding only when the farmer makes ready to claim his own rights to its use, whether in the field or at home or market.

A. *Tractate Maaserot before 70*

The tractate's one dispute attributed to the period before 70, M. Ma. 4:2, appears to be pseudepigraphic, for it depends upon the Ushan idea that once produce is designated for a meal it must be tithed (M. Ma. 4:3). The specific problem addressed by the Houses is a subtle development of that idea, concerning whether the intention to use produce in a meal has a generalized effect upon the produce or whether it applies to the specified meal alone.

B. *Maaserot in the Time of Yavneh*

While comprised of only four pericopae, the Yavnean material presents the tractate's underlying idea, that produce must be tithed to be used in a meal. Yavneans develop this notion in only a minor way. They assume that produce normally will be tithed when it is brought into the individual's home, where he has his meals, and they ask whether or not a courtyard is comparable to a home (M. Ma. 3:5A-D, 3:9). Yavneans answer that this depends upon whether or not the courtyard offers protection and privacy such as a home provides. Ushans will develop this issue to state that all depends upon the householder's own feelings about the courtyard.

The two other Yavnean pericopae make minor points. A seed-

---

[19] Ibid., pp. 4-5.

crop is not subject to tithes at all, since it is not eaten, M. Ma. 4:5E-H. Yavneans dispute how foods that must be tithed are defined, M. Ma. 4:6. One side holds that we take into account only the fact of the item's edibility: anything that can be eaten must be tithed. The opposing view follows communal behavior: only things that people normally eat are tithed. Ushans, M. Ma. 1:1, deem the latter view normative. Rather than botanical characteristics, the Israelite's attitude determines what is or is not a food.

C. *Tractate Maaserot in the Time of Usha*

Ushans hold that the requirement to tithe is activated through the desires and perceptions of the Israelite who readies produce for use in a meal. This is expressed in the rule that, to be subject to tithes at all, produce must not only be edible but must be cultivated purposely by Israelites for use as food and must be privately owned (M. Ma.1:1, 2-3, 4). Only food that in these ways is subject to the desires of Israelites enters the system of tithes.

With this much established, Ushans, like Yavneans, want to know when produce that is subject to tithes *must* be tithed. In the Yavnean stratum, the single consideration for determining liability to tithes is that the individual has brought the produce home. Ushans greatly expand this discussion, reviewing other cases in which it is clear that the individual considers the food ready for use in a meal. Meir, for instance, holds that a sale renders the produce subject to tithes; the new owner has, in a formal way, acquired the produce as his own (M. Ma. 2:1, 2, 5, 8D-J). Ushans further apply here a principle familiar from the designation of agricultural gifts, in which physical actions indicate the individual's intentions. They hold that in the case of the liability to tithe as well we judge what the Israelite is thinking by the way he handles the produce. If he snacks on unprocessed food—an act not normally subject to tithes—in a way that prevents him from returning the surplus to the processing vat, we can be certain that he views what he has taken as a little meal unto itself, and he must tithe (M. Ma. 2:4).

Two other rules highlight the centrality of the Israelite's attitudes. A traveler's home is a place in which he feels at ease, as he would in his own house. This is known, for instance, by the fact that he prepares to spend the Sabbath there (M. Ma. 2:3). Similarly, Ushans carry forward the Yavnean discussion of the status of a courtyard (M. Ma. 3:5E-I, 7). But unlike Yavneans, who are concerned with the courtyard's function, Ushans examine the individual's attitude towards it, treating it as a home only if he feels as comfortable in it as he does in his own house.

Conclusion

Systematic exposition of this tractate's foundational idea comes in the Ushan period, when a full list of the classes of produce subject to tithes and the conditions under which agricultural taxes must be separated is developed. The point ultimately made by the tractate as a whole is also Ushan: God's claim for portions of the produce of the land of Israel is effective only upon food that Israelites purposely cultivate and then take for their own use in the meals that provide their sustenance. The Israelites' exploitation of the land for the production of food, that is to say, brings with it the obligation to set aside agricultural dues, which recognize God's role in the growing of crops. Food that grows without the intervention of Israelites or that Israelites do not desire for a meal is exempt from God's claim, the individual essentially not having appropriated for himself God's blessings.

When we recall Mishnah Terumot's understanding of the role of the Israelite in the processes of sanctification, we see how that tractate along with this one create a unitary picture. Tractate Terumot depicts the pivotal role of the Israelite in the consecration of a specific quantity of produce. Tractate Maaserot enhances this picture by stating firmly that, just as Israelites control what will and will not be holy, so their own desire for produce and their intention in growing and processing crops determine what food is in the first place subject to sanctification. A food's being subject to the Israelite's will is a precondition of holiness, Tractate Maaserot tells us. The logical counterpart to that idea is Tractate Terumot's claim that, through the application of their intention, Israelites designate part of the crop as holy. Israelites' intentions and desires thus account for all aspects of the system of sanctification described in the Division of Agriculture. God, to be sure, is the ultimate source of holiness. Only what is owned by or dedicated to him can, in the first place, take on a status of sanctification. The fundamental theological datum of this division, however, is that, in actually establishing what is consecrated and what is secular, God acts and wills only in response to the intentions of common Israelites.

Tractate Maaser Sheni

Second tithe is separated from the crop and carried to Jerusalem to be eaten "before the Lord," so that Israelites will "learn to fear the Lord your God always" (Deut. 14:23). The Mishnah's interest in this offering parallels the long middle section of Tractate Terumot, concerning Israelites' responsibility to maintain consecrated produce in their secular domain before it actually is eaten. Indeed, the topic of second tithe allows analysis of the handling of holy food from a distinctive angle. A person who lives far from Jerusalem may sell second tithe (Deut. 14:24-25). The money he receives takes on the consecrated status of the original produce and is carried to Jerusalem and used there to purchase food, eaten in place of the original. Exposition of this topic gives the Mishnah's authorities the opportunity to stipulate the powers of the Israelite who transfers the status of holiness from one object to another, desanctifying the first and sanctifying the second in its place.

As we have come to expect, Maaser Sheni's distinctive point is found in its Ushan materials, which comprise almost all of the tractate's long middle section. Repeating ideas known from Tractate Terumot, Ushans state that the designation of produce or other objects to be holy depends upon the Israelite's intentional declaration that he deems them to be sanctified. In the Ushan view, the validity of the transfer of the status of second tithe from produce to coins and back does not depend upon a physical act of sale or exchange. The transfer depends, rather, upon the designation of the Israelite, who indicates what object, food, or money he intends to be holy.

This is not to say that the Israelite's ability to impose a status of sanctification has no limits. As we know from Tractate Maaserot, only produce grown through the partnership between God and Israel is subject to sanctification in the first place. Yet just as in Tractate Maaserot the conditions that allow for sanctification depend upon the Israelite's own actions and desires, so in Tractate Maaser Sheni, the limits of the individual's ability to impose a status of sanctification revolve around his own perceptions and hopes. Israelites determine exactly what can and should be holy and, in the case of second tithe, establish the monetary value of holy food. The tractate thus deepens the points made by Tractates Terumot and Maaserot, teaching that nothing is intrinsically holy and that the worth of objects deemed holy is a reflex of the Israelite marketplace. Israelites, not God, have full control over the process of sanctification. The possibility of sanctification is contingent upon the existence of God; but holiness does not exist as a transcendent and ongoing quality in the world. Its presence, rather, is a function of the actions and desires of Israelites.

A. *Tractate Maaser Sheni before 70*

The Houses argue a major point of the tractate, M. M.S. 2:7, 8A-C, and 9F-H, disputing whether coins used in the purchase of second tithe are actually sanctified with the status of that offering or whether they simply represent the value of the consecrated produce. The Hillelites take the latter view. If second-tithe and regular coins are mixed together, the householder simply collects a value in coins equal to the second tithe-money that was lost. He need not worry that he has the original coins. This view dominates in the material before us (M. M.S. 2:5, 8D-E, 9I-L).

Other issues attributed to the Houses cannot be firmly verified to the period before 70 and do not play roles in the unfolding of the Mishnah's law. The Houses argue whether produce that can be used either as food for humans or as animal fodder is treated as an edible, subject to the rules of uncleanness and the separation of tithes (M. M.S. 2:3B-D, 4F-J). Later authorities assume that, if known, the owner's intention regarding use of the produce determines its status. The Houses dispute whether or not produce of the fourth year of growth of a vineyard is in all respects comparable to second tithe (M. M.S. 5:3) and whether or not agricultural gifts that have been cooked are subject to removal (M. M.S. 5:6H-J). The list of ordinances attributed to Yohanan the High Priest does not concern matters referred to elsewhere in the Mishnah, such that its origin in Second Temple times cannot be evaluated through an analysis of the logical unfolding of the law.[20]

---

[20] Cf., Aharon Oppenheimer, *The Am Ha-Aretz* (Leiden, 1977), pp. 34-35, and Saul Lieberman, *Hellenism in Jewish Palestine* (New York, 1950), pp. 139-143.

B. *Maaser Sheni in the Time of Yavneh*

The Yavneans' central concern is that the full value of produce designated second tithe is transferred to the money for which it is sold and that, later, when food is purchased in place of the original tithe, the full value again is received. In a sale, therefore, the individual must accept only proper coins (M. M.S. 1:2G) and the purchase of non-food items does not transfer to those items the status of consecration held by the coins (M. M.S. 1:5A-C, 2:3A, 4A-E). While in line with the general Yavnean picture of the processes of sanctification, these rules are quite different from Ushan ones, which hold that anything an Israelite intentionally purchases with consecrated coins takes on the money's status of sanctification.

Aqiba introduces a point assumed throughout the Division of Agriculture. At the time of removal, one need not separate and remove heave-offering and tithes from produce that only later will become subject to those offerings. Aqiba thus holds that offerings are in no physical sense present in produce that is not yet subject to their separation (M. M.S. 5:8). This view is in line with the understanding of Tractate Maaserot that agricultural gifts are not separated from produce that is not yet processed and ready for consumption.

A final Yavnean pericope introduces another important idea. One who, at the time of removal, cannot physically distribute agricultural gifts he has gathered may make an oral declaration designating those gifts for their rightful recipients (M. M.S. 5:9). Yavneans thus initiate for this special case a mode of designating heave-offering and tithes that, in Ushan times, becomes commonplace. Such designations are accepted by Ushans for use in the separation of heave-offering (M. Ter. 3:5) and for accounting for agricultural gifts that may not have been separated from doubtfully tithed produce (M. Dem. 5:1, 2).

C. *Tractate Maaser Sheni in the Time of Usha*

The Ushans' development of Yavnean ideas is by now predictable. They hold that, as in the designation of heave-offering, proper intention is central in the designation of second tithe and determines whether or not produce purchased with second tithe-coins actually takes on the status of second tithe (M. M.S. 1:3, 4, 5D-E, 6, 7, 3:12,

13). Contrary to Yavneans, Ushans hold that, when purchased intentionally, even non-edibles take on the status of this tithe. They further hold that a householder's intention to consecrate something as second tithe is effective even in a case in which an actual exchange of produce and coins does not occur (M. M.S. 2:10, 3:3, 4).

Like other consecrated offerings, that which has the status of second tithe must be put to its normal use (M. M.S. 2:1A-H, 2A-F). This assures that normally eaten produce does not go to waste. Yet, as in Tractate Terumot, Ushans here are clear that sanctified produce or coins of insignificant value lose their status of consecration and may be put to secular use (see M. Ter. 4:8G-I). An object's value to Israelites determines whether or not it retains a consecrated status.

The tractate's long middle section parallels the chief Ushan concern of Tractate Terumot for the time during which sanctified produce is in Israelite hands, such that it might be misused. One who finds produce of uncertain status treats it as consecrated only if he has good reason to believe it is in fact holy (so Yose, M. M.S. 4:11, and the anonymous rule at M. M.S. 4:9 against Judah, M. M.S. 4:10, 12). So long as there are any grounds for claiming what he has found is not sanctified, it may be treated as secular. The familiar point is that the objective status of the produce is of no real weight. What matters, rather, is the attitude of the Israelite who finds it. This same approach controls the value at which produce in the status of second tithe is bought and sold (M. M.S. 4-1, 2, 6, 8A-F): the market at the time and place of the sale prevails. The value of sanctified produce is determined by what an Israelite would pay for it at any given moment if it were secular food.

Conclusion

Tractate Maaser Sheni explains how a status of holiness is transferred to and from objects in the secular world. Its point is that these processes depend upon the attitudes of Israelites and the everyday workings of the Israelite economic system. The factors of supply and demand determine the value of consecrated produce. Normal procedures used in all sales establish who has purchased—and therefore deconsecrated—produce in the status of second tithe. In Jerusalem, these same procedures apply to the purchase of produce to be eaten in conditions of holiness. The processes of sanctification thus are under Israelite control and correspond to the Israelite community's own, secular, economic system. Holiness is not conceived as a power that transcends the common Israelite's control. While what is holy is set apart and subject to special treatment, still, it comes into existence and is maintained as an ordinary commodity within Israelite economic life. Holiness functions within the Israelite world like all other commodities produced upon the land of Israel, traded in the Israelite marketplace, and eaten on the Israelite table.

Only in one respect do food or coins in the status of second tithe differ from other market-goods. The difference is the requirement that, in trading or selling that which is holy, the Israelite recognize that he is engaged in a sacred act. He does this by formulating the intention to deconsecrate one object and to impart a status of sanctification to another. This requirement, familiar from Tractates Terumot and Maaserot, highlights the distinctive perspective that the Division of Agriculture brings to its description of the source and nature of holiness. The possibility of sanctification ultimately depends upon the presence of God. The deepest message of the Mishnah, however, is that God acts only in response to the Israelite's specific desires and actions. The potential for sanctification is, in the first place, a response to the Israelite's desire to use the produce of the land of Israel. The designation of specific food to be holy, further, is in the hands of the individual Israelite who, through his actions and intentions, determines all aspects of the processes of sanctification and desanctification.

Tractate Hallah

Israelites living in the land of Israel must separate from dough they prepare an offering to the Lord (Num. 15:17-21). The Mishnah's interest in this agricultural gift parallels its concern in Tractate Maaserot for the conditions under which dough is subject to the separation of dough offering. The answers the tractate proposes likewise are familiar. Yavneans argue that liability depends solely upon the class of grain from which the dough is made. If it is made from grain that normally becomes leavened, dough offering must be separated. While not rejecting the Yavnean idea, Ushans add their usual perspective: in cases of ambiguity or doubt, the Israelite's own perception of the dough determines whether or not it is subject to dough offering. Thus the ideas presented here by both Yavneans and Ushans correspond closely with their generation's perspectives elsewhere in the Division of Agriculture.

A. *Tractate Hallah before 70*

The one dispute attributed to the Houses shows evidence of being a late creation (M. Hal. 1:6A-F). The issue concerns whether or not the batter used in making certain types of dumplings is subject to dough offering. The dispute assumes the Yavnean or post-Yavnean notion that all grains prepared like bread-dough are subject to this offering, regardless of the purpose to which the dough ultimately will be put (see M. Hal. 1:5, 7, and 6G-I).[21] This being the case, there is no evidence that work on the topic of dough offering began before Yavnean times.

B. *Tractate Hallah in the Time of Yavneh*

The tractate's central Yavnean idea is that any grain that becomes leavened is subject to dough offering, without regard for the intentions and perceptions of the Israelite who produces it. Liability to dough offering thus begins at the point at which a grain that leavens is made into dough, and it continues even if the dough ultimately is used for some purpose other than the baking of bread (M. Hal. 1:1, 5, 7). Dough is subject to dough offering even if it is not in the class of produce subject to other agricultural tithes or if it is in the status of a different agricultural gift (M. Hal. 1:3). All that matters to Yavneans is that grain is made into dough. They exempt from the offering only very small quantities of dough, which never are made into bread (M. Hal. 2:3, 6). Unlike Ushans, who in other contexts hold that such exemption depends upon an Israelite's perception that the produce is insignificant (see, e.g., M. Ter. 11:4-8), Yavnean apply this principle without regard to the Israelite baker's purpose or sense of the usefulness of the particular batch of dough.

---

[21] See Abraham Havivi in Jacob Neusner, *Judaism: The Evidence of the Mishnah* (Chicago, 1981), p. 299.

C. *Tractate Hallah in the Time of Usha*

The tractate's few Ushan rules repeat ideas familiar from elsewhere in the division: at each point in the designation and separation of dough offering, the effects of the Israelite's actions are judged in light of his intentions and perceptions. This is stated in general terms by the rule that dough offering, which is designated for the exclusive use of the priest, is treated according to the same rules that apply to heave-offering (M. Hal. 1:9). Other rules make the same point. In cases of ambiguity, for instance, only dough that the Israelite deems edible is subject to dough offering (M. Hal. 1:8). In the same way, dough made from a mixture of leavened and non-leavened grains is subject only if it tastes like dough made from grains that normally are subject to the offering (M. Hal. 3:7, 10). The concern is not the actual edibility of the dough or the fact that it contains grains that are subject. Liability to dough offering, rather, like liability to the other agricultural gifts, occurs only in response to the perceptions of common Israelites.

Normally, agricultural gifts may be given only to priests known to eat their foods in conditions of cleanness. Ushans rule that this does not apply to offerings separated from produce that might not have been subject to those particular gifts in the first place (M. Hal. 4:9). Since these offerings might not have a sanctified status, Ushans are not concerned that they are consumed by priests who are not careful to eat food under conditions of cultic purity.

Conclusion

Yavnean materials here repeat the common Yavnean perspective: liability of produce to agricultural gifts is determined on the basis of the botanical classification of the grain and in light of the physical actions of the Israelite who handles it. To the extent that these Yavnean materials set the tractate's issues and provide the bulk of its assigned traditions,[22] this tractate, more than any other in the Division of Agriculture, must be deemed a Yavnean creation.

While it is unclear why Ushans had so little to offer here, what

---

[22] Eleven of the tractate's thirty-seven entries (29%) are attributed to Yavneans, compared to only five (13%) bearing Ushan names. Ten of the twenty anonymous rules appear to be Yavnean. Only six are clearly Ushan.

they do say expresses ideas familiar from Ushan materials throughout the Division of Agriculture. The householder's own perspective determines what batch of dough is subject to dough offering and his intentions in separating the offering define whether or not the separation is valid. The tractate's anonymous rules also repeat ideas commonly found in the mouths of Ushans, that, in cases of doubt, the perceptions and intentions of Israelites must be taken into account. This Ushan point, derived directly from Tractates Maaserot and Terumot, suggests again that Israelites' desire for the produce of the land determines the liability of that produce to agricultural offerings. God demands a share only as a reflex of the Israelites' desire to use the produce of the land of Israel. While God is the ultimate source of holiness, specific portions of produce become susceptible to sanctification and are actually sanctified only through the actions and intentions of Israelites.

Tractate Orlah

Lev. 19:23 states: "When you come into the land and plant all kinds of trees for food, then you shall count their fruit as forbidden; three years it shall be forbidden to you, it must not be eaten." Tractate Orlah 1) clarifies what are to be classified as fruit trees, 2) defines what produce of such trees comprises their fruit, and 3) indicates whether or not an old tree that is uprooted and replanted is deemed a new growth, so as again to be subject to the three-year restriction. Finally, 4) several rules discuss neutralization and the loss of the forbidden status of Orlah-produce.

Yavnean and Ushan deliberations on these topics reflect the legal perspectives common in these periods. The few Yavnean rules concern the botanical characteristics of the tree and its produce. Since a tree that is uprooted and replanted begins to grow anew, Yavneans deem it again subject to the restriction of Orlah. This is the case unless a root remained in the ground while the tree was being transplanted. Yavneans thus disregard the Israelite's perception to be planting the tree as a new growth or simply to be moving an old tree. Ushans, by contrast, judge matters in light of the intentions of the Israelite. Thus they hold that only a tree planted purposely for its fruit is subject to the restriction of Orlah. If the tree is planted for lumber or as a fence, it is not classified as a fruit tree at all. Even in its first years of growth an Israelite may eat its produce.

If the particular laws presented here are not surprising, viewed as a whole, the tractate is note-worthy. Concerned with basic matters of definition, its rules lack a single, generative issue such as characterizes other tractates in the Division of Agriculture. Furthermore, rules on the topic of Orlah comprise no more than half the tractate's laws. The rest discuss tangentially related matters, concerning the status of mixtures of forbidden and permitted produce. Yet even the question of what determines the status of a mixture is not answered in the materials before us. It therefore is impossible to locate an overriding point of the tractate as a whole. Unlike the other tractates in this division, Tractate Orlah lacks an identifiable problematic or even a single topical theme.[23] This is a set of loosely connected chapters on tangentially related topics, only in part discussing the very area of law that, in the first place, called for their compilation.

A. *Tractate Orlah before 70*

The one dispute attributed to the Houses makes use of ideas known, in Tractate Terumot, to derive only from the period of Usha. These concern whether or not forbidden produce that leavens or flavors permitted produce renders that permitted produce forbidden for consumption (M. Or. 2:4-7). In light of its dependence upon late ideas, the dispute cannot be authentic to the early period.

B. *Tractate Orlah in the Time of Yavneh*

Yavneans define a new tree, subject to the restrictions of Orlah, as any tree that has been newly planted. Thus an old tree that is completely uprooted and replanted again becomes subject to these restrictions (M. Or. 1:4). Eliezer and Joshua dispute whether the restrictions of Orlah apply to all edible products of a tree or only to the primary fruit (M. Or. 1:7). Eliezer follows the view commonly found in his name. He takes no account of the Israelite's attitude

---

[23] See Howard Essner, "Mishnah Tractate 'Orlah," in W.S. Green, ed., *Approaches to Ancient Judaism* (Chico, 1981), p. 105.

but, instead, deems all of the tree's edible products to be forbidden. Joshua, as elsewhere, takes into account the Israelite's perspective, and he therefore exempts a tree's secondary products from the restrictions of Orlah. Ushans, as we shall see, accept Joshua's view and develop it to its most striking conclusion.

One Yavnean item, unrelated to the specific topic of this tractate, forms the basis for an extended Ushan discussion of mixtures of more than one type of forbidden produce in a large quantity of permitted food. The specific Yavnean issue remains moot at Usha. This concerns whether or not we attribute dough's being leavened to heave-offering even if unconsecrated leaven may in fact have acted upon the dough (M. Or. 2:11-12, 13).

C. *Tractate Orlah in the Time of Usha*

While following the Yavnean's basic theory of what constitutes a new tree, Ushans add their own, distinctive perspective. They define a fruit tree, subject to the restrictions of Orlah, as a tree that Israelites purposely plant in order to use its fruit. A tree planted for lumber or as a fence is exempt, even if it does, incidentally, produce fruit (M. Or. 1:1). In such a case, Israelites may even eat the fruit of that tree during its first three years of growth. In the Ushan view, the tree's classification and status are not determined by botanical genus but by the use to which Israelites put it.

Ushans are clear that, like heave-offering, Orlah-produce that is mixed with unconsecrated food loses its forbidden status. The mixture as a whole then may be consumed (M. Or. 1:6). Yet here again the perceptions of the Israelite are central. Meir, for instance, holds that Orlah-produce already subject to processing by an Israelite no longer is rendered permitted through neutralization (M. Or. .3:1-2, 6-8). Having come under the Israelite's careful attention and desires, the produce has irrevocable value. It never may be deemed an insignificant portion of the mixture and, therefore, is not subject to neutralization.

The discussion of neutralization accounts for the appearance here of other materials concerning mixtures of two or more types of forbidden produce and permitted food. As in the Yavnean stratum, the question of the status of the three-part mixture remains moot (M. Or. 2:10, 14, 15-16). Ushans clarify only one situation. If heave-offering leaven and unconsecrated leaven are mixed with unconsecrated dough, the dough's rising is attributed to the heave-offering (M. Or. 2:8), and it becomes forbidden for consumption by non-priests. Ushans dispute whether or not this is the case if it can be proven that only the unconsecrated leaven accounts for the dough's rising (M. Or. 2:9). In these cases the theory that in matters of doubt we avoid an impairment of status (see, e.g., M. Ter. 7:5-7) is not applied.

Conclusion

While lacking a single sustained topic, Tractate Orlah has a unifying theme that deserves recognition. This concerns the classification of ambiguous objects that fall into two or more different legal categories. More than anything else, the tractate's materials concern how to determine the status of something that is equally like two different things. The old tree that is uprooted and replanted and products of a tree that may or may not called its fruit are classic examples of objects that elude clear-cut classification. This concern for ambiguous cases is highlighted in the long section of the tractate concerning mixtures. In consistently turning to such gray areas in the law, Tractate Orlah fits firmly within the larger program of inquiry that characterizes the Division of Agriculture and the Mishnah as a whole.[24] Thus, while Tractate Orlah's lack of a single program of inquiry regarding its topic is unusual, that which it has to say about the various issues it raises is fully in line with what we have come to expect within the Division of Agriculture as a whole.

Tractate Bikkurim

The tractate's first unit lists the prerequisites for separating first fruits and reciting the confession required by Deut. 26:1-11. The third unit's narrative describes the actual procedures through which this offering is designated, separated, and carried to the Jerusalem Temple, where it is presented to the priests. Constructed almost exclusively of Ushan materials, these units supply all the Israelite needs to know in order to designate and dispose of first fruits. Concerned primarily with the mechanics of this operation, they discuss few of

---

[24] See on this Neusner, *Judaism*, pp. 256-270.

the theoretical issues familiar from the rest of the division. While the Mishnah's authorities deemed it important to discuss this Scriptural offering, they did not identify an agendum of issues deeper than the surface question of what the Israelite must do to fulfill the requirement described in Scripture.

The tractate's middle unit compares the rules that apply to each of the several agricultural offerings referred to in the Division of Agriculture. While unrelated to the specific topic of first fruits, this material comprises a fitting conclusion to and summary of this division as a whole. It is unclear why it has been redacted between the tractate's two units on the laws of first fruits instead of in the more apt position at the end of the tractate and Mishnaic division.

A. *Tractate Bikkurim before 70*

The tractate contains no materials assigned to authorities who lived before 70.

B. *Tractate Bikkurim in the Time of Yavneh*

Yavneans refer to three areas of concern, leaving it to Ushans to provide a larger framework within which the laws of first fruits are systematically expounded. Basing their considerations upon Scripture, Yavneans establish when in the agricultural year the Israelite may bring first fruits and recite the accompanying confession (M. Bik. 1:3, 6). They dispute whether or not Trans-Jordan was part of God's gift of land to the Israelites, such that first fruits may be brought from there (M. Bik. 1:10). Finally, they ask whether or not the decorations with which farmers adorn the baskets of first fruits are comparable in status to the first fruits themselves (M. Bik. 3:9).

C. *Tractate Bikkurim in the Time of Usha*

Ushans explore the conditions under which an individual may bring first fruits and recite the confession, delineate the procedure for the actual designation of the first fruits, and describe the procession in which the fruits are carried to Jerusalem and presented in the Temple. Two issues of interest arise. Anonymous law holds that in order to bring first fruits, the individual must own the land upon which the produce grew (M. Bik. 1:1-2, 6, 7, 11). In this view, the recitation's statement, "The first fruits of the ground which you, Lord, have given me" (Deut. 26:10), refers to a specific Israelite's ownership of the land at the moment at which the confession is recited. Judah, by contrast, holds that this is not a concern. The confession, he says, thanks God for giving the land of Israel as a whole to all of the people of Israel. In this view, presently owning an area of land does not determine the right of individual Israelites to bring first fruits and recite. Even those who do not own land may do so, an important idea in the land of Israel in the second century.

The second issue of Ushan concern is familiar from Tractate Demai and elsewhere. Judah states that the farmer may give first fruits only to priests scrupulous regarding matters of purity. The anonymous law disagrees, holding that, like other Temple offerings, first fruits are divided among all of the priests serving in the Temple (M. Bik. 3:12). While the materials before us offer no resolution to this issue, it is important to note that, again, the notion that observance of the purity laws divides the people of Israel into distinct groups occurs only in the Ushan period,

The middle unit of the tractate compares and contrasts the rules that apply to the agricultural offerings referred to in the Division of Agriculture as a whole. Synthesizing a wide range of facts familiar from other tractates, these materials come at the end of the formation of the law.

Conclusion

Tractate Bikkurim details the mechanics of the separation of first fruits and describes the processional to the Jerusalem Temple. In this regard, it is parallel in concern to Tractate Peah, which describes how poor offerings are designated and transmitted to the poor, and to the introduction to Tractate Terumot, which describes the designation and separation of heave-offering. Unlike these other tractates, which detail the metaphysical aspects of the consecration of produce to be an agricultural offering, Tractate Bikkurim concentrates primarily upon matters of ritual. In describing this Temple ritual, its concluding narrative is particularly effective.

Most notable, though, is that Tractate Bikkurim lacks the sort of single issue that, in other tractates in this division, forms the foundation of the Mishnah's authorities' theoretical perspectives upon the rights and obligations of Israelites in relation to God. While Tractate Bikkurim fills in details left open by Scripture and makes one important point about the right of Israelites to bring first fruits despite the current ownership of the land, it does not leave the framework of Scripture's own law so as to describe, as Tractates Terumot and Peah do, the deeper processes through which produce comes to have the status of an agricultural offering,

Like Tractate Orlah, Tractate Bikkurim suggests that decisions regarding what topics should be included in the Division of Agriculture preceded the actual work done on those topics. Tractates Orlah and Bikkurim appear in this division, creations of the Ushan period,[25] despite the absence in them of important theoretical concepts comparable to those found in their companion tractates.

CONCLUSION: HUMAN WILL AND THE SYSTEM OF AGRICULTURE

Analysis of the content and development of the Division of Agriculture allows us to draw a number of important conclusions regarding the character of the Mishnah and the specific ways in which the rabbis responded to the questions they faced in the period following the two failed wars against Rome. These conclusions are as follows:

1) The materials in the Division of Agriculture have no identifiable context or significance prior to their inclusion in the Mishnah. This is not a collection of laws deriving from Israelite antiquity and transmitted to Mishnaic rabbis who formed them into the tractates that stand before us today. Each tractate, rather, forms a cogent essay on a specific legal problem, beginning with the basic questions and ideas that instigated discussion and containing signs of a development in legal thinking that took place over the several periods of the emergence of Mishnaic law. Were we to claim that the law as a whole, or even significant parts of it, were the creations not of the Mishnah's rabbis but of Israelite antiquity, it would be difficult to explain the basic level of inquiry found in the Yavnean stratum or the fact that almost all of the Ushan materials take up questions first posed by Yavneans. Even if the Mishnah's rabbis did inherit certain laws or concepts from Second Temple times, their work in

---

[25] Only six of Tractate Orlah's thirty-seven units and six of Tractate Bikkurim's thirty-five units are attributed to Yavneans.

developing and structuring these materials is so innovative as completely to efface all signs of the original inheritance. These conclusions apply to the Mishnah's anonymous statements as much as to those assigned to specific authorities. There is no evidence that the anonymous materials comprise an earlier, inherited layer of the law.

2) The Mishnah's rabbis present careful essays designed to facilitate application of the agricultural law. This is not a collection of random topics but a systematic treatment of all topics related to Israelites' planting, harvesting, and eating the produce of the land of Israel. In all of this, the predominant interest is the processes of sanctification, an interest taken up already at Yavneh and developed throughout the formation of the law.

3) Just as the division reveals narrowly defined topical concerns, so each generation of authorities explores a particular theoretical issue. Yavnean materials as a whole detail matters of definition, with Ushans taking up the role of human motivation and the impact of extenuating circumstances. Again, we have every evidence of a carefully considered program of inquiry, not the result of wide ranging and random discussions or the product of a simple reporting of agricultural practices already in use.

4) Underlying the Mishnaic rabbis' treatment of these topics is the assertion that all of Scripture's rules regarding the land of Israel must still be followed. With this proclamation, beginning in the period of the destruction of the Jerusalem Temple in 70 C.E. the rabbis forcefully assert that things have not changed so much as the events of history might suggest. Just as when the Temple stood, the priests and Levites retain their special privileges. By affirming their status, the Mishnah's framers make the deeper claim that God still is owner of the land of Israel and Lord over the Israelite people. Only for this reason do the priests and Levites retain the right to a portion of the produce grown on the land. Only because of God's continued rule must the other agricultural laws still be followed. Despite Israel's defeat by Rome, God still owns the land and has the right to determine how it and its produce are used. Only for this reason do the agricultural laws need still to be observed, the priests and Levites need still to be supported.

5) In making this statement, the earliest generations of Rabbinic authorities and those living in Yavnean times present a unitary theory of law, consistently excluding attention to the motivations or perceptions of the Israelite whose deeds are under scrutiny. The rea-

sons or perceptions that lead an individual to act have no bearing upon the permissibility of that behavior. The status of a deed, rather, depends solely upon the nature of the actions through which it is carried out. It does not matter to Yavneans why an Israelite collects stones in his field during the Sabbatical year. The fact is that, in doing so, he makes possible the cultivation of the land, which is forbidden during the Sabbatical. Such actions therefore are forbidden. This is the case, as we saw, even if the individual simply desires to build a stone fence, a deed that itself is permitted.

Ideas such as this reveal the Yavneans' understanding of the existence of a foreordained order in the world, of an objective reality separate from any individual's perceptions of how things are or should be. Correct acts are those that conform completely to the ideal. Behavior, not intention, counts. The result of the action, not its underlying motivation, is determinative. By adhering to and promoting this reality, Israelites will return the world to the state of cosmic perfection in which God, at the time of creation, first sanctified it.

6) The Bar Kokhba revolt signifies a major watershed in Rabbinic thinking about the law. In developing the Yavneans' larger theory of God's continued rule over the land and people of Israel, Ushans develop an approach that significantly distinguishes the Mishnah's ideology from that of Scripture. Unlike those at Yavneh, these rabbis analyze actions in light of the intentions of the individual who performs them and on the basis of the perceptions of those who witness and interpret them. They thus understand the permissibility of field labor in the Sabbatical year, for instance, to depend upon the Israelite's intentions in carrying it out. An action is permitted so long as the individual does not intend to break the Sabbatical rules and so long as he works in a way that prevents others from assuming that he proposes to break the law. Unlike Yavneans, Ushans thus recognize no order or standard of behavior in the world other than that imposed by Israelites who, through their own intentions and perceptions, give meaning to their activities in planting, tilling, and harvesting produce on the land of Israel.

7) Through this approach, Ushans identify an entirely new locus of holiness within Israelite life. They do this by placing cultic observance in the hands of common Israelites. As we have seen again and again, by the Ushan period, common Israelites are seen as responsible for all aspects of the sanctification of agricultural offer-

ings, for the proper maintenance of food deemed holy, and for the determination of the point at which the sanctified food is deemed deconsecrated and so available for secular use. The Ushan response to the loss of the Temple and the devastation of the land of Israel was to say that God's rule and the potential for the sanctification of Israelite life remains, but is to be recognized now not in the Temple cult and priestly prerogatives but in the ability of common Israelites to identify and manipulate the holiness that emerges from their partnership with God in the cultivation of the land. A particularly striking example of this is Judah's view in Tractate Bikkurim that temporal ownership of the land is not at all a factor in the system of consecrated agricultural offerings. Whereas Yavneans held that only a person who now owns the land may bring first fruits and thank God for possession of the land, Judah holds that even possession of the land is metaphysical and continues without regard for property's temporal ownership. No matter who temporarily claims ownership of the land or controls the people's political destiny, all Israelites farming the land of Israel may bring first fruits and recite the confession. In doing this and in adhering to the remainder of the agricultural laws, they have the power to recreate a world of order and, hence, of sanctity.

In all, we see that the Rabbinic plan for Judaism after the destruction of the Temple was in large part about imagination. The plan depends upon the Mishnaic rabbis' ability to imagine that their small, powerless nation actually is at the center of God's plan for the world, and that, through their intentions and perceptions, the Israelite people could create a model of holiness and perfection equal to that plotted out by God when the universe was created. The Mishnah's rabbis place common Israelites at the center of creation, claiming that, through their perceptions and intentions, they impose meaning upon a world otherwise seen to be in a state of chaos. In this way Israelites are empowered themselves to recreate the world out of the ashes.

The Mishnah's law responds to the events of the first centuries by reaffirming the validity of the scriptural covenant, subject here to intense examination and systematization. In the context of this affirmation, however, the Mishnaic Rabbis also articulate a system of theology that uniquely symbolizes their own historical, political, and religious situation. This theology replaces the lost cult and its priesthood with new foci, first, the rabbis themselves, viewed as the bearers of revelation, and, second, the common Israelites, whose thoughts and deeds are made primary to the creation of a perfected world. In this regard, the Mishnah's message is poignant. For, as is clear, with the Temple destroyed and the land defiled, Israelites' intentions and perceptions were all that remained to deny the events of history and affirm God's Lordship.[26]

---

[26] See [Avery-]Peck, *The Priestly Gift in Mishnah*, p. 7. For similar interpretations of individual tractates of the Division of Agriculture, see Jaffee, *Mishnah's Theology of Tithin*, pp. 3-6; Mandelbaum, *Kilaim*, pp. 3-4; Roger Brooks, *Support for the Poor in the Mishnaic Law of Agriculture: Tractate Peah* (Chico, 1983), pp. 35-36; and Newman, *The Sanctity of the Seventh Year*, pp. 17-20. For one of the original statements of this thesis, see Jacob Neusner, *Judaism: The Evidence of the Mishnah* (Chicago, 1981), p. 271.

THE MISHNAH IN RABBINIC CONTEXT: TOSEFTA AND SIFRA

JACOB NEUSNER

Bard College

Alongside Scripture, the Mishnah stands at the head of the canonical documents of Rabbinic literature in the formative age, particularly those of the Halakhah. After Scripture, no document of Rabbinic Judaism reached closure prior to the Mishnah. Its nearest companions, the Tosefta and Sifra, provide perspective on the character of the foundation-document. They cite the Mishnah verbatim and gloss its words. Each forms a response to the Mishnah, a systematic reading thereof. A process of comparison and contrast between the Mishnah and the Tosefta, or the Mishnah and Sifra, shows how the character of the Mishnah represents a set of decisions. It emerges as the realization of a policy of law and theology, to which heirs of the document would respond in time. From the comparison, the Tosefta stands forth as a commentary and complement, amplifying the language of the Mishnah and also supplying legal statements that complete the Mishnah's account of matters. Sifra, for its part, takes up a position of criticism of the Mishnah's generative logic. What the Tosefta and Sifra in relationship to the Mishnah demonstrate is the capacity of the heirs of the Mishnah both to take up the Mishnah's intellectual discipline and to frame a critical, analytical program in response to it.

1. The Mishnah and the Tosefta

A single instance suffices to show that the Mishnah declares the law, the Tosefta gives the reasons, clarifies the details, and otherwise complements and supplements the Mishnah's statements. We deal with M. Ber. 8:1ff., given in bold-face, and the Tosefta's complement, in regular type:

M. 8:1 In reciting the sequence of blessings for wine and the Sabbath, one blesses over the wine, and afterward one blesses over the day.

T. 5:25 The reason is that it is [the presence of the cup of] wine [at the table] that provides the occasion for the Sanctification of the Day to be recited. The benediction over the wine is usual, while the benediction for the day is not usual [and that which is usual takes precedence over that which is infrequent].

M. **8:2-4 In preparing to recite the Grace after the Meal, they mix the cup and afterward wash the hands. He dries his hands on the cloth and lays it on the pillow. They wash the hands, and afterward they clean the house.**

M. **8:5 The sequence of blessings at the end of the Sabbath is: Light, and spices, and food, and Havdalah.**

T. 5:29 One who enters his house after the end of the Sabbath recites the benediction over the wine, the light, the spices and [then] recites [the] Havdalah [benediction]. And if he has but one cup [of wine], he sets it aside until after the meal and strings together all [these benedictions] after it [i.e., after the benediction for the meal]. One recites Habdalah at the end of the Sabbath, and at the end of festivals, and at the end of the Day of Atonement, and at the end of the Sabbath [which immediately precedes] a festival, and at the end of a festival [preceding] the intermediate days of the festival. One who is fluent [or, accustomed to doing so] recites many Habdalot [i.e., enumerates many kinds of separations in his Havdalah benediction, e.g., "Praised be Thou, O Lord...(1) who separates the holy from the profane, (2) who separates Israel from the nations, (3) who separates light from darkness...," and one who is not fluent recites one or two.

If we read the Tosefta as though there were no Mishnah, we should have no formidable problems in understanding the Tosefta. But that begs the question. We do have the Mishnah, and we do have ample evidence that the framers of compositions located in the Tosefta responded to the program and detailed contents and wording of the Mishnah.

The Problem of Mishnah-Tosefta Relationships

How does the Tosefta relate to the Mishnah? In completed research,[1] I maintained that the Tosefta forms a problem in the unfolding of

---

[1] *A History of the Mishnaic Law of Purities* (Leiden, 1974-1977: I-XXII); *A History of the Mishnaic Law of Holy Things* (Leiden, 1979: I-VI); *A History of the Mishnaic Law*

the writings of Judaism, since its importance lies in its relationship to three other documents, the Mishnah, which came earlier, and the Talmud of the Land of Israel and the Talmud of Babylonia, which were completed later on. The Tosefta does not present a system of its own, as does the Mishnah, nor does it present both an inherited system and one of its own, as do both Talmuds. Rather, like a vine on a trellis, the Tosefta rests upon the Mishnah, having no structure of its own; but it also bears fruit nourished by its own roots. A small fraction of the Tosefta's contents can have reached final formulation prior to the closure of the Mishnah, but most of the document either cites the Mishnah verbatim and comments upon it, or—the Mishnah in hand—can be fully and completely understood only in light of the Mishnah even though the Mishnah is not cited verbatim. The Tosefta's materials, some formed into cogent composites, most incoherent and cogent not among themselves but only in relationship to the Mishnah, serve as the Mishnah's first commentary, first amplification, and first extension—that is, the initial Talmud, prior to the one done in the land of Israel by ca. 400 and the one completed in Babylonia by ca. 600.

The Tosefta, defined in relationship to the Mishnah contains three types of materials, two of them secondary to, therefore assuredly later than, the Mishnah's materials, the third autonomous of the Mishnah and therefore possibly deriving from the same period as do the sayings compiled in the Mishnah.

The first type of materials contains a direct citation of the Mishnah followed by secondary discussion of the cited passage. That type of discourse certainly is post-Mishnaic, hence by definition Amoraic, as much as sayings of Samuel, Rab Judah, and R. Yohanan, are Amoraic.

The second sort of materials depends for full and exhaustive meaning upon a passage of the Mishnah, although the corresponding statements of the Mishnah are not cited verbatim. That sort of discussion probably is post-Mishnaic, but much depends upon our exegesis. Accordingly, we may be less certain of the matter.

---

of Women (Leiden, 1979-1980: I-V); *A History of the Mishnaic Law of Appointed Times* (Leiden, 1981-1983: I-V); *A History of the Mishnaic Law of Damages* (Leiden, 1983-1985: I-V). The forty-three volumes are now reprinted by Global Publications, SUNY Binghamton, in its Classics of Judaic Studies series. My graduate students of that period did the work on the Mishnaic Law of Agriculture. The detailed analysis of Mishnah-Tosefta relationships for the whole of the Mishnah and the Tosefta therefore has been in print from 1974.

The third type of passage in the Tosefta stands completely independent of any corresponding passage of the Mishnah. This is in one of two ways. First, a fully-articulated pericope in the Tosefta may simply treat materials not discussed in a systematic way, or not discussed at all, in the Mishnah. That kind of pericope can as well reach us in the Mishnah as in the Tosefta, so far as the criterion of literary and redactional theory may come to apply. Second, a well-constructed passage of the Tosefta may cover a topic treated in the Mishnah but follow a program of inquiry not dealt with at all in the Mishnah. What the statements of the Tosefta treat, therefore, may prove relevant to the thematic program of the Mishnah but not to the analytical inquiry of the framers of the Mishnah. Such a passage, like the former sort, also may fit comfortably into the Mishnah. If any components of the received Tosefta derive from the second century, that is, the time of the framing of the Mishnah, it would be those of the third type.

In proportion, a rough guess (based on the Sixth Division) would place less than a fifth of the Tosefta into this third type, well over a third of the whole into the first. In all, therefore, the Tosefta serves precisely as its name suggests, as a corpus of supplements—but of various kinds—to the Mishnah.

The Tosefta depends upon the Mishnah in yet another way. Its whole redactional framework, tractates and subdivisions alike, depends upon the Mishnah's. The Mishnah provides the lattice, the Tosefta, the vines. The rule (though with many exceptions) is that the Tosefta's discussion will follow the themes and problems of the Mishnah's program, much as the two Talmuds' treatments of the passage of the Mishnah are laid out along essentially the same lines as those of the Mishnah. The editorial work accordingly highlights the exegetical purpose of the framers of both the two Talmuds and the Tosefta. The whole serves as a massive and magnificent amplification of the Mishnah. In this regard, of course, the framers of the Tosefta may claim considerably greater success than those of the two Talmuds, since the Tosefta covers nearly all the tractates of the Mishnah, while neither Talmud treats more than two-thirds of them (and then not the same two-thirds).

But the Tosefta's redactors or arrangers tend to organize materials, within a given tractate, in line with two intersecting principles of arrangement. First, as I said, they follow the general outline of the Mishnah's treatment of a topic. Accordingly, if we set up a block of materials in the Tosefta side-by-side with a corresponding block of those of the Mishnah, we should discern roughly the same order of discourse. But, second, the Tosefta's arrangers also lay out their materials in accord with their own types. That is to say, they will tend

(1) to keep as a group passages that cite and then comment upon the actual words of the Mishnah's base-passage, then

(2) to present passages that amplify in the Tosefta's own words opinions fully spelled out only in response to the Mishnah's statements, and, finally,

(3) to give at the end, and as a group, wholly independent and autonomous sayings and constructions of such sayings.

I stress that that redactional pattern may be shown only to be a tendency, a set of not uncommon policies and preferences, not a fixed rule. But when we ask how the Tosefta's editors arranged their materials, it is not wholly accurate to answer that they follow the plan of the Mishnah's counterparts. There will be some attention, also, to the taxonomic traits of the units of discourse of which the Tosefta itself is constructed. That is why two distinct editorial principles come into play in explaining the arrangement of the whole.

When we turn from the definition of the Tosefta and of its editorial and redactional character to the contents of the document as a whole, the Mishnah once more governs the framework of description. For the Tosefta, as is already clear, stands nearly entirely within the circle of the Mishnah's interests, rarely asking questions about topics omitted altogether by the Mishnah's authors, always following the topical decisions on what to discuss as laid down by the founders of the whole. For our part, therefore, we cannot write about the Tosefta's theology or law, as though these constituted a system susceptible of description and interpretation independent of the Mishnah's system. At the same time, we must recognize that the exegetes of the Mishnah, in the Tosefta, and in the two Talmuds, stand apart from, and later than, the authors of the Mishnah itself.

Accordingly, the exegetes systematically say whatever they wish to say by attaching their ideas to a document earlier than their own and by making the principal document say what they wish to contribute. The system of expressing ideas through re-framing those of predecessors preserves the continuity of tradition and establishes a deep stability and order upon the culture framed by that tradition.

Let me now review a single text-problem to show in concrete terms the relationship between the two documents. To see how the Tosefta fits into the sweep of the Rabbinic literature extending from the

Mishnah, we follow a single passage. What is important, we shall observe, is how the Tosefta receives the Mishnah and transmits it forward. The following presents Mishnah Berakhot Chapter Eight. I then give the Tosefta to that chapter, following the text of Saul Lieberman. The main point I wish to register here is the position of the Tosefta in relationship to the Mishnah.

I

8:1.A. These are the things which are between the House of Shammai and the House of Hillel in [regard to] the meal:

B. The House of Shammai say, "One blesses over the day, and afterward one blesses over the wine."

And the House of Hillel say, "One blesses over the wine, and afterward one blesses over the day."

8.2.A. The House of Shammai say, "They wash the hands and afterward mix the cup."

And the House of Hillel say, "They mix the cup and afterward wash the hands."

8:3.A. The House of Shammai say, "He dries his hands on the cloth and lays it on the table."

And the House of Hillel say, "On the pillow."

8:4.A. The House of Shammai say, "They clean the house, and afterward they wash the hands."

And the House of Hillel say, "They wash the hands, and afterward they clean the house."

8:5.A. The House of Shammai say, "Light, and food, and spices, and Havdalah."

And the House of Hillel say, "Light, and spices, and food, and Havdalah."

B. The House of Shammai say, "'Who created the light of the fire.'"

And the House of Hillel say, "'Who creates the lights of the fire.'"

II

8:6.A. They do not bless over the light or the spices of gentiles, nor the light or the spices of the dead, nor the light or the spices which are before an idol.

B. And they do not bless over the light until they make use of its illumination.

III

8:7.A. He who ate and forgot and did not bless [say Grace]—

B. The House of Shammai say, "He should go back to his place and bless."

And the House of Hillel say, "He should bless in the place in which he remembered."

C. Until when does he bless? Until the food has been digested in his bowels.

8:8.A. Wine came to them after the meal, and there is there only that cup—

B. The House of Shammai say, "He blesses the wine, and afterward he blesses the food."

And the House of Hillel say, "He blesses the food, and afterward he blesses the wine."

C. They respond Amen after an Israelite who blesses, and they do not respond Amen after a Samaritan who blesses, until hearing the entire blessing.

The Mishnah-chapter goes over rules on the conduct of meals, first for Sabbaths and festivals, then in general, with special concern for preserving the cultic purity of the meal. That means the people at the meal keep the laws of cultic cleanness set forth in the book of Leviticus, as these are interpreted by the sages of the Torah. Here is how the Tosefta confronts the same themes and also cites some of the passages verbatim.

5:21 (Lieberman, p. 28, ls. 41-2).

A. They answer Amen after a gentile who says a blessing with the divine name. They do not answer Amen after a Samaritan who says a blessing with the divine name until they have heard the entire blessing.

5.25 (Lieberman, p. 29, ls. 53-57).

A. [The] things which are between the House of Shammai and the House of Hillel in [regard to] the meal:

B. The House of Shammai say, "One blesses over the day, and afterward he blesses over the wine, for the day causes the wine to come, and the day is already sanctified, but the wine has not yet come."

C. And the House of Hillel say, "One blesses over the wine, and afterward he blesses over the day, for the wine causes the Sanctification of the day to be said.

"Another explanation: The blessing over the wine is regular [= always required when wine is used], and the blessing over the day is not continual [but is said only on certain days]."

D. And the law is according to the words of the House of Hillel.

5:26 (Lieberman, pp. 29-30, ls. 57-61).

A. The House of Shammai say, "They wash the hands and afterward mix the cup, lest the liquids which are on the outer surface of the cup be made unclean on account of the hands, and in turn make the cup unclean."

B. The House of Hillel say, "The outer surfaces of the cup are always deemed unclean.

"Another explanation: The washing of the hands must always take place immediately before the meal."

C. "They mix the cup and afterward wash the hands."

5:27 (Lieberman, p. 30, ls. 61-65).

A. The House of House of Shammai say, "He dries his hand on the napkin and leaves it on the table, lest the liquids which are in the napkin be made unclean on account of the cushion, and then go and make the hands unclean."

B. And the House of Hillel say, "A doubt in regard to the condition of liquids so far as the hands are concerned is resolved as clean."

C. "Another explanation: Washing the hands does not pertain to unconsecrated food.

D. "But he dries his hands on the napkin and leaves it on the cushion, lest the liquids which are in the napkin be made unclean on account of the table, and they go and render the food unclean."

5:28 (Lieberman, p. 30, ls. 65-68).

A. The House of Shammai say, "They clean the house, on account of the waste of food, and afterward they wash the hands."

B. The House of Hillel say, "If the waiter was a disciple of a sage, he gathers the scraps which contain as much as an olive's bulk.

C. "And they wash the hands and afterward clean the house."

5:29 (Lieberman, p. 30, ls. 68-72).

A. The House of Shammai say, "He holds the cup of wine in his right hand and spiced oil in his left hand."

He blesses over the wine and afterward blesses over the oil.

B. And the House of Hillel say, "He holds the sweet oil in his right hand and the cup of wine in his left hand."

C. He blesses over the oil and smears it on the head of the waiter. If the waiter was a disciple of a sage, he [the diner] smears it on the wall, because it is not praiseworthy for a disciple of a sage to go forth perfumed.

5:30 (Lieberman, pp. 30-31, ls. 72-75).

A. R. Judah said, "The House of Shammai and the House of Hillel did not dispute concerning the blessing of the food, that it is first, or concerning the Habdalah, that it is at the end.

"Concerning what did they dispute?

"Concerning the light and the spices, for—

"The House of Shammai say, 'Light and afterward spices.'"
"And the House of Hillel say, 'Spices and afterward light.'"

5:30 (Lieberman, p. 31, ls. 75-77).

B. He who enters his home at the end of the Sabbath blesses the wine, the light, the spices, and then says Habdalah.

C. And if he has only one cup [of wine] he leaves it for after the meal and then says all [the liturgies] in order after [reciting the blessing for] it.

5:31 (Lieberman, p. 31, ls. 81-85).

A. If a person has a light covered in the folds of his garment or in a lamp and sees the flame but does not use its light, or uses its light but does not see its flame, he does not bless [that light]. [He says a blessing over the light only] when he both sees the flame and uses its light.

As to a lantern—even though he had not extinguished it [that is, it has been burning throughout the Sabbath], he recites a blessing over it.

B. They do not bless over the light of gentiles. One may bless over [the flame of] an Israelite kindled from a gentile, or a gentile who kindled from an Israelite.

5:32 (Lieberman, p. 31, ls. 80-81).

A. In the house of study—
The House of Shammai say, "One [person] blesses for all of them."
And the House of Hillel say, "Each one blesses for himself."

Clearly, the Tosefta has a variety of materials. Some of this is freestanding, but some simply cites and glosses the Mishnah. We see in the following comparison just how these things come to the surface.

THE TOSEFTA AND THE MISHNAH COMPARED

Mishnah	Tosefta
M. 8:1. A. These are the things which are between the House of Shammai and the House of Hillel in [regard to] the meal:	T. 5:25. [The] things which are between the House of Shammai and the House of Hillel [as regards] the meal:
B. The House of Shammai say, "One blesses the day, and afterward one blesses over the wine."	The House of Shammai say, "One blesses the day, and afterward one blesses over the wine, for the day causes the wine to come, and the day is already sanctified, but the wine has not yet come."

And the House of Hillel say, "One blesses the wine, and afterward one blesses over the day."

M. 8:2.A. The House of Shammai say, "They wash the hands and afterward mix the cup."

And the House of Hillel say, "They mix the cup and afterward wash the hands."

8:3.A. The House of Shammai say, "He dries his hands on the napkin and lays it on the table." And the House of Hillel say, "On the cushion."

And the House of Hillel say, "One blesses over the wine, and afterward one blesses the day, for the wine causes the Sanctification of the day to be said."

"Another matter: The blessing of the wine is continual, and the blessing of the day is not continual."

And the law is according to the words of the House of Hillel.

T. 5:26. The House of Shammai say, "They wash the hands and afterward mix the cup, lest the liquids which are on the outer surfaces of the cup may be made unclean on account of the hands, and they may go back and make the cup unclean."

The House of Hillel say, "The outer surfaces of the cup are perpetually unclean. "Another matter: The washing of the hands is only [done] near [at the outset of] the meal. "They mix the cup and afterward wash the hands."

T. 5:27. The House of Shammai say, "He dries his hand on the napkin and lays it on the table, lest the liquids which are in the napkin may be made unclean on account of the pillow, and they may go and make the hands unclean. The House of Hillel say, A doubt in regard to the condition of liquids so far as the hands are concerned is clean.

"Another matter: Washing the hands does not pertain to unconsecrated food. But he dries his hands on the napkin and leaves it on the cushion lest the liquids which are in the pillow may be made unclean on account of the table, and they may go and render the food unclean."

M. 8:4.A. The House of Shammai say, "They clean the house and afterward wash the hands." And the House of Hillel say, "They wash the hands and afterward clean the house."

8:5.A. The House of Shammai say, "Light, and food and spices, and Habdalah."
And the House of Hillel say, "Light, and spices, and food, and Habdalah."

B. The House of Shammai say, "'Who created the light of the fire.'"
And the House of Hillel say, "'Who creates the lights of the fire.'"

M. 8:8.A. Wine came to them after the meal, and there is there only that cup —
B. The House of Shammai say, "He blesses over the wine and afterward he blesses over the food."
And the House of Hillel say, "He blesses over the food and afterward he blesses over the wine."
[If wine came to them after the meal and] there is there only that cup House of Shammai say, "He blesses the wine and then the food."

T. 5:28. The House of Shammai say, "They clean the house on account of the waste of food and afterward wash the hands." The House of Hillel say, "If the waiter was a disciple of a sage, he gathers the scraps which contain as much as on olive's bulk.
"They wash the hands and afterward clean the house."

T. 5:30. R. Judah said, "The House of Shammai and the House of Hillel did not dispute concerning the blessing of the food, that it is first, and concerning the Habdalah that it is the end. Concerning what did they dispute? Concerning the light and the spices, for the House of Shammai say, 'Light and afterward spices,' and the House of Hillel say, 'Spices and afterward light.'"

[No equivalent.]

T. 5:30. A. He who enters his home at the end of the Sabbath blesses over the wine, the light, the spices, and then says Habdalah.

B. And if he has only one cup [of wine], he leaves it for after the meal and then says them all in order after [blessing] it.
If he has only one cup [of wine] [he leaves if for after the meal and then says them all in order, thus:] Wine, then food.

(House of Hillel say, "He blesses the food and then the wine.")

M. 8:6.A. They do not bless the light or the spices of gentiles, nor the light or the spices of the dead, nor the light or the spices which are before an idol. B. And they do not bless the light until they make use of its illumination.	T. 5:31.B. They do not bless the light of gentiles. An Israelite who kindled [a flame] from a gentile, or a gentile who kindled from an Israelite—one may bless [such a flame]. T. 5:31 A. If a person has a light covered in the folds of his garment or in a lamp, and he sees the flame but does not use its light, or uses its light but does not see its flame, he does not bless. [He blesses only] when he both sees the flame and uses its light.
M. 8:8.C. They respond Amen after an Israelite who blesses, and they do not respond Amen after a Samaritan who blesses, until one hears the entire blessing.	T. 5:21 They answer "Amen" after a blessing with the divine name recited by a gentile. They do not answer Amen after a Samaritan who blesses with the divine name until they hear the entire blessing.

The pattern is now clear. We simply cannot understand many lines of the Tosefta without turning to the Mishnah. That means that the Tosefta-passage before us must have been composed with the Mishnah in hand, that is, after 200, and that the authorship of the Tosefta had in mind the clarification of the received document, the Mishnah. Its judgment upon the program and plan of the Mishnah becomes transparent when we set the two documents up side by side. The Tosefta turns out to play three roles: a complement, a supplement, and a critique, all carried out systematically and completely. The two Talmuds would pick and choose, deal with some tractates, omit many others, and they would pursue their own program, which vastly transcended that of the Mishnah. The Tosefta, serving nearly the whole of the Mishnah and responding to the greater part of its propositions, made itself the Mishnah's indispensable companion, its first guide.

2. Sifra's Critique of Mishnaic Logic

The authorship of Sifra, ca. 300 C.E., a line by line commentary to the book of Leviticus, undertook a vast polemic against the logic of classification that forms the foundation of the system of the Mishnah. This they did two ways. The first, and less important, was to demonstrate that the Mishnah's rules required exegetical foundations. The second, and paramount, way was to attack the very logic by which the Mishnah's authorship developed its points. To understand the polemic of Sifra, therefore, we have to grasp the fundamental logical basis of the Mishnah. Then we shall see in its polemical context the recurrent statement of the authorship of Sifra: classification does not work, because there is no genus, but only species. The Mishnah's Listenwissenschaft, its insistence that things are either like one another, and follow the same rule, or opposite to one another, therefore follow the opposite rule—these fundamental building blocks of Mishnaic thought prove deeply flawed. For if nothing is ever really like something else, we cannot classify different things together, as the same thing. And, it follows, we also can make no lists of things that, whether in a polythetic or a monothetic framework, follow the same rule and therefore generate a generalization. Since, as we shall now see, the logic of the Mishnah begins with the premise that diverse species form a single genus, so can be subjected to comparison and contrast, that dogged insistence, time and again, upon the incomparability of species, forms a fundamental critique of the practical reason of the Mishnah. A full appreciation of matters requires that we dwell at some length upon the system of the Mishnah.

The System of the Mishnah and Its Logic of Classification

The Mishnah's authorship invariably invokes the philosophical logic of syllogism, the rule-making logic of lists. Like good Aristotelians, they would uncover the components of the rules by comparison and contrast, showing the rule for one thing by finding out how it compared with like things and contrasted with the unlike. Then, in their view, the unknown would become known, conforming to the rule of the like thing, also to the opposite of the rule governing the unlike thing.² That purpose is accomplished, in particular, though list-making, which places on display the data of the like and the unlike and implicitly (ordinarily, not explicitly) then conveys the rule. That is why, in exposing the interior logic of its authorship's intellect, the Mishnah had to be a book of lists, with the implicit order, the nomothetic traits, dictating the ordinarily unstated general and encompassing rule. And all this why? It is in order to make a single statement, endless times over, and to repeat in a mass of tangled detail precisely the same fundamental judgment.

The Mishnah in its way is as blatantly repetitious in its fundamental statement as is the Pentateuch. But the power of the Pentateuchal authorship, denied to that of the Mishnah, lies in their capacity always to be heard, to create sound by resonance of the surfaces of things. The Pentateuch is a fundamentally popular and accessible piece of writing. By contrast, the Mishnah's writers spoke into the depths, anticipating a more acute hearing than they ever would receive. So the repetitions of Scripture reinforce the message, while the endlessly repeated paradigm of the Mishnah sits too deep in the structure of the system to gain hearing from the ear that lacks acuity or to attain visibility to the untutored eye. So much for the logic. What of the systemic message? Given the subtlety of intellect of the Mishnah's authorship, we cannot find surprising that the message speaks not only in what is said, but in what is omitted.

When we listen to the silences of the system of the Mishnah, as much as to its points of stress, we hear a single message. It is a message of a system that answered a single encompassing question, and the question formed a stunning counterpart to that of the sixth century B.C.E. The Pentateuchal system addressed one reading of the events of the sixth century, highlighted by the destruction of the Jerusalem Temple in 586 B.C.E. At stake was how Israel as defined by that system related to its land, represented by its Temple, and the message may be simply stated: what appears to be the given is in fact a gift, subject to stipulations. The precipitating event for the Mishnaic system was the destruction of the Jerusalem Temple in 70, but at stake now was a quite fresh issue. It was, specifically, this: what, in the aftermath of the destruction of the holy place and holy

---

² Compare G.E.R. Lloyd, *Polarity and Analogy. Two Types of Argumentation in Early Greek Thought* (Cambridge, 1966). But the core-logic of Listenwissenschaft extends back to Sumerian times.

cult, remained of the sanctity of the holy caste, the priesthood, the holy land, and, above all, the holy people and its holy way of life? The answer was that sanctity persists, indelibly, in Israel, the people, in its way of life, in its land, in its priesthood, in its food, in its mode of sustaining life, in its manner of procreating and so sustaining the nation.

The Mishnah's system therefore focused upon the holiness of the life of Israel, the people, a holiness that had formerly centered on the Temple. The logically consequent question was, what is the meaning of sanctity, and how shall Israel attain, or give evidence of, sanctification. The answer to the question derived from the original creation, the end of the Temple directing attention to the beginning of the natural world that the Temple had (and would again) embodied. For the meaning of sanctity the framers therefore turned to that first act of sanctification, the one in creation. It came about when, all things in array, in place, each with its proper name, God blessed and sanctified the seventh day on the eve of the first Sabbath. An orderly nature was a sanctified and blessed nature. So to receive the blessing and to be made holy, all things in nature and society were to be set in right array. Given the condition of Israel, the people, in its land, in the aftermath of the catastrophic war against Rome led by Bar Kokhba in 132-135, putting things in order was no easy task. But that is why, after all, the question pressed, the answer proving inexorable and obvious. The condition of society corresponded to the critical question that obsessed the system-builders.

Once we discern that message, we shall also understand the logic necessary for its construction and inner structure. For the inner structure set forth by a logic of classification alone could sustain the system of ordering all things in proper place and under the proper rule. The like belongs with the like and conforms to the rule governing the like, the unlike goes over to the opposite and conforms to the opposite rule. When we make lists of the like, we also know the rule governing all the items on those lists, respectively. We know that and one other thing, namely, the opposite rule, governing all items sufficiently like to belong on those lists, but sufficiently unlike to be placed on other lists. That rigorously philosophical logic of analysis, comparison and contrast, served because it was the only logic that could serve a system that proposed to make the statement concerning order and right array that the Mishnah's authorship wished to set forth. To the urgent question, what of the holiness of Israel after the destruction of the Temple in 70, therefore, the system of the Mishnah provided the self-evidently valid answer and gave that answer in ineluctable and compelling logical form. That sanctification, as a matter of fact, from the viewpoint of the system now endured and transcended the physical destruction of the building and the cessation of sacrifices. For Israel the people was holy, enduring as the medium and the instrument of God's sanctification. The system then instructed Israel so to act as to express the holiness that inhered in the people. This Israel would accomplish by the right ordering, in accord with a single encompassing principle, of all details of the common life of the village and the home, matching the Temple and the cult.

The diverse topical program of the Mishnah, time and again making the same points on the centrality of order, works itself out in a single logic of cogent discourse, one which seeks the rule that governs diverse cases. And, as we now see, that logic states within its interior structure the fundamental point of the document as a whole. The correspondence of logic to system here, as in the Pentateuch viewed overall, hardly presents surprises. To see how this intellect does its work we turn to Mishnah Sanhedrin, Chapter Two, to see the more subtle way in which list-making yields a powerfully-argued philosophical theorem. The Mishnah's authorship here wishes to say that Israel has two heads, one of state, the other of cult, the king and the high priest, respectively, and that these two offices are nearly wholly congruent with one another, with a few differences based on the particular traits of each. Broadly speaking, therefore, our exercise is one of setting forth the genus and the species. The genus is head of holy Israel. The species are king and high priest. Here are the traits in common and those not shared, and the exercise is fully exposed for what it is, an inquiry into the rules that govern, the points of regularity and order, in this minor matter, of political structure. My outline, imposed in bold-face type, makes the point important in this setting.

1. **The rules of the high priest: subject to the law, marital rites, conduct in bereavement**

2:1A. A high priest judges, and [others] judge him;

B. gives testimony, and [others] give testimony about him;

C. performs the rite of removing the shoe [Deut. 25:7-9], and [others] perform the rite of removing the shoe with his wife.

D. [Others] enter levirate marriage with his wife, but he does not enter into levirate marriage,
E. because he is prohibited to marry a widow.
F. [If] he suffers a death [in his family], he does not follow the bier.
G. "But when [the bearers of the bier] are not visible, he is visible; when they are visible, he is not.
H. "And he goes with them to the city gate," the words of R. Meir.
I. R. Judah says, "He never leaves the sanctuary,
J. "since it says, 'Nor shall he go out of the sanctuary' (Lev. 21:12)."
K. And when he gives comfort to others
L. the accepted practice is for all the people to pass one after another, and the appointed [prefect of the priests] stands between him and the people.
M. And when he receives consolation from others,
N. all the people say to him, "Let us be your atonement."
O. And he says to them, "May you be blessed by Heaven."
P. And when they provide him with the funeral meal,
Q. all the people sit on the ground, while he sits on a stool.

2. The rules of the king: Not subject to the law, marital rites, conduct in bereavement

2:2A. The king does not judge, and [others] do not judge him;
B. does not give testimony, and [others] do not give testimony about him;
C. does not perform the rite of removing the shoe, and others do not perform the rite of removing the shoe with his wife;
D. does not enter into levirate marriage, nor [do his brother] enter levirate marriage with his wife.
E. R. Judah says, "If he wanted to perform the rite of removing the shoe or to enter into levirate marriage, his memory is a blessing."
F. They said to him, "They pay no attention to him [if he expressed the wish to do so]."
G. [Others] do not marry his widow.
H. R. Judah says, "A king may marry the widow of a king.
I. "For so we find in the case of David, that he married the widow of Saul,
J. "For it is said, 'And I gave you your master's house and your master's wives into your embrace' (2 Sam. 12:8)."
2:3A. [If] [the king] suffers a death in his family, he does not leave the gate of his palace.

- B. R. Judah says, "If he wants to go out after the bier, he goes out,
- C. "for thus we find in the case of David, that he went out after the bier of Abner,
- D. "since it is said, 'And King David followed the bier' (2 Sam. 3:31)."
- E. They said to him, "This action was only to appease the people."
- F. And when they provide him with the funeral meal, all the people sit on the ground, while he sits on a couch.

3. Special rules pertinent to the king because of his calling

- 2:4A. [The king] calls out [the army to wage] a war fought by choice on the instructions of a court of seventy-one.
- B. He [may exercise the right to] open a road for himself, and [others] may not stop him.
- C. The royal road has no required measure.
- D. All the people plunder and lay before him [what they have grabbed], and he takes the first portion.
- E. "He should not multiply wives to himself" (Deut. 17:17)—only eighteen.
- F. R. Judah says, "He may have as many as he wants, so long as they do not entice him [to abandon the Lord (Deut. 7:4)]."
- G. R. Simeon says, "Even if there is only one who entices him [to abandon the Lord]—lo, this one should not marry her."
- H. If so, why is it said, "He should not multiply wives to himself"?
- I. Even though they should be like Abigail [1 Sam. 25:3].
- J. "He should not multiply horses to himself" (Deut. 17:16)—only enough for his chariot.
- K. "Neither shall he greatly multiply to himself silver and gold" (Deut. 17:16)—only enough to pay his army.
- L. "And he writes out a scroll of the Torah for himself" (Deut. 17:17)
- M. When he goes to war, he takes it out with him; when he comes back, he brings it back with him; when he is in session in court, it is with him; when he is reclining, it is before him,
- N. as it is said, "And it shall be with him, and he shall read in it all the days of his life" (Deut. 17:19).
- 2:5A. [Others may] not ride on his horse, sit on his throne, handle his scepter.
- B. And [others may] not watch him while he is getting a haircut, or while he is nude, or in the bath-house,
- C. since it is said, "You shall surely set him as king over you"

(Deut. 17:15)—that reverence for him will be upon you.

The Mishnaic authorship's philosophical cast of mind is amply revealed in this essay, which in concrete terms effects a taxonomy, a study of the genus, national leader, and its two species, king and high priest: how are they alike, how are they not alike, and what accounts for the differences. The premise is that national leaders are alike and follow the same rule, except where they differ and follow the opposite rule from one another. But that premise also is subject to the proof effected by the survey of the data consisting of concrete rules, those systemically inert facts that here come to life for the purposes of establishing a proposition. By itself, the fact that, e.g., others may not ride on his horse, bears the burden of no systemic proposition. In the context of an argument constructed for nomothetic, taxonomic purposes, the same fact is active and weighty.

No natural historian can find the discourse and mode of thought at hand unfamiliar; it forms the foundation of all disposition of data in quest of meaning, of making connections, drawing conclusions. For if I had to specify a single mode of thought that established connections between one fact and another, it is in the search for points in common and therefore also points of contrast. We seek connection between fact and fact, sentence and sentence in the subtle and balanced rhetoric of the Mishnah, by comparing and contrasting two things that are like and not alike. At the logical level, too, the Mishnah falls into the category of familiar philosophical thought. Once we seek regularities, we propose rules. What is like another thing falls under its rule, and what is not like the other falls under the opposite rule. Accordingly, as to the species of the genus, so far as they are alike, they share the same rule. So far as they are not alike, each follows a rule contrary to that governing the other. So the work of analysis is what produces connection, and therefore the drawing of conclusions derives from comparison and contrast: the and, the equal. The proposition then that forms the conclusion concerns the essential likeness of the two offices, except where they are different, but the subterranean premise is that we can explain both likeness and difference by appeal to a principle of fundamental order and unity. To make these observations concrete, we turn to the case at hand. The important contrast comes at the outset. The high priest and king fall into a single genus, but speciation, based on traits particular to the king, then distinguishes the one from the other. In a treatise on government, organizing details into unifying rules, the propositions of the present passage will have been stated differently. But the mode of thought, the manner of reaching conclusions, the mind-set that sees connections in one way rather than some other, that draws conclusions in this wise, not in that—these will have found an equally familiar place in the mind of both philosophy, of Aristotle's kind in particular, and the Jewish intellect represented by the Mishnah.

But comparing the intellect of the Mishnah's system-builders to that of Aristotle diverts our gaze from the still more apt likeness, the one with which we commenced. Like the authorship of the Pentateuch, the framers of the Mishnah have drawn together diverse materials in a single, nearly-seamless fabric. And in them they have made a single statement, many times over, in the setting of an extraordinarily vast range of topics. Once authorship has registered the statement it wishes to make, it finds possible the expression of that same statement through what seems to me an unlimited range of topical media. Not only so, but just as in the Pentateuch a single logic of cogent discourse joins fact to fact and sentence to sentence into proposition and paragraph respectively, the same takes place in the Mishnah. That logic of list-making, which brings to the surface a deeper intellectual structure formed of comparison and contrast, classification and exclusion, predominates throughout. Accordingly, a single logic serves to make a single statement, in behalf of both the authorship of the Pentateuch and the framers of the Mishnah.

Speaking anonymously, collectively, and authoritatively, each set of system-builders has followed precisely the same rules of intellect, that, stated very simply, require a logic of a single taxon to make a statement. of a singular character. And, as in the Pentateuch, so in the Mishnah, the form of the logic must fit the framework of the statement: teleology for a statement made up of connections between events and lessons drawn from events, philosophical syllogism for a statement made up of rules governing (or deriving from) a variety of cases. And that brings us to the final issue of systemic analysis in quest of insight into intellect: both authorships leave open the question of tradition, since, as we see with great clarity, each group of system-builders has chosen to do one thing only: set forth a system, without laying claim to the authority of tradition. And that is surely a trait of intellect of system-builders, so persuaded of the compelling character of their statement as to deny need to invoke the authority of tradition. Logic takes the place of tradition, argument and powerful rhetoric, of the argument of precedent and an authoritative past. It is one thing to claim God said it all to Moses, who wrote it down. It is another to say that the unbroken chain of tradition from Sinai stands behind the document, and the Pentateuchal Judaism affirms the one and rejects the other. The Pentateuchal compositors claimed their system came not through tradition but from Sinai, dictated whole and complete by God to Moses. Given their extraordinary achievement, as I said, we need hardly find surprising the claim that, with enormous but entirely ordinate pride, they made in behalf of that achievement.

But the Mishnah's authorship claimed no less. For, in the very face of the Torah of God revealed to Moses at Sinai, they built and set forth a system resting wholly on the foundations of logic and order set forth within the systemic statement itself. That is to say, theirs was a statement standing on the firm two feet of the systemic authorship itself. The authorship of the Pentateuch appealed to Sinai for authority. The framers of the Mishnah kept silent about why people should keep the rules of their document and so construct out of an inchoate and chaotic world that system that they set forth. The systemic statement contained its own authority. That, at any rate, is what they seem to me implicitly to have said through those silences that invite us, in the end, to join in the conversation they inaugurated. Logic, compelling and uncompromising, sustained the system; an appeal to tradition would have contradicted that proud claim of the system-makers of the Mishnah, and it is a claim that they did not deign to put forth. True, others alleged in their behalf that their authority, if not their exact positions, set them into a chain of tradition commencing with Moses at Sinai. But that claim came only in the context of debates following the closure of the Mishnah and made necessary by the character of the Mishnah. To state the upshot simply, the framers of the Mishnah set forth a system that, in its very nature, demanded to be transformed into a tradition.

Sifra's Critique of the Logic of the Mishnah

Now the intellectual labor of relating system to tradition and also of finding an appropriate logic of cogent discourse for the composition of a system could be accomplished in more than one way. And that brings us to the position of the authorship of Sifra. To state matters simply, what we shall now see in Sifra is a two-pronged polemic against the Mishnah, one a mere feint, the other the main attack.

[1] The authorship of Sifra commonly invokes the exact language of the Mishnah or the Tosefta, asks whether the position presented in that language, lacking all proof-texts drawn from Scripture, is not a matter of mere logic, and proves that it is not. That shows that what is required is law resting on scriptural proof.

[2] The authorship of Sifra, time and again, systematically demonstrates the futility of the logic of Listenwissenschaft, classification or taxonomy, comparison and contrast. This it does in a very simple way. It shows that species that look as though they form a common genus do not in fact form such a genus. Therefore it is not possible to compare and contrast two species to find the law common to the two of them, if they compare, or the law that differentiates one from the other, if they contrast.

A systemic statement could be woven into the cloak of tradition by its presentation as (mere) exegesis of a received text. The urgent question and self-evidently valid answer, not stated openly as a proposition for demonstration and argument, but merely repeated endlessly in the form of commentary, bore its own power of persuasion. Repeating the point gains for the message a self-evident that argument and therefore counter-argument can deny it. And that is the first of the two attacks of Sifra's authorship on the Mishnah, the feint. What about the other? While I should claim that the whole of the document is composed as a sustained demonstration of the improbability of the logic of classification, let me give two examples, the first from the opening pages of the document (Sifra I:I.1):

I:I.1.A. "The Lord called [to Moses] and spoke [to him from the tent of meeting, saying, 'Speak to the Israelite people and say to them']" (Lev. 1:1):
B. He gave priority to the calling over the speaking.
C. That is in line with the usage of Scripture.
D. Here there is an act of speaking, and in connection with the encounter at the bush [Exod. 3:4: "God called to him out of the bush, 'Moses, Moses'"], there is an act of speaking.
E. Just as in the latter occasion, the act of calling is given priority over the act of speaking [even though the actual word, "speaking" does not occur, it is implicit in the framing of the verse], so here, with respect to the act of speaking, the act of calling is given priority over the act of speaking.

2.A.	No [you cannot generalize on the basis of that case,] for if you invoke the case of the act of speaking at the bush, which is the first in the sequence of acts of speech [on which account, there had to be a call prior to entry into discourse],
B.	will you say the same of the act of speech in the tent of meeting, which assuredly is not the first in a sequence of acts of speech [so there was no need for a preliminary entry into discourse through a call]?
C.	The act of speech at Mount Sinai [Exod. 19:3] will prove to the contrary, for it is assuredly not the first in a sequence of acts of speech, yet, in that case, there was an act of calling prior to the act of speech.
3.A.	No, [the exception proves nothing,] for if you invoke in evidence the act of speech at Mount Sinai, which pertained to all the Israelites, will you represent it as parallel to the act of speech in the tent of meeting, which is not pertinent to all Israel?
B.	Lo, you may sort matters out by appeal to comparison and contrast, specifically:
C.	The act of speech at the bush, which is the first of the acts of speech, is not of the same classification as the act of speech at Sinai, which is not the first act of speech.
D.	And the act of speech at Sinai, which is addressed to all Israel, is not in the same classification as the act of speech at the bush, which is not addressed to all Israel.
4.A.	What they have in common, however, is that both of them are acts of speech, deriving from the mouth of the Holy One, addressed to Moses, in which case, the act of calling comes prior to the act of speech,
B.	so that, by way of generalization, we may maintain that every act of speech which comes from the mouth of the Holy One to Moses will be preceded by an act of calling.
5.A.	Now if what the several occasions have in common is that all involve an act of speech, accompanied by fire, from the mouth of the Holy One, addressed to Moses, so that the act of calling was given priority over the act of speaking, then in every case in which there is an act of speech, involving fire, from the mouth of the Holy One, addressed to Moses, should involve an act of calling prior to the act of speech.
B.	But then an exception is presented by the act of speech at the tent of meeting, in which there was no fire.
C.	[That is why it was necessary for Scripture on this occasion

to state explicitly,] "The Lord called [to Moses and spoke to him from the tent of meeting, saying, 'Speak to the Israelite people and say to them']" (Lev. 1:1).

D. That explicit statement shows that, on the occasion at hand, priority was given to the act of calling over the act of speaking.

I:II.1.A. ["The Lord called to Moses and spoke to him from the tent of meeting, saying, 'Speak to the Israelite people and say to them'" (Lev. 1:1)]: Might one suppose that the act of calling applied only to this act of speaking alone?

B. And how on the basis of Scripture do we know that on the occasion of all acts of speaking that are mentioned in the Torah, [there was a prior act of calling]?

C. Scripture specifies, "from the tent of meeting,"

D. which bears the sense that on every occasion on which it was an act of speaking from the tent of meeting, there was an act of calling prior to the act of speaking.

2.A. Might one suppose that there was an act of calling only prior to the acts of speech alone?

B. How on the basis of Scripture do I know that the same practice accompanied acts of saying and also acts of commanding?

C. Said R. Simeon, "Scripture says not only, '...spoke...,' but '...and he spoke,' [with the inclusion of the 'and'] meant to encompass also acts of telling and also acts of commanding."

The exercise of generalization addresses the character of God's meeting with Moses. The point of special interest is the comparison of the meeting at the bush and the meeting at the tent of meeting. And at stake is asking whether all acts of God's calling and talking with, or speaking to, the prophet are the same, or whether some of these acts are of a different classification from others. In point of fact, we are able to come to a generalization, worked out at I:I.5.A. And that permits us to explain why there is a different usage at Lev. 1:1 from what characterizes parallel cases. I:II.1-2 proceeds to generalize from the case at hand to other usages entirely, a very satisfying conclusion to the whole. I separate I:II from I:I because had I:I ended at 5, it could have stood complete and on its own, and therefore I see I:II as a brief appendix.

My second example derives from Parashat Vayyiqra Dibura Denedabah Parashah 9. It shows how in the context of defining norms, the same polemic is carried forward (Sifra XVI:I.3):

XVI:I.3.A.	"[and present it to Aaron's sons,] the priests. The priest shall scoop out of it a handful [of its choice flour and oil]:"
B.	This teaches that the taking up of a handful of meal-offering requires the action of a priest [and may not be done by an outsider] (T. Men. 1:2G).
C.	Is that not [the contrary proposition] a matter of logic? [Proof of the foregoing requires scriptural demonstration, since logic cannot have produced that result.]
D.	If the slaughter of a beast for sacrifice, which is assigned a place at the northern side of the altar, is not assigned the services of a priest, the act of taking the handful, which is not assigned a place at the north side of the altar, surely should not be assigned the services of a priest?
E.	The act of pinching the nerve will prove the contrary, for it has not been assigned a place at the northern side of the altar, but it has been assigned the requirement that only a priest do it.
F.	No, if you have stated such a rule with reference to the pinching of a bird's neck, which is assigned a position at the altar itself, will you so state of the taking of a handful of meal offering, which is not assigned a position at the altar [but may be done anywhere in the courtyard]?
G.	Since it has not been assigned a place at the altar, it also should not be assigned the action of an officiating priest.
H.	[Because logic proves the opposite of the fact, it was necessary for Scripture to state matters explicitly, as follows:] "[and present it to Aaron's sons,] the priests. The priest shall scoop out of it a handful [of its choice flour and oil]:"
I.	This teaches that the taking up of a handful of meal-offering requires the action of a priest [and may not be done by an outsider] (T. Men. 1:2G).
4.A.	Might one suppose that while taking up a handful of meal offering requires the action of a priest, if it is done by an outsider, it should be acceptable?
B.	Scripture says, "The priest shall scoop out."
C.	Scripture has so ordained matters that if a non-priest should scoop out the handful, the offering is invalid.

The polemic of No. 3 is against logic, not merely against the a-scriptural presentation of the law by the authorship of the Tosefta. That is a secondary consideration. The minor clarification at No. 4 of course is tacked on. Now we shall see a handsome demonstration of the impossibility of relying upon the logic of Listenwissenschaft, precisely the logic of the Mishnah, as we have seen:

XVIII:II.1A. "The priest shall scoop out of it a handful:"
B. Is the rule that a single handful suffices not only for a single tenth ephah of the offering, but a single handful also suffices for sixty tenth ephahs?
C. Or is the rule that a single handful serves only a single tenth ephah, while there must be sixty handfuls taken up out of sixty tenth ephahs?
D. Lo, I reason as follows:
E. The meal offering requires the taking up of a handful, and it also requires frankincense. Just as in the case of frankincense, a single handful serves for a single tenth ephah, and a single handful serves also for sixty tenth-ephahs, so in the case of the taking up of the handful, a single handful serves for one tenth ephah, and a single handful serves for sixty tenth ephahs.
F. Or try taking this route:
G. The meal offering requires the taking up of a handful, an it also requires oil. Just as in the case of the oil, a single log of oil serves for a single tenth ephah, while sixty logs of oil are required for sixty tenth ephahs, so in the case of a handful, the taking up of a handful serves a single tenth ephah, while for sixty tenth ephahs, there must be sixty taking ups of handfuls.
H. Let us then see to the correct analogy:
I. We should establish an analogy from something which is wholly offered up on the altar fire to something that is wholly offered up on the altar fire, but oil should not then enter the picture, since it is not wholly burned up on the altar fire.
J. Or take this route:
K. We should establish an analogy from something in which the smaller portion is indispensable to the validity of the entire portion [for instance, if any of the required fine flour or oil is lacking, the entire meal offering is null], but let us not propose proof from the example of frankincense, in which the lack of a smaller portion of the whole is not indispensable to the validity of the entire portion.
L. [Accordingly, we appeal to Scripture to settle matters, as it does when it says:] "The priest shall scoop out of it a handful:"
M. It is the rule that a single handful suffices not only for a single tenth ephah of the offering, but a single handful also suffices for sixty tenth ephahs.

This elegant exercise once more proves the falsity of appealing to classification for settling a moot point, because taxonomy yields contradictory results.

Let me give yet another example, because it shows a much more subtle critique of the logic of classification. It indicates that Sifra's authorship was prepared to concede the possibility of polythetic, not merely monothetic, classification—and to destroy that possibility as well! We proceed directly to the immediately following pericope, because it goes through the same process and then reverts to the more familiar attack on the very possibilities of classificatory or taxonomic logic. I present Parashat Vayyiqra Dibura Denedabah Pereq 13:

Sifra XXIII:I.1

> A. [Continuing the foregoing: R. Simeon says, "'When you present to the Lord a meal offering that is made in any of these ways, it shall be brought [to the priest who shall take it up to the altar'— that statement serves to encompass under the rule of waving also the sheaf of first grain, for it is said, 'When you come into the land which I give you and reap its harvest, you shall bring the sheaf of the first fruits of your harvest to the priest, [and he shall wave the sheaf before the Lord, that you may find acceptance]' (Lev. 23:10), '...who shall take it up to the altar' serves to encompass the meal offering of the wife accused of adultery, that that too requires being brought near: 'who shall take it up to the altar' [parallel to Num. 5:25]:"
> B. is that proposition not a matter of logic?
> C. if the meal offering brought by a sinner, which does not require waving, does require drawing near, the meal offering of a wife accused of adultery, which does require waving, surely should require drawing near.
> D. No, if you have invoked that rule in the case of the sinner's meal offering, which derives from wheat, will you invoke the same rule in the case of the meal offering of an accused wife, which does not derive from wheat [but from barley, and therefore falls into a different genus]?
> E. The meal offering of the sheaf of first brain will prove the contrary, for it too does not derive from wheat [but rather from barley] and yet it does require being brought near!
> F. No, if you have invoked that rule in the case of the meal offering of the sheaf of first grain, which requires also oil and frank incense, will you place into that same category and subject to

that same rule the meal offering of an accused wife, which does not require oil and frank incense?

G. Lo, you must therefore reason by appeal to a polythetic analogy [in which not all traits pertain to all components of the category, but some traits apply to them all in common]:

H. The sinner's meal offering, which derives from wheat, is not in all respects equivalent to the meal offering of the sheaf of first grain, which after all does not derive from wheat, nor is the meal offering of the sheaf of first grain, which requires oil and frank incense, equivalent in all respects to the meal offering of the sinner, which does not require oil and frankincense. But the common trait that pertains to them both is that they both require the taking up of a handful, and, furthermore, they both require being brought near.

I. So I shall invoke the case of the meal offering of an accused wife, which is equivalent to them in that the taking up of a handful is required. It should also be equivalent to them in being brought near.

J. Or perhaps what they have in common is that they are not valid if they derive from coarse meal and they require drawing near. Then that would exclude the meal offering of the accused wife, which indeed is valid when it derives from coarse meal, and which, therefore, should not require drawing near.

K. [Accordingly, Scripture is required to settle the matter, which it does when it states,]"..who shall take it up to the altar,"

L. which then serves to encompass the meal offering of the wife accused of adultery, and indicates that that too requires being brought near.

Precisely the same mode of argument worked out in XXII:I now applies to Simeon's proposition, with the same satisfactory result. I need hardly repeat the point that is already familiar.

Conducting a sustained and brilliant polemic against the Mishnah, the authorship of Sifra presents, in a systemic and orderly way, an amazing, subtle demonstration that there is no such thing as a genus, but only species. Then, it follows for our authorship, Scripture serves as the sole source for rules governing otherwise incomprehensible, because incomparable, species. A critical corollary is that the Mishnah not only rests upon false logic, but in failing to tie its propositions to Scripture, its authorship has set the law of the Torah upon unreliable foundations. The framers of Sifra then correct the errors of logic, on the one side, and set forth solid foundations in revelation, there alone, on the other. All of this they do while working their way through what will seem, on the surface, somewhat remote facts indeed. My hope is that the reader will find as compelling as I do the powerful, sustained, and amazingly cogent argument our authorship sets forth only in the minutia of cultic law.

The authors of Sifra, working on the book of Leviticus, have given us a mélange of materials, some of them exegetical in a narrow sense, others more broadly speculative Since all named authorities are supposed to have lived before the publication of the Mishnah in ca. 200, the work is assigned to the same period as the formation of the Mishnah. But passages in the Sifra cite verbatim both the Mishnah and the Tosefta, so the document as we have it certainly reached closure some time after ca. 200. It is an Amoraic text as much as the Tosefta and the Talmud of the Land of Israel. That fact is shown not only by the document's citing the Mishnah verbatim and pursuing an exegetical program vis-à-vis the Mishnah. There is a still more telling consideration. The polemic of the work takes account of the character of the Mishnah as a piece of writing essentially autonomous of Scripture and repeatedly claims one thing. It is that the rules of the Mishnah demand scriptural support, through exegesis. They cannot stand on their own as the result of a mere exercise in logic and reason. Accordingly, one principal purpose in the formation of the document addresses the issue of the standing of the Mishnah in relationship to Scripture (in theological terms: the Oral Torah in relationship to the Written Torah). It must follow that the document in its fundamental focus and stress derives from the period from ca. 200 to ca. 400. That is the age that also yielded the Tosefta, supplements to the Mishnah; the commentaries to Genesis and Leviticus called Genesis Rabbah and Leviticus Rabbah; the Talmud of the Land of Israel; and some of the formative layers of the Talmud of Babylonia.

Sifra has its own, strikingly polemical, purposes, for which the laws pertinent to, and even shared with, the Mishnah and the Tosefta are reshaped. Sifra proposes to present a kind of gemara, that is, an essay, worked out dialectically through questions and answers, rapidly and with great economy of expression and thought, moving from point to point within discrete thematic structures. While it often enough simply cites a verse and adds a few words about its interpretation, it much more commonly then goes on to raise a series of logical questions about that primary citation and original interpretation. These questions may vary, but predominant among them, the common one is, Might one think the opposite? How do we know that the original interpretation may withstand the test of reason, the consideration of different, mostly contrary, propositions? This, I think is the definitive characteristic of gemara and justifies our calling Sifra a sort of the Bavli, or Babylonian Talmud, in its own right. But I should claim that our authorship has given us a far more engaging statement than did the framers of the Bavli, because of the stunning coherence of their recurrent and methodical exercise.

One critical polemic, fundamental to Sifra's purpose, is to demonstrate the inadequacy of reason unaided by revelation. Time and again Sifra asks, Does this proposition, offered with a proof-text, really require the stated proof of revelation? Will it not stand firmly upon the basis of autonomous reason, unaided by Scripture? Sometimes Scripture will show that the opposite of the conclusion of reason is the result of exegesis. Therefore the truth is to be discovered solely through exegesis. At other times Sifra will show that reason by itself is flawed and fallible, not definitive. At important points it will seek to prove not only a given proposition, but also that that proposition is to be demonstrated solely through revelation, through exegesis of Scripture. In all it is difficult to avoid the impression that the primary purpose of the compilers of Sifra is to criticize the Mishnah and the Tosefta, documents only episodically interested in the exegetical foundations of their laws.

The Tosefta and Sifra look backward, toward the Mishnah. Only when we come to the Talmuds, the one of the land of Israel, ca. 400 C.E., the other of Babylonia, ca. 600 C.E., do we encounter a systematic response to the Mishnah that does not restrict itself to the framework defined by the Mishnah. But that next act of intellectual independence requires attention in its own terms, and,—by definition—they are not dictated by the Mishnah.

THE MISHNAH IN ROMAN AND CHRISTIAN CONTEXTS

JACOB NEUSNER

Bard College

The outmost context of comparison brings the Mishnah into juxtaposition with Roman legal codification, on the one side, and with Christian encounters with the law of Judaism, on the other. In the former exercise we ask a simple question: is the Mishnah like, or unlike, its Roman counterparts? In the latter we enter into the substance of the debate on the norms of Scripture conducted between Christianity and Judaism, now with special attention to the Mishnah's (and the Tosefta's) reading of the Sabbath commandments of Scripture and the interpretation of the same commandments set forth by Jesus.

I. THE MISHNAH IN THE CONTEXT OF ROMAN LEGAL CODIFICATION OF THE SECOND CENTURY

Since critics have dismissed out of hand my entire systematic representation of the Mishnah as the foundation-document, alongside Scripture, of Judaism, and since they have insisted it is nothing more than a law code like other law codes of its time and place, I decided to look into the matter further. It is commonly alleged that the Mishnah fits into the context of Roman legal codification of the second century. Is this the fact?

The answer matters, because it is further inferred that because the Mishnah (supposedly) finds its place within the framework of Roman legal codification of its time and place, it is to be read as a law code like other law codes, *in the genre of law codes*. It is not to be seen as I see it, that is, in its own terms and encompassing framework. I maintain that the Mishnah is *sui generis*. Others place it into the genre of law code. A genre is not defined by a single exemplar. The genre of law code is amply set forth by the Roman codification-process of the second century. And that brings us to the issue at hand. Is the Mishnah in general—process, premise, structure—

sufficiently like Roman legal codification to sustain comparison, hence also contrast, as part of a single genre? Or have the points of intersection and comparison been misconstrued or flagrantly misrepresented? Readers will answer for themselves.

The questions then are these: Is it true that the Mishnah fits into the context of Roman legal codification in the second century? Must or may we assign the Mishnah to the genre, law code, as defined by Roman law codes of the same century? To find out, I consulted a classicist for an account of Roman legal codification of the second century.[1] The result is partial but one-sided. Stephen A. Stertz touches on a variety of issues that pertain directly to problems of legal codification but that scarcely intersect in character or in contents with the Mishnah.[2] But at five points his account of Roman legal codification in the age in which the Mishnah took shape does afford perspective upon the Mishnah. Specifically, he treats five questions that may be addressed equally to the Mishnah and to the Roman process of codification. These points at which the Mishnah intersects with its Roman counterpart, not in detail but in large proportions, allow us to determine whether or not the Mishnah falls into the genre, legal code, as defined in its time and place, the Roman Empire of the second century.

Concerning myself not with details of comparing a particular Roman law with a particular Mishnah-law, but rather with the large and fundamental questions of literary redaction, I systematically compare the Mishnah with the Roman counterpart as Stertz portrays matters. I italicize the main pertinent result of Stertz's account of Roman legal codification, then comment on the Mishnah's counterpart, if any. At only one point does the Mishnah intersect with its Roman counterpart: it deals with some of the same subjects. But the Mishnah deals with a great many subjects that the Roman codes of its day ignore.

---

[1] Steven Stertz, "Roman Legal Codification in the Second Century," presented as an appendix in the following chapter.

[2] I also consulted Catherine Hezser, "The Codification of Legal Knowledge in Late Antiquity. The Talmud Yerushalmi and Roman Law Codes," in Peter Schaefer, ed., *The Talmud Yerushalmi and Graeco-Roman Culture*, pp. 581-641. But the Mishnah in particular is not at issue in that fine paper.

1. *The Institutional Foundations of Legal Codification: Who Determines the Law and on What Foundations?*

By the second century—Hadrian's day—the Emperor possessed the authority to make the law, hence to codify it.

A law code derives from an institutional sponsor, finding its authority in the standing of the one who determines the law. Does the Mishnah qualify as a law code by defining its institutional foundations and by specifying the politics that sustain the code, whether in fact or in myth?

So far as the genre, law code, involves a clear statement of sponsorship, the Mishnah does not fit. It rarely cites prior authoritative sources of the law, the Pentateuch for example. If we relied on the Mishnah's internal evidence, we could not answer the question for the document, who says? And why should anyone conform?

That is to say, unlike the Roman law codes, the Mishnah does not tell us who has determined the law and on what institutional basis he has done so. True, Judah the Patriarch is credited in the continuation-documents with promulgating the Mishnah. But not a single piece of evidence internal to the document itself supports that allegation. It is further taken for granted that the Patriarchate, recognized as the Jewish ethnic government in the land of Israel, formed the institutional basis for enforcing the law of the Mishnah.

The Mishnah does set forth a fantasy-sponsorship, out of relationship with the politics that sustained the document itself. The Mishnah assumes that the King, High priest, and Sanhedrin took charge of law-enforcement, so tractate Sanhedrin, e.g., Chapter 2 for High priest and King. But the Mishnah acknowledges that the Temple lies in ruins and knows no Israelite monarch. So the Mishnah contains no counterpart to the Roman emperor as sponsor of the system, and its authorities are fictive, perhaps eschatological.

What about the patriarch (*nasi*)—is he not the sponsor of the Mishnah within the framework of the Mishnah? The evidence that the Patriarch sponsored the Mishnah, employed sages educated in its law, and enforced their decisions, is difficult to discern in the details of the Mishnah. To be sure, the Mishnah knows "the nasi," ordinarily assumed to refer to the patriarch. But by "nasi" is sometimes meant "head of the sages' court" (e.g., M. Hag. 2:2), sometimes, "head of the local Jewish community" (e.g., M. Ta. 2:1).

More to the point, there is a disjuncture between the representation of the Nasi and his alleged position in sponsorship of the

Mishnah or of the Halakhah in general. Where we do have a political power called patriarch (*nasi*), his alleged sponsorship of the Mishnah does not figure. The one context in which the ethnarch does figure is Tractate Horayot, where "*nasi*" clearly pertains to the principal authority of the community of Judaism in the land of Israel. The context is errors of instruction or decision-making made by the high priest or the *nasi*. None of this suggests that the Mishnah is credited to the Jewish ethnarch or patriarch. From the discussion in Mishnah- and Tosefta Horayot, we should have no reason to attribute the Mishnah as a law-code to the sponsorship of the patriarch/*nasi*, in the way in which we have ample reason to attribute the Roman law codes of the second century to the sponsorship of the emperor. A genre to encompass both the Mishnah and the Roman law codes would have to accommodate both a total fantasy-system with a practical account of how a powerful government administers the civil order.

To sum up: the Mishnah does not explain itself or account for its institutional foundations. We do not know who determines the law and on what foundations. If we take for granted that the document speaks for the consensus of the sages who collected or made up its laws, our supposition is no more solidly grounded. In this aspect of matters, Stertz's account of Roman law codes in this aspect yields no common ground with the Mishnah.

2. *Of What Does a Code Consist?*

What occurred under Hadrian? The law was collected and fixed. Various documents were brought together and redacted, with some reorganization but minor changes in actual content.

The Mishnah represents its contents not as a compilation of various documents that have been brought together and redacted, but as a free-standing system, resting on its own foundations of applied reason and practical logic. The document only rarely preserves the indicators of a prior piece of writing. It ordinarily obscures the markings of origin in autonomous tradition. It rarely collects and sets forth opinions of a given school or authority or prior document. It homogenizes whatever language of individuality it has received and commonly lays out all opinion in a uniform rhetoric. Form-analysis of the Mishnah is complete and detailed and leaves no doubt whatsoever as to these facts. So while the Mishnah may have collected and fixed the laws of received documents, nothing in the document as we have it signals that fact, and the prevailing literary policy of the framers of the document contradicts it. So if the mark of the genre, law code, as defined by the Roman laws was to highlight the diverse origins of law now collected and reorganized with minor changes—a law code as collection and arrangement of existing law—the Mishnah simply does not exhibit the indicative traits of a law code.

Let us then consider the facts of the matter, which those who assign the Mishnah to the genre, law code, do not address when they criticize the systemic reading of the Mishnah (and Tosefta). Is the Mishnah comprised of collections of laws, various documents brought together and redacted with some reorganization? It is difficult to answer with any certainty. The answer is, rarely and not as a paramount characteristic of the formal definition of the document. On the one hand, we can pick out anomalous compositions that clearly form a free-standing collection, for example, Tractate Kelim Chapter Twenty-Four, representing a particular authority on a given set of closely-related problems. There are, moreover, formal composites that cohere not on topic or problem, as is the norm for the Mishnah, but around formulations of language. These, which are uncommon in the Mishnah in general, are represented by M. Meg. 1:4ff. So they do exist. These anomalous compositions are organized not by topic, as is characteristic of the Mishnah, but by principle or by verbal pattern. Clearly, a theory of writing up the law other than the one that prevails in the Mishnah is in play here (M. Meg. 1:4-1:11):

1:4 A.		[If] they read the Scroll in the first Adar, and then the year was intercalated, they read it [again] in the second Adar.
I B.		There is no difference between [the fourteenth or fifteenth of] the first Adar and [the same dates in] the second Adar except for the reading of the Scroll and giving gifts to the poor [which must be done in the second Adar, not in the first Adar, but in both Adars on the fourteenth or fifteenth, lamentations and fasts are prohibited].
1:5 II A.		There is no difference between a festival day and the Sabbath day except for preparing food alone [M. Bes. 5:2].
III B.		There is no difference between the Sabbath and the Day of Atonement except that deliberately violating this one is punishable at the hands of an earthly court, while deliberately violating that one is punishable through extirpation.

1:6 IV A. There is no difference between one who is prohibited by vow from deriving [general] benefit from his fellow, and one who is prohibited by vow from deriving food from his fellow, except for setting foot in his house and using utensils of his which are not for preparing food [permitted in the former case].

V B. There is no difference between vows and freewill offerings, except that for animals designated in fulfillment of vows one is responsible, while for animals set aside in fulfillment of freewill offerings one is not responsible [should the animal be lost].

1:7 VI A. There is no difference between a Zab who suffers two appearances of flux and one who suffers three except for the requirement of an offering [for the latter].

VII B. There is no difference between a mesora who is shut up and one who has been certified except for the requirement to mess up the hair and tear the clothing.

VIII C. There is no difference between [a mesora] declared clean having been shut up and one declared clean having been certified [unclean] except for the requirement of shaving and of bringing a bird offering.

1:8 IX A. There is no difference between sacred scrolls and phylacteries and mezuzot except that sacred scrolls may be written in any alphabet ["language"], while phylacteries and mezuzot are written only in square ["Assyrian"] letters.

B. Rabban Simeon b. Gamaliel says, "Also: in the case of sacred scrolls: they have been permitted to be written only in Greek."

1:9 X A. There is no difference between a priest who is anointed with anointing oil and one who wears many garments except in the bullock which is offered for unwitting transgression of any of the commandments [required only of the former].

XI B. There is no difference between a [high] priest presently in service and [high] priest [who served) in times past except for the bullock which is offered on the Day of Atonement and the tenth of the ephah [cf., M. Hor. 3:4].

1:10 XII A. There is no difference between a major high place and a minor high place except for Passover offerings.

B. This is the governing principle: Whatever is offered in fulfillment of a vow or as a freewill offering may be offered on a high place,

C.	And whatever is not offered in fulfillment of a vow or as a freewill offering may not be offered on a high place.
1:11 A.	There is no difference between Shilo and Jerusalem except that in Shilo they eat Lesser Holy Things and second tithe in any place within sight [of the place], while in Jerusalem [they eat the same things only] within the wall.
B.	And in both places Most Holy Things are eaten [only] within the area encompassed by the veils.
C.	[After] the sanctification of Shilo it was permitted [to set up high places elsewhere], but after the sanctification of Jerusalem it was not permitted [to set up high places elsewhere] [M. Zeb. 14:4-8].

This protracted abstract suffices to show what a distinct source, freestanding and autonomous of the Mishnah, looks like in the context of the Mishnah. The upshot is, the document does encompass selections from various legal documents. But these are anomalous, few and unrepresentative. So if the case serves, then it underscores the uniformity of the bulk of the Mishnah, which is characterized by two traits. First, it is composed in highly disciplined language and adheres to a few, uniform rules of rhetoric. Second, it is organized by topic, and it sets forth its topical program in accord with the dictates of the problematics of a given topic—the specific issues concerning the topic at hand that engage the framers of the law.

The document is, over all, marked by recurrent formal traits, and these obscure the origin of law in prior compilations. It suffices to point out, for example, that the Mishnah forms its completed units of discourse in groups of threes or fives. The numerical patterns render inaccessible any supposed prior law collections that have now been formed into a single code.

So I maintain that Stertz's account of the second century law codes gives us a kind of legal writing—collection of prior documents—that does not characterize the Mishnah. If a genre is formed by common policies of rhetoric or topical program—construction and organization and exposition—that characterize two distinct kinds of writing then the Mishnah and the second century Roman law codes simply do not belong together in a common genre. Those who categorize the Mishnah as a law code like Roman law codes have yet to do more than allege their reading of matters. They have not validated it.

To show what a labor of verification and falsification requires, let me summarize the criteria of formalization and organization of the Mishnah, criteria that apply throughout. These are the traits of the writing—the policies of composition and formalization—that we should expect to find characteristic of other documents that are supposed to share the common genre.

The first of the two criteria of formalization and organization derives from the nature of the principal divisions themselves: theme. It is along thematic lines that the redactors organized vast corpora of materials into principal divisions, tractates. These fundamental themes themselves were subdivided into smaller conceptual units. The principal divisions treat their themes in units indicated by the sequential unfolding of their inner logical structure. Accordingly, one established criterion for the deliberation of an aggregate of materials from some other, fore or aft, will be a shift in the theme, or predominant and characteristic concern, of a sequence of materials. The second fundamental criterion is the literary character, the syntactical and grammatical pattern, which differentiates and characterizes a sequence of primitive (that is, undifferentiable, indivisible) units of thought. Normally, when the subject changes, the mode of expression, the formal or formulary character, the patterning of language, will change as well.

From the basic traits of large-scale organization, which appeal to the characteristics of subject-matter, we turn to the way in which sentences and paragraphs are put together. By a "paragraph" (which is a metaphor drawn from our own circumstance), I mean a completed exposition of thought, the setting forth of a proposition whole and complete, now without regard to the larger function, e.g., in a sustained discourse of argument or proposition, served by that thought. Two or more lapidary statements, e.g., allegations as to fact, will make up such a sustained cognitive unit. The cognitive units in the Mishnah in particular resort to a remarkably limited repertoire of formulary patterns, and the document as a whole exhibits remarkable formal uniformity.

For the authorship of the Mishnah manages to say whatever it wants in one of the following ways:
1. the simple declarative sentence, in which the subject, verb, and predicate are syntactically tightly joined to one another, e.g., he who does so and so is such and such;
2. the duplicated subject, in which the subject of the sentence is stated twice, e.g., He who does so and so, lo, he is such and such;

3. mild apocopation, in which the subject of the sentence is cut off from the verb, which refers to its own subject, and not the one with which the sentence commences, e.g., He who does so and so..., it [the thing he has done] is such and such;
4. extreme apocopation, in which a series of clauses is presented, none of them tightly joined to what precedes or follows, and all of them cut off from the predicate of the sentence, e.g., He who does so and so..., it [the thing he has done] is such and such..., it is a matter of doubt whether...or whether...lo, it [referring to nothing in the antecedent, apocopated clauses of the subject of the sentence] is so and so...
5. In addition to these formulary patterns, in which the distinctive formulary traits are effected through variations in the relationship between the subject and the predicate of the sentence, or in which the subject itself is given a distinctive development, there is yet a fifth. In this last one we have a contrastive complex predicate, in which case we may have two sentences, independent of one another, yet clearly formulated so as to stand in acute balance with one another in the predicate, thus, He who does...is unclean, and he who does not...is clean.

It naturally will be objected, is it possible that "a simple declarative sentence" may be asked to serve as a formulary pattern, alongside the rather distinctive and unusual constructions which follow? True, by itself, a tightly constructed sentence consisting of subject, verb, and complement, in which the verb refers to the subject, and the complement to the verb, hardly exhibits traits of particular formal interest. Yet a sequence of such sentences, built along the same gross grammatical lines, may well exhibit a clear-cut and distinctive pattern. And here the mnemonics of the document enter into consideration. The Mishnah is not a generalizing document; it makes its points by repeating several cases that yield the same, ordinarily unarticulated, general principle. Accordingly, the Mishnah, as I said, utilizes sets of three or five repetitions of cases to make a single point. Now when we see that three or five "simple declarative sentences" take up one principle or problem, and then, when the principle or problem shifts, a quite distinctive formal pattern will be utilized, we realize that the "simple declarative sentence" has served the formulator of the unit of thought as aptly as did apocopation, a dispute, or another more obviously distinctive form or formal pattern. The contrastive predicate is one example; the Mishnah contains many more.

The important point of differentiation, particularly for the simple declarative sentence, therefore appears in the intermediate or the whole cognitive unit, thus in the interplay between theme and form. It is there that we see a single pattern recurring in a long sequence of sentences, e.g., the X which has lost its Y is unclean because of its Z. The Z which has lost its Y is unclean because of its X. Another example will be a long sequence of highly developed sentences, laden with relative clauses and other explanatory matter, in which a single syntactical pattern will govern the articulation of three or six or nine exempla. That sequence will be followed by one repeated terse sentence pattern, e.g., X is so and so, Y is such and such, Z is thus and so. The former group will treat one principle or theme, the latter some other. There can be no doubt, therefore, that the declarative sentence in recurrent patterns is, in its way, just as carefully formalized as a sequence of severely apocopated sentences or of contrastive predicates or duplicated subjects. None of the Mishnah's secondary and amplificatory companions, e.g., the Tosefta, the Talmud of the Land of Israel or Yerushalmi, the Talmud of Babylonia or Bavli, exhibits the same tight and rigidly-adhered-to rhetorical cogency.

It follows that the Mishnah is mainly, though not exclusively, the work of its final redactors. Whatever laws they have collected, whatever opinions they have amassed, they have formalized and presented as a stylistically cogent whole. We cannot say that various documents have been brought together and cobbled into a single statement. If that is what Hadrian's lawyers did, then the Mishnah's counterparts engaged in an altogether different enterprise—no common genre here.

3. *What Is the Standing of the Code?*

There was one uniform, permanent, unalterable edition from Hadrian's reign. What was done was to edit the received laws, forbidding alterations.

If a law code is published in writing, then the Mishnah does not belong to the genre, law code, because it was not published in writing. I invite the proponents of the view that the Mishnah is a law code like other Roman law codes of the time and place to explain how the Mishnah qualifies in this fundamental trait of the alleged genre: publication in conventional form.

The Mishnah was not published in writing, True, there was a uniform text. But it was not generally accessible, as a law code in the Roman model was, to its constituency. Saul Lieberman maintains: "Since in the entire Talmudic literature we do not find that a book of the Mishnah was ever consulted in the case of controversies or doubt concerning a particular reading, we may safely conclude that the compilation was not published in writing, that a written ekdosis [edition] of the Mishnah did not exist." The Mishnah was published in a different way:

> A regular oral ekdosis, edition, of the Mishnah was in existence, a fixed text recited by the Tannaim of the college. The Tannaite authority ('repeater, reciter') committed to memory the text of certain portions of the Mishnah which he subsequently recited in the college in the presence of the great masters of the Law. Those Tannaim were pupils chosen for their extraordinary memory, although they were not always endowed with due intelligence.... When the Mishnah was committed to memory and the Tannaim recited it in the college, it was thereby published and possessed all the traits and features of a written ekdosis... Once the Mishnah was accepted among the college Tannaim (reciters) it was difficult to cancel it.

Lieberman's evidence for these conclusions is drawn from two sources, first, sayings within the rabbinical corpus and stories about how diverse problems of transmission of materials were worked out, second, parallels, some of them germane but none of them probative, drawn from Greco-Roman procedures of literary transmission.

Considerably more compelling evidence of the same proposition derives from the internal character of the Mishnah itself. But if stylization and formalization testify to a mnemonic program, then absence of the same traits must mean that some materials were not intended to be memorized. The Mishnah, and the Mishnah alone, was the corpus to be formulated for memorization and transmitted through "living books," Tannaim, to the coming generations. The Tosefta cannot have been formulated along the same lines. Accordingly, the Mishnah is given a special place and role by those who stand behind it.

The Mishnah's publication represents a unique procedure, with no counterpart in the Roman practice of the second century as Stertz lays it out. If, as I say, the Roman codes belong to the genre, law code, then the Rabbinic one does not.

4. *How Is the Code Organized?*

The codified praetor's edict is set forth topically. First come rules of procedure and jurisdiction, actions before the actual trial, then come legal remedies. The topics of the law encompass property of various classifications, e.g., consecrated for religious purposes, belonging to wives (inclusive of divorce), stolen property, wills, guardianship, water rights, property destroyed in fires and shipwrecks, the execution of judgment, legal formulae, public property.

The Mishnah also is organized topically, and that is an important point in common with the Roman code of its day. In this aspect the Mishnah certainly does compare with the Roman counterpart. But it also compares with those Pentateuchal codes that are organized topically, Leviticus 1-15, for example, and with the Qumran library's law code, with its (truncated) topical construction as well. Tractates Niddah-Zabim and Negaim exactly correspond with Leviticus 12-15, to take a blatant example, and Parah to Numbers 19, to take another. So the topical construction on its own does not establish a common genre, law code, encompassing the Mishnah and the Roman codes—unless we assign to the same genre other law codes of other communities of Judaism. More to the point, the topics of the Mishnah intersect with those of the Roman codes only at some few points. If for convenience' sake we call "secular" the topics of the Roman code, then the Mishnah's topical program vastly transcends the "secular," and the "sacred" ones vastly outweigh the secular. Then there is no topical indicator that would tell us what belongs and what does not belong in the genre, law code. What is left is any compilation of norms whether of behavior or of belief, whether of a sacred or a secular character, qualifies for the genre, law code.

But then the genre has no use; it tells us any statement of how things should be done, whatever its formal traits, whatever its logical qualities, whatever its topical program, constitutes a "law code." What does not tell us what does not belong cannot tell us what does. Then the traits shared in common by the Roman codes of the second century and the Mishnah prove abstract, trivial, and unenlightening. Stated simply: the allegation that both the Mishnah and the Roman codes belong to the proposed genre, codes, makes no difference at all in our understanding of either code or both. What they have in common is nothing consequential, and we cannot then explain a trait of the one by appeal to a counterpart trait of the other.

So the supposed common genre does not allow us to answer the question, why this, not that? The upshot, in a word, is this: genre by topic—so what?

5. *The Purpose of the Code*

The code was meant to collect and organize the law, to order the received materials, annual accretions, repetitions and ambiguities.

The traits of the Roman codes permit us to state the purpose of those that made them. The Mishnah contains not a hint about what its authors conceive their work to be. Is it a law-code? Is it a school-book? Since it makes statements describing what people should and should not do, or rather, do and do not do, we might suppose it is a law-code. Since it covers topics of both practical and theoretical interest, we might suppose it is a school-book. But the Mishnah never expresses a hint about its authors' intent. The reason is that the authors do what they must to efface all traces not only of individuality but even of their own participation in the formation of the document. So it is not only a letter from utopia to whom it may concern. It also is a letter written by no one person—but not by a committee, either. If the genre, law-code, serves to tell people what the law is, then the Mishnah certainly does not qualify. If the genre, law-code, provokes theorizing on the deeper philosophical issues embodied by practical cases, e.g., issues of causation or of theology, then the Roman codes do not qualify within the genre, a law code, as exemplified by most of the Mishnah. For the Roman codes, the Mishnah encompasses too much within the genre it is supposed to embody, for the Mishnah, the Roman counterpart encompasses too little.

6. *The Upshot: Does the Mishnah Belong to the Genre, Law Code?*

If the genre, law code, is defined by the Roman codes as Stertz portrays them, then the Mishnah does not belong. A genre cannot be defined by a unique document, and in the contexts treated here, the Mishnah emerges without counterpart. No other document sufficiently compares to afford the occasion of defining a genre encompassing the Mishnah and some other compilation of social norms, including laws on topics treated in law codes—none.

Let me be clear. I recognize that comparative study of Roman law and the law of Judaism yields illuminating results. But here at issue is not details of the Halakhah contained in the Mishnah in comparison with details of Roman law contained in the codes. A vast and valuable corpus of detailed work has compared and contrasted the Halakhah (transcending that contained in the Mishnah to be sure) and Roman law. But with what result for the categorization of the Mishnah? I see none whatsoever. For the Mishnah's Halakhah intersects with that of the Pentateuch, the Elephantine Papyri, the Gospels, and the Dead Sea Scrolls—not to mention legal formulas and traditions of Sumer, Akkad, and Babylon! And no one has then insisted that we read the Halakhah of the Mishnah, let alone the Mishnah as a whole, in the context of ancient Israel, Elephantine, earliest Christian communities, Qumran, Sumer, Akkad, or Babylon. If the Mishnah is not *sui generis*, no one has yet established the genre to which, viewed whole and complete, it belongs. The burden of defining that genre encompassing the Mishnah with other documents belongs on the shoulders of those who do not see the document, as I do, *as sui* generis—even in the context of Rabbinic Judaism to its time and for a thousand years afterward as well.

II. Mishnah and the Gospels

The other exterior context pertinent to Mishnah-interpretation is the Christian one, broadly construed. Just as for Catholic, Orthodox Christianity, the Gospels form the starting point and foundation-stone for all else, so, for normative Judaism, the Mishnah and its associated traditions in the Tosefta serve the same function. When we align the two foundation-documents side by side, we establish a point of comparison and contrast for the religious systems constructed on the foundations of each one, Rabbinic Judaism and Catholic, Orthodox Christianity, respectively.

Not only so, but the two documents further intersect in the Hebrew Scriptures of ancient Israel, which both religious systems claim for their own, the one as the Written part of the one whole Torah of our rabbi, Moses, the other as the Old Testament, prefiguring the new. And both compilations concur that the Hebrew Scriptures set forth authoritative teachings, but need not be emulated. Neither pretends to recapitulate the traits of Scripture. The Mishnah's laws are given no revelation-myth ("the Lord spoke to

Moses say, Speak to the children of Israel and say to them"), and the Gospel's accounts of the life and teachings of Jesus draw upon—but do not copy—any of the Israelite Scripture's lives. Each document, then, pays profound respect to that Scripture while going its own way. The acutely logical organization of the Mishnah, the Passion Narrative at the climax of the Gospels—neither imitates any prior Israelite writing, whether Scripture or otherwise, and both inaugurate a length and vital tradition, each of its own character and quality.

And, it further follows, the two foundation-writings—the Mishnah and the Gospels—share a common aspiration: to make an autonomous statement, free-standing and not exegetical in form. Rather than citing a verse of the Hebrew Scriptures and commenting on it in such a way as to make a fresh point—displaying such ideas as the framers wished to lay out, both the Mishnah and the Gospels define their own organizing structures, even while utilizing exegetical forms here and there, at Matthew 2-3, Mishnah-tractate Sotah chapter eight, for instance.

Viewed as foundation-documents for the religious community to which each is addressed—each a group claiming to embody the "Israel" of Scripture—they part company from one another, but predictably so. The Mishnah bears a social message, aiming at a restorationist vision of the heart of the Torah's vision of humanity—how Adam and Eve will regain Eden in the embodiment of Israel restoring the Land of Israel to perfection. Necessarily, therefore, its authorship (those responsible for the document as we now know it) chooses the form of a systematic law code, laying out whatever theological ideas it wishes to present in the form of detailed rules. The Gospels, representing their "Israel" in the embodiment of God, through Christ as the Last Adam, the model of humanity in God's image, after God's likeness ("God incarnate") frame their messages around the biography of the principal figure of the faith. But Rabbinic Judaism makes its principal statements through describing the norms of the Israelite social order, and the Gospels, theirs through appealing to the figure and the model of Jesus Christ, whom the faithful are to emulate. So matters of virtue, theological convictions, formulations of the holy, in the Mishnah find their place in a large legal system, and in the Gospels, in a counterpart biographical structure.

A. *Dating, Provenience, and Purpose of the Literature*

The canonical Gospels reached closure a century before the Mishnah was concluded, the former around 100 at the latest, the latter around 200 at the earliest. The provenience of the Gospels, all scholarship concurs, finds its location in the communities of Christianity who treasured the remembered model of the earthly life of their "risen Lord." The purpose of the Gospels was to set forth what it means for God to take the form of man, so providing the model for the Christian communities themselves to aspire to live Godly lives in the interim until Christ returns. These well-established readings of the Gospels underscore the social character of the Gospels, their power to make a systemic statement of the faith through their portrayal of the founder thereof.

The same aspiration to lay out the shape and structure of the holy community of the faithful characterizes the formation of the traditions attributed to oral tradition from Sinai that are recorded in the counterpart foundation documents of Rabbinic Judaism. The Mishnah, the Tosefta, and a third corpus of kindred traditions, external to the Mishnah and called by an Aramaic word meaning, "external traditions," Baraitot, systematically cite authorities who flourished in the first and second centuries C.E. Some of these laws and teachings may well originate in the period in which the named authorities flourished. But the first documentary evidence we have of them is the Mishnah, the Tosefta, and for the corpus of Baraitot, the two Talmuds, the Talmud of the Land of Israel of ca. 400 C.E., and the Talmud of Babylonia of ca. 600 C.E. Consequently, we cannot take for granted that the Mishnah, Tosefta, and baraita-literature informs us about the state of the law that sages put forth in first two centuries.

The compilations find a common provenience in the circles of masters and disciples who are described as links in the chain of oral tradition beginning with Moses at Sinai and concluding with named authorities who appear in the Mishnah itself. The upshot is, the Mishnah and related legal traditions are assigned a place in the ongoing chain of oral tradition, commencing with God to Moses "our rabbi," and ultimately transcribed in the Mishnah, Tosefta, and the baraita-corpus of the Talmuds. That provenience is best described for us in the following account of how the Mishnah-traditions were formulated from ancient times onward to the Mishnah itself (B. Erub. 5:1 I.43/54b):

> A. Our rabbis have taught on Tannaite authority:
> B. What is the order of Mishnah teaching? Moses learned it from the mouth of the All-Powerful. Aaron came in, and Moses repeated his chapter to him and Aaron went forth and sat at the left hand of Moses. His sons came in and Moses repeated their chapter to them, and his sons went forth. Eleazar sat at the right of Moses, and Ithamar at the left of Aaron.
> D. Then the elders entered, and Moses repeated for them their Mishnah chapter. The elders went out. Then the whole people came in, and Moses repeated for them their Mishnah chapter. So it came about that Aaron repeated the lesson four times, his sons three times, the elders two times, and all the people once.
> E. Then Moses went out, and Aaron repeated his chapter for them. Aaron went out. His sons repeated their chapter. His sons went out. The elders repeated their chapter. So it turned out that everybody repeated the same chapter four times.

The Mishnah is represented, therefore, as a document that was orally formulated and orally transmitted in a process of memorization. The principle of imitating God here is embodied in the master-disciple relationship; for each master himself was a disciple, each a link backward in the chain of tradition to Moses, God's disciple on Sinai, so states tractate Abot, the Mishnah's first apologetic, of ca. 250 C.E. (M. Abot 1:1):

> A. Moses received Torah at Sinai and handed it on to Joshua, Joshua to elders, and elders to prophets. And prophets handed it on to the men of the great assembly.
> B. They said three things: (1) "Be prudent in judgment. (2) Raise up many disciples. (3) Make a fence for the Torah."

Here we see two allegations, the first, oral tradition, the second, oral tradition is not the same as the tradition of the Written Torah; the three sayings are not citations of Scripture but statements of sages themselves. Each link in the chain of tradition, from God to Moses, from master to disciple, bears its own inscription, and every statement forms part of that same tradition, orally formulated and orally transmitted through human memory, of Sinai.

If the dating and provenience of the great foundation-code prove difficult to ascertain, the purpose is blatant. When we realize that the Mishnah took shape in the aftermath of the destruction of the

Temple in 70 C.E. and the defeat of Bar Kokhba and the definitive closure of Jerusalem to Jewry in ca. 135 C.E., the topical program of the Mishnah attests to its purpose. The Mishnah, and the entire legal code given its classical formulation in the Mishnah, forms a systematic, sustained essay on the sanctification of Israel, the people, in its enduring realization of God's rule in the Torah. The Mishnah and related compilations make the opening statement of a large and coherent theological structure, which animates the entirety of the Rabbinic writings of late antiquity and imparts cogency to the message of each with the messages of all the others. No consideration of the provenience of the Mishnah in relationship to the Gospels can ignore the theology that is embodied in the law of the Mishnah as much as in the lore and exegesis of its counterpart documents, the Midrashim. The theological system built upon the Mishnah, Tosefta, and baraita-corpus rests on four propositions, all of them variations on the authorized history of Scripture from Genesis through Kings:

1. God formed creation in accord with a plan, which the Torah reveals. World order can be shown by the facts of nature and society set forth in that plan to conform to a pattern of reason based upon justice. Those who possess the Torah—Israel—know God and those who do not—the gentiles—reject him in favor of idols. What happens to each of the two sectors of humanity, respectively, responds to their relationship with God. Israel in the present age is subordinate to the nations, because God has designated the gentiles as the medium for penalizing Israel's rebellion, meaning through Israel's subordination and exile to provoke Israel to repent. Private life as much as the public order conforms to the principle that God rules justly in a creation of perfection and stasis.

2. The perfection of creation, realized in the rule of exact justice, is signified by the timelessness of the world of human affairs, their conformity to a few enduring paradigms that transcend change. Involved here is a theology of history, an account of how God works through what happens to man. No present, past, or future marks time, but only the recapitulation of those patterns. Perfection is further embodied in the unchanging relationships of the social commonwealth. What is required here is a theology of political economy, which assures that scarce resources, once allocated, remain in stasis. In that way the politics and economics of the social order will correspond to that perfection that was attained at Eden. A further

indication of perfection lies in the complementarity of the components of creation, on the one side, and, finally, the correspondence between God and man, in God's image (theological anthropology), on the other. At stake here is an account of God's view of man, a systematic investigation of how God intended man to be.

3. Israel's condition, public and personal, marks flaws in creation. What disrupts perfection is the sole power capable of standing on its own against God's power, and that is man's will. What man controls and God cannot coerce is man's capacity to form intention and therefore choose either arrogantly to defy, or humbly to love, God. Because man defies God, the sin that results from man's rebellion flaws creation and disrupts world order. The paradigm of the rebellion of Adam in Eden governs, the act of arrogant rebellion leading to exile from Eden thus accounting for the condition of humanity. But, as in the original transaction of alienation and consequent exile, God retains the power to encourage repentance through punishing man's arrogance. In mercy, moreover, God exercises the power to respond to repentance with forgiveness, that is, a change of attitude evoking a counterpart change. Since, commanding his own will, man also has the power to initiate the process of reconciliation with God, through repentance, an act of humility, man may restore the perfection of that order that through arrogance he has marred.

4. God ultimately will restore that perfection that embodied his plan for creation. In the work of restoration death that comes about by reason of sin will die, the dead will be raised and judged for their deeds in this life, and most of them, having been justified, will go on to eternal life in the world to come. In the paradigm of man restored to Eden is realized in Israel's return to the Land of Israel. In that world or age to come, however, that sector of humanity that through the Torah knows God will encompass all of humanity. Idolators will perish, and humanity that comprises Israel at the end will know the one, true God and spend eternity in his light.[3]

Now, recorded in this way, the story told by the Mishnah proves remarkably familiar, with its stress on God's justice (to which his mercy is integral), man's correspondence with God in his posses-

---

[3] I have shown that these four propositions encompass the entire system of Rabbinic Judaism in my *Theology of the Oral Torah: Revealing the Justice of God* (Kingston, 1998).

sion of the power of will, man's sin and God's response. But the Mishnah and the other Halakhic compilations do not tell their story through narrative but through law. The story that the law means to translate into normative rules of conduct turns out to account for the condition of the world and also to adumbrate the restoration of humanity to Eden through the embodiment of Israel in the Land of Israel. So much, in brief terms, for the purpose of the Mishnah and related Rabbinic documents. No one has ever alleged that the Mishnah and the Gospels form a common genre of writing.

B. *Questions in, and Methods of, Comparison with the Gospels*

Now that we have dealt with the hermeneutics, we may reasonably translate the result into exegesis. Comparison of how major components of the Mishnah's law and doctrine address issues taken up by the Gospels' traditions of Jesus affords perspective on the systems that build through those components. And that perspective affords insight into two fundamental traits of Catholic, Orthodox Christianity and Rabbinic Judaism: how they sort out the heritage of a shared Scripture, where and why they part company in their respective systems for human salvation. It is time for the comparison of wholes:[4] large constructs of a systematic character concerning normative conviction and conduct, the one set forth in the Gospels, read not only discretely but also as a whole composite of Christian con-

---

[4] Until the appearance of E.P. Sanders, *Paul and Palestinian Judaism* (Philadelphia, 1975) no one had ever shown what a coherent picture of several distinct Judaisms, each examined in its own terms, would look like, either each on its own or all seen side by side. So far as I know, Sanders was the first to portray as sustained and crafted religious systems, without attempting to harmonize, or correlate, or explain away differences among them, the Judaism of the Dead Sea community, the Judaism of the rabbis, and the Judaism of Paul. The work exhibited profound flaws, since it was undertaken on a narrowly-historical and historicistic base and therefore required that all of the Judaisms flourish on the same plane of time. The advantages of the comparative study of religions applied to the study of different systems of the same genus of religions (here: Judaism) were lost. And, unfortunately, Sanders himself repudiated the entire approach in his *Judaism*, published two decades later, which portrays a supposed unitary Judaism, encompassing all sources, whatever their systemic provenience. But in his first and most important work on Judaism, Sanders opened up an entirely new approach to the study of ancient Judaism, and in systematically differentiating between and among the formations of a single religion, he provoked thought on an entirely fresh set of questions.

viction, the other set forth in the counterpart construction of the Mishnah and associated legal traditions.

What is the alternative to the kind of holistic comparison of theological and even legal (normative) constructions characteristic of the Christianity and the Judaism represented by Gospels and Mishnah, respectively? A century of exegetical work leaves in obscurity few points of intersection at details. Everyone now knows that Jesus concurs with the House of Shammai as to grounds for divorce, that Hillel and Jesus agree on Lev. 19:18 as the center-piece of faith, and much else. If Jesus has been described as a Sadducee and also as a Pharisee, as a member of the House of Shammai and also as a member of the House of Hillel, as a rabbi who said especially well what rabbis were supposed to say and as an anti-rabbi whose authentic sayings can only be those not found in the Rabbinic corpus, then matters have pretty well run their course. But that is not only because a method that yields everything and its opposite provides flawed guidance in the study of the privileged documents, in the present instance, the Gospels and the figure of Jesus portrayed therein. It is also because nearly everybody in Gospels- and Rabbinic-scholarship today recognizes the problem of critical history: the Mishnah comes to closure a century after the Gospels. How then are we supposed to open the Mishnah for an account of "Jewish law" or "Pharisaic law" a century earlier?

The labor-saving response—"they must have had a tradition"—no longer compels broad credence. In fact, if we want to know the state of "Jewish law" in the first century, we begin not with the Mishnah and its attributions of sayings to first century figures—these are beyond all tests of verification or falsification—but with the Gospels' stories themselves. These stand far closer to the events of which they speak than the Mishnah's counterpart laws. Not only so, but until the Mishnah enjoys a privileged position in the shared enterprise of biblical studies concerning New Testament times, the Gospels will always define the governing agenda, dictating the points of inquiry. And, finally, the kind of history of Mishnaic law that the Mishnah (and the Tosefta) itself makes possible allows us to identify conceptions that, logically, must precede and precipitate subordinate conceptions; then we have a logical sequence, A must come before B, which can correspond to a temporal sequence, A was set forth, and then, confronted with the inner tensions contained by A,

B was formulated.[5] That is to say, before we can conduct an argument on how to divide an apple, we have to affirm that we have an apple to divide. Before sages can debate secondary questions, they have to have in hand primary principles subject to refinement later on. All that the test at hand does is search out anachronism of an intellectual character, for instance, attributing to an early authority an opinion on a question that is systematically investigated only much after that authority flourished.

But these logical- and possibly-temporal-sequences hardly correspond to a social history of how the law actually was set forth and practiced. The upshot is, unless we accept at face value the attributions of sayings to named authorities and further take as fact that the authorities really said what is attributed to them at that particular time, we cannot assume that the Mishnah and related documents tell us about the state of law or theology in the time in which Jesus lived, on the one side, or in the age in which the Evangelists wrote the Gospels, on the other.

The comparison of large-scale theological constructs yields insight into the theological structure set forth by the respective religious systems that afford a place for those constructs, for in comparison, we gain perspective on the traits of each system, on the choices its framers have made. Such a comparison means, then, to afford a deeper understanding not so much for detail pertinent to a given, one-time historical moment, but for the sustaining religious worldview and way of life embodied, also, in a given construct. The basis for comparison is, Catholic, Orthodox Christianity and Rabbinic Judaism appeal to the same Scriptures. Now, even though, commonly enough, they quote each its own repertoire of verses of Scripture, still, as my theological reprise indicates, they accept as the foundation for all else the Israelite Scriptures' account of humanity and of Israel within humanity: Adam and the Last Adam, for Christianity, Adam and Eve and Israel, Eden and the Land of Israel, for Rabbinic Judaism. In the end we may conclude, the purpose of studying the Gospels and Rabbinic counterparts is to understand the religion that the Gospels and the Rabbinic writings, respectively, put forth. It is now time to undertake the religious study of the

---

[5] I have systematically set forth the logical sequences of primary and subsidiary laws for the entirety of the Mishnah-Tosefta in my *History of the Mishnaic Law* (Leiden, 1974-1986) in forty-three volumes.

religions of Catholic, Orthodox Christianity, represented by the Gospels, and Rabbinic Judaism, represented by the Mishnah, the Tosefta, and the baraita-collections, not only severally but, by reason of their shared heritage, jointly as well.

C. *An Example of an Illuminating Comparison: Healing on the Sabbath*

Take the case of Jesus's healing on the Sabbath, for instance. There we see how profound walls of incomprehension separate New Testament exegesis from the Rabbinic sources supposedly drawn upon to sustain that exegesis. What we see here is that the same topic, healing on the Sabbath, in the Gospels makes one point, in the halakhah of the Mishnah and the Tosefta makes an entirely different point, and treating the same subject the two bodies of tradition simply part company. But that fact affords striking insight into the issues that inhere in the whole of the two religious systems, respectively.

Matt. 12:9-14 = Mark 3:1-6 = Lk. 6:6-11 show Jesus challenged to heal on the Sabbath. Mark has, "Is it lawful on the Sabbath to do good or to do harm, to save life or to kill?" In Matthew he answers, "What man of you, if he has one sheep and it falls into a pit on the Sabbath, will not lay hold of it and lift it out? Of how much more value is a man than a sheep. So it is lawful to do good on the Sabbath." The premise throughout is, it is lawful on the Sabbath to save life, as indeed, the law of the Mishnah and the Tosefta and the exegetical readings of the pertinent passages in the Written Torah all concur is the fact. But saving life is not at issue in the story, only doing good. And that brings us to the specific premise in the version of Matthew, that one may lift a sheep out of a pit on the Sabbath. The Tosefta (among many documents) is explicit that one saves life on the Sabbath, and any show of piety is hypocrisy (T. Shab. 15:11-12):

> They remove debris for one whose life is in doubt on the Sabbath. And the one who is prompt in the matter, lo, this one is to be praised. And it is not necessary to get permission from a court. How so? [If] one fell into the ocean and cannot climb up, or [if] his ship is sinking in the sea, and he cannot climb up, they go down and pull him out of there. And it is not necessary to get permission from a court.
>
> If he fell into a pit and cannot get out, they let down a chain to him

> and climb down and pull him out of there. And it is not necessary to get permission from a court. A baby who went into a house and cannot get out—they break down the doors of the house for him, even if they were of stone, and they get him out of there. And it is not necessary to get permission from a court. They put out a fire and make a barrier against a fire on the Sabbath [cf. M. Shab. Chap. 16]. And one who is prompt, lo, this one is to be praised. And it is not necessary to get permission from a court.

But what about the animal in a pit (T. Shab. 14:3L)?

> For a beast that fell into a pit they provide food in the place in which it has fallen, so that it not die, [and they pull it up after the Sabbath].

The rule is given anonymously; it is not subject to dispute but is normative. But then how are we to understand the certainty with which Jesus asks, "What man of you, if he has one sheep and it falls into a pit on the Sabbath, will not lay hold of it and lift it out? Of how much more value is a man than a sheep. So it is lawful to do good on the Sabbath"?

Clearly, the Synoptic picture of Jesus deems the critical issue to concern whether or not it is lawful to do good on the Sabbath, and the answer is, it is indeed lawful to do good, and the Pharisees do not understand the law. But what if, to the framers of the Mishnah,[6] the Sabbath involves other issues entirely, so that when they speak of the Sabbath, they use a theological language that simply does not intersect with the language of doing work on the Sabbath or doing good on the Sabbath? After all, even the parallelism, do good or do harm, save life or kill, hardly is commensurate; sages concur, one must save life, and everyone knows, one may never murder, not on a week day, not on the Sabbath. So the framing of the question, sensible in the setting of Jesus's teaching, proves disingenuous in the setting of the sages' system. But then in what context do sages consider healing on the Sabbath? It is not a matter of (excess) labor—and the story strikingly does not represent Jesus as having done an act of labor, for no labor is involved in the healing. Jesus tells the man, "Come here." He said to the man, "Stretch out your hand." He stretched it out, and his hand was restored. In fact, Jesus has done nothing; labor is not the issue.

---

[6] The role of Pharisees before 70 in the framing of Rabbinic Judaism afterward sets forth its own set of problems, which I have discussed in *Eliezer ben Hyrcanus. The Tradition and the Man* (Leiden, 1973), 2 vols.

Now with regard to the Sabbath, let me specify what as I examine the halakhah of the Mishnah and related writings I conceive to be the encompassing principles, the generative conceptions that the laws embody and that animate the law in its most sustained and ambitious statements. They concern three matters, [1] space, [2] time, and [3] activity, as the advent of the Sabbath affects all three. The advent of the Sabbath transforms creation, specifically reorganizing space and time and reordering the range of permissible activity. First comes the transformation of space that takes effect at sundown at the end of the sixth day and that ends at sundown of the Sabbath day. At that time, for holy Israel, the entire world is divided into public domain and private domain, and what is located in the one may not be transported into the other. What is located in public domain may be transported only four cubits, that is, within the space occupied by a person's body. What is in private domain may be transported within the entire demarcated space of that domain. All public domain is deemed a single spatial entity, so too all private domain, so one may transport objects from one private domain to another. The net effect of the transformation of space is to move nearly all permitted activity to private domain and to close off public domain for all but the most severely limited activities; people may not transport objects from one domain to the other, but they may transport objects within private domain, so the closure of public domain for most activity, and nearly all material or physical activity, comes in consequence of the division of space effected by sunset at the end of the sixth day of the week.

When it comes to space, the advent of the Sabbath divides into distinct domains for all practical purposes what in secular time is deemed divided only as to ownership, but united as to utilization. Sacred time then intensifies the arrangements of space as public and private, imparting enormous consequence to the status of what is private. There, and only there, on the Sabbath, is life to be lived. The Sabbath assigns to private domain the focus of life in holy time: the household is where things take place then. When, presently, we realize that the household (private domain) is deemed analogous to the Temple or tabernacle (God's household), forming a mirror image to the tabernacle, we shall understand the full meaning of the generative principle before us concerning space on the Sabbath. Second comes the matter of time and how the advent of sacred time registers. Since the consequence of the demarcation on the Sabbath of all space into private and public domain effects, in particular, transporting objects from one space to the other, how time is differentiated will present no surprise. The effects concern private domain, the household.

Specifically, what turns out to frame the Halakhic issue is what objects may be handled or used, even in private domain, on the Sabbath. The advent of the Sabbath thus affects the organization of space and the utilization of tools and other objects, the furniture of the household within the designated territory of the household. The basic principle is simple. Objects may be handled only if they are designated in advance of the Sabbath for the purpose for which they will be utilized on the Sabbath. But if tools may be used for a purpose that is licit on the Sabbath, and if those tools are ordinarily used for that same purpose, they are deemed ready at hand and do not require reclassification; the accepted classification applies. What requires designation for Sabbath use in particular is any tool that may serve more than a single purpose, or that does not ordinarily serve the purpose for which it is wanted on the Sabbath. Designation for use on the Sabbath thus regularizes the irregular, but is not required for what is ordinarily used for the purpose for which it is wanted and is licitly utilized on the Sabbath.

The Sabbath then finds all useful tools and objects in their proper place. But what are the implications for practical behavior? That may mean, they may not be handled at all, since their ordinary function cannot be performed on the Sabbath. That is, useful tools are to be left alone. Or it may mean, they may be handled on the Sabbath exactly as they are handled every other day, the function being licit on the Sabbath. That is to say, since they may be used on the Sabbath, they may be used in the same way in which they are used on ordinary days. Or it may mean, they must be designated in advance of the Sabbath for licit utilization on the Sabbath. On Friday one must form the intention in his heart to utilize the utensil on the Sabbath. And that may mean, to use the utensil in a common manner. That third proviso covers utensils that serve more than a single function, or that do not ordinarily serve the function of licit utilization on the Sabbath that the householder wishes them to serve on this occasion. The advent of the Sabbath then requires that all tools and other things be regularized and ordered.

The rule extends even to utilization of space, within the household, that is not ordinarily used for a (licit) purpose for which, on the Sabbath, it is needed. If guests come, storage-space used for food may be cleared away to accommodate them, the space being conceived as suitable for sitting even when not ordinarily used for that purpose. But one may not clear out a store room for that purpose. One may also make a path in a store room so that one may move about there. One may handle objects that, in some way or another, can serve a licit purpose, in the theory that that purpose inheres. But what is not made ready for use may not be used on the Sabbath. So the advent of the Sabbath not only divides space into public and private, but also differentiates useful tools and objects into those that may or may not be handled within the household.

We come to the third generative problematic that is particular to the Sabbath. The influence upon activity that the advent of the Sabbath makes concerns constructive labor. I may state the generative problematic in a simple declarative sentence: Normally one may not carry out entirely on his own a completed act of constructive labor, which is to say, work that produces enduring results. That is what one is supposed to do in profane time. What is implicit in that simple statement proves profound and bears far-reaching implications. No prohibition impedes performing an act of labor in an other-than-normal way, e.g., in a way that is unusual and thus takes account of the differentiation of time. Labor in a natural, not in an unnatural, manner is prohibited. But that is not all. A person is not forbidden to carry out an act of destruction, or an act of labor that produces no lasting consequences. Nor is part of an act of labor, not brought to conclusion, prohibited. Nor is it forbidden to perform part of an act of labor in partnership with another person who carries out the other requisite part. Nor does one incur culpability for performing an act of labor in several distinct parts, e.g., over a protracted, differentiated period of time. The advent of the Sabbath prohibits activities carried out in ordinary time in a way deemed natural: acts that are complete, consequential, and in accord with their accepted character.

What is the upshot of this remarkable repertoire of fundamental considerations having to do with activity, in the household, on the holy day? The halakhah of Shabbat in the aggregate concerns itself with formulating a statement of how the advent of the Sabbath defines the kind of activity that may be done by specifying what may not be done. That is the meaning of repose, the cessation of activity, not the commencement of activity of a different order. To carry out the Sabbath, one does nothing, not something. And what is that "nothing" that one realizes through inactivity? One may not carry out an act analogous to one that sustains creation. An act or activity for which one bears responsibility, and one that sustains creation, is [1] an act analogous to one required in the building and maintenance of the tabernacle, [2] that is intentionally carried out [3] in its entirety, [4] by a single actor, [5] in the ordinary manner, [6] with a constructive and [7] consequential result—one worthy of consideration by accepted norms. These are the seven conditions that pertain, and that, in one way or another, together with counterpart considerations in connection with the transformation of space and time, generate most of the halakhah of Shabbat.

Like God at the completion of creation, so is Israel on the Sabbath: the halakhah of the Sabbath defines the Sabbath to mean to do no more, but instead to do nothing. At issue in Sabbath rest is not ceasing from labor but ceasing from labor of a very particular character, labor in the model of God's work in making the world. Then why the issues of space, time, and activity? Given the division of space into public domain, where nothing much can happen, and the private domain of the household, where nearly everything dealt with in the law at hand takes place, we realize that the Sabbath forms an occasion of the household in particular. There man takes up repose, leaving off the tools required to make the world, ceasing to perform the acts that sustain the world. The issue of the Sabbath is the restoration of Eden, the realization of Eden in the household of holy Israel.

To that issue, the matter of how much effort is involved in saving the beast proves monumentally irrelevant. Nor can sages have grasped what someone meant in saying, "The son of man is the Lord of the Sabbath." When set alongside the Gospels' framing of issues, we realize, the two pictures of the Sabbath and the issues that inhere therein scarcely intersect. But knowing that fact affords perspective on both the figure of Jesus and the Torah of the sages that seeing each on its own does not provide. Small details turn out to recapitulate large conceptions, and that, in the end, ought to define the hermeneutics, and the consequent exegesis, of the next phase of study of both the Gospels and the Mishnah.

APPENDIX: ROMAN LEGAL CODIFICATION IN THE SECOND CENTURY

STEPHEN A. STERTZ

Dowling College; Mercy College

Although Roman law is commonly thought to have reached its culmination with the *Code of Justinian*, the collection and organization dating from the sixth century C.E., scholars since at least the time of Gibbon have placed the golden age of the Empire in general,[1] and the most creative period in the writing and interpretation of Roman law, much earlier, in the second century.[2]

In this century, the foundations were laid for both the Theodosian Code, dating from the late fourth century, the earliest codification of the entire corpus of the Roman law, and for the attitude of humanitarian reform characterizing this code and the later one of Justinian.[3] During this period, especially under Hadrian (117-138), the Emperor became the sole lawgiver.[4] The most important feature of this period of legal rationalization, modernization, and reform, influenced by Greek philosophy and Hellenistic ideas of universal monarchy, was the so-called codification of the praetor's edict, which is generally believed to have organized and stabilized, under

---

[1] Edward Gibbon, *The Decline and Fall of the Roman Empire* (New York, 1932), I, p. 1.

[2] Cf., e.g., Fritz Schulz, *History of Roman Legal Science* (Oxford, 1946; corrected reprint, 1953), p. 99.

[3] Elmar Bund, "Salvius Iulianus, Leben und Werk," in *Aufstieg und Niedergang der Römischen Welt*, II, *Principat*, Vol. 15, *Recht (Methoden, Schulen, einzelne Juristen;* Berlin, 1976), p. 423, notes that forbidding alterations in the praetor's edict (see text, below) was the closest approach to codification along Theodosian lines possible in the age of Hadrian; on humanitarianism see, e.g., Bernard d'Orgeval, *L'empereur Hadrien, oeuvre législative et administrative* (Paris, 1950), p. 39; Wolfgang Waldstein, "Entscheidungsgrundlagen der klassischen römischen Juristen," *Aufsteig...*, op. cit., II, 15, pp. 147 and 154-157.

[4] See D'Orgeval, op. cit., [n. 3], p. 22; the gradual nature of this process, "like water wearing away rocks," is emphasized by Tullio Spagnuolo Vigorita and Valerio Marotta, "La legislazione imperiale. Forme e orientamenti," in *Storia di Roma*, vol. II, *L'impero mediterraneo*, part III, *La cultura e l'impero* (Turin, 1992), p. 145; nevertheless the same authors emphasize the decisive nature of legal changes under Hadrian at p. 148, while asserting at p. 108 that the innovative character of Hadrian's principate has been exaggerated.

the direction of the Emperor Hadrian and the general execution of the great jurist Salvius Iulianus, a substantial portion of written Roman law, arguably setting the stage for later and fuller codification.[5] Full codification was impossible in the second century because of the great conservatism of the Roman law and because the Emperor was not yet the sole lawgiver in both theory and practice.[6]

The nature and organization of this codification, together with related events necessary to understand the second-century context, form the subject matter of this paper.

Under the Empire, new sources of Roman law were coming into being, taking the place of older sources, which were no longer legislating.[7] The *princeps* (emperor), in theory a magistrate of the Republic, would not openly be called an absolute monarch (*dominus*), at least in the Western Empire, until the late third century, but had in practice, and even to some extent in theory, assumed such a status by Hadrian's reign.[8] Historically, the resolutions of the Roman senate (*senatusconsulta*) had had the *de facto* status of law because of the personal and family influence (*auctoritas*) of the senators. Under the early Empire, although the senate in practice could no nothing contrary to the emperor's will, it still had some power in certain judicial and legislative areas, including those involving the so-called senatorial provinces, which in theory were still under the control of that body (the emperor directly controlled the imperial provinces, which generally were located in areas where a heavy military presence was considered necessary).[9] In addition, certain magistrates and jurists,

---

[5] On the use of the word "codification" in this context see above, n. 3. Primary sources will be discussed below. The secondary literature on this topic is voluminous. There is a long bibliography at the end (pp. 448-454) of Bund's article (cited, n. 3), on Salvius Iulianus and the codification; some earlier works are cited by D'Orgeval, op. cit. [n. 3], pp. 41-49, *passim*.

[6] See, e.g., *Digest* 5.3.22: Hadrian tells the senators: "You must decide..." in a case involving possession of property; on the conservatism of the Roman law in this period see, e.g., H.F. Jolowicz and Barry Nicholas, *Historical Introduction to the Study of Roman Law* (Cambridge, U.K., 1972), pp. 411-413.

[7] The last known "law of the Roman people," passed by the Republican assemblies, dated from 97 C.E., under Nerva (*Digest* 47.21.3); see, e.g., John Crook, *Law and Life of Rome* (Ithaca, 1967), p. 19, and literature there cited.

[8] Cf., Gaius *Institutes* 1.5 ; for secondary literature see Jean-Pierre Coriat, *Le prince législateur. La technique législative des Sévères et les méthodes de creation du droit impérial à la fin du Principat*. (Bibliothèque des Écoles Françaises d'Athènes et de Rome, fasc. 294; Rome, 1997), p. 3 and numerous items there cited.

[9] Cf., *Digest* 5. 3. 20. 6; Crook, op. cit. [n. 7], p. 22; D'Orgeval, op. cit. [n. 3], pp. 22; 40-41.

largely by force of custom in the latter case, had the *ius (publice) respondendi*, the right to make law through precedent-forming decisions in particular cases, somewhat comparable to decisions of higher courts in the present-day United States, although in Rome certain very prominent law professors, because of their prestige (*auctoritas*), seem also to have held this right.[10]

By the time of Hadrian, the *ius respondendi* had gradually passed almost entirely to the Emperor alone; in the second half of the first century, although less had changed in theory, in practice the Emperor was the sole lawgiver, generally acting through the imperial *consilium*, which now included many of the leading legal experts (jurisconsults).[11] In accordance with legislation passed under Augustus, the Emperor, still in theory a republican magistrate, used his *imperium* as a high magistrate and his tribunician power (tribunes had substantial veto power under the Republic) to act as sole *de facto* legislature, powers that were taken advantage of very gradually in the first and second centuries.[12] Modern scholars have asserted that there was no real legal justification for so great extension of imperial power, and that the jurists use circular language in attempting to justify it.[13]

Under Hadrian, the Emperor presented legislation to the Senate, but his speech introducing the legislation, the *oratio in senatu*, was in itself the *de facto* promulgation of the new law.[14] Although dis-

---

[10] Aspects of *ius respondendi*, including the power of law professors in this respect, are discussed by O.F. Robinson, *The Sources of Roman Law: Problems and Methods for Ancient Historians* ("Approaching the Ancient World," ed., Richard Stoneman; London, 1997), p. 25; 45; Olga Tellegen-Couperus, *A Short History of Roman Law* (London, 1993), p. 95.

[11] On the emperor and the *ius respondendi* in the second century see Gaius *Institutes* 1.2.27; Jolowicz and Nicholas, op. cit. [n. 6], p. 361 and literature there cited; Robinson, op. cit. [n. 10], p. 11, interprets *Digest* 1.2.2.35 to mean that jurists still had the *ius respondendi* during Hadrian's reign, but notes that the text is corrupt; see also D'Orgeval, op. cit. [n. 3], p. 40; Tellegen-Couperus, op. cit. [n. 10], p. 97; on the imperial *consilium*, see generally John A. Crook, *Consilium Principis* (Cambridge, U.K., 1955).

[12] See, for example, the jurist Pomponius, writing in the mid-second century, cited in *Digest* 1.2. 2.48-50; for background see Jolowicz and Nicholas, op. cit. [n. 6], p. 359.

[13] Gaius, *Institutes* 1.5 says that "that which has been decided by the Emperor has the force of law" because "the Emperor himself is given his *imperium* by a law." Gaius wrote in the mid-second century, but several scholars, notably John Crook, op. cit. [n. 7], p. 20, believe that this passage may be a later (perhaps third-century) intrerpolation.

[14] Crook, op. cit. [n. 7], p. 23; Jolowicz and Nicholas, op. cit. [n. 6], p. 362;

tinctions continued to be made between sources of law, the Emperor was at least in practice the sole source of law.[15] The edict was a major source of law under the Republic, and of particular importance was the praetor's edict. Praetors were elected officials in both the Republic and the Empire, in charge of the judicial system. Their number continually increased; under the early Empire they continued to be elected by the Roman assembly (*comitia centuriata*) for one-year terms, but they were in practice appointed by the Emperor. At the beginning of their terms in office, they issued edicts, stating what they intended to do as praetors. These edicts gradually, during the Republic, assumed the force of law. It is believed that at first (for how long is disputed) these edicts had the force of law only during the praetor's term of office. The *praetor urbanus*, in charge of the legal system at first in Rome and later in Italy (in the second century his jurisdiction was again reduced to the area surrounding Rome), and among Roman citizens especially, was the most important praetor, and his annual edict was the "praetor's edict" *par excellence*.[16]

As early as 67 B.C.E., a *lex Cornelia de edictis praetorum*, mentioned by Asconius (*In Cornelium* 1, p. 48, in Stangl's edition) and the historian Dio Cassius (36.40.1-2), appealed to the praetors not to alter the edicts of their predecessors, but this was a nonbinding request and there are difficulties with the texts.[17]

What is believed by most scholars to have occurred under Hadrian is the compulsory, imperially-ordered "freeze" of the text of the edict of the *praetor urbanus*, and possibly other documents of this nature, together with the redaction, probably with changes in the order of presentation of material, with minor changes in actual content, under the direction of the eminent jurist and member of the imperial *consilium*, Salvius Iulianus, thus setting a precedent for the later codes

---

D'Orgeval, op. cit. [n. 3], p. 51, cites modern literature on this topic.

[15] There were imperial constitutions, subdivided into edicts (the emperor, like any magistrate, could make his orders and intentions known, but his sphere alone was unlimited as to topic), decrees (the judgments of the emperor acting as judge), and epistulae (instructions to and answers to questions of, usually, subordinate officials; the rescript, one type of epistula, was another form of imperial law). The senatusconsulta were still another type of law. These are discussed in detail in all surveys of Roman law, including those cited above.

[16] See, e.g., D'Orgeval, op. cit. [n. 3], pp. 40-42, and literature there cited; Schulz, op. cit. [n. 2], p. 127.

[17] For discussion see Antonio Guarino, "La formazione dell'editto perpetuo," in *Aufsteig und Niedergang...*, op. cit. [n. 3], II, vol. 13, *Recht (Normen, Verbreitunf, Materien*; Berlin, 1980), p. 70, and material there cited.

of Theodosius (two other codes, of which only quotations are extant, apparently date from the earlier fourth century),[18] and Justinian. Unfortunately the evidence is far from complete and highly ambiguous in several respects.[19]

The *Digest* or *Pandects* presents important evidence. This work was a summary of the major legal teachings of famous jurists, prefixed to the Code of Justinian and written at that emperor's orders. It is preceded by three "constitutions," dealing with legal education and other matters and giving the Code the force of law. These are referred to by their first words. The constitution *Tanta*, which gives the Code the force of law, is in Latin and is repeated in the text of the Code itself (1.17.2), but there is a slightly differing version in Greek, Devdwken, which is a little more detailed and is believed by some scholars to contain material from independent sources.[20]

According to this material, the Emperor Hadrian proposed this codification of the praetor's edict in an oration to the senate; it gained the force of law through a senatusconsultus amounting in fact to an automatic ratification of the emperor's proposal, as was becoming customary at this period; the prominent jurist Salvius Iulianus was entrusted with this codification, which involved the elimination of ambiguities in this set of legal texts.[21] Other evidence may be found in the writings of two fourth-century historians, Eutropius (*Breviarium* 8.17), who says that Salvius Iulianus, a very noble and expert man, composed the *edictum perpetuum* under Hadrian, and Aurelius Victor, 19.1-2, who says that Iulianus first composed into order the previously varying edicts issued by the praetors. The *Chronicle* of St. Jerome says in the entry on the "year of Abraham" 2147,[22] which corresponds to 131 C.E., Iulianus composed the *edictum perpetuum*. Jerome's sources for this information are believed to be Eutropius and Aurelius Victor.[23]

Among the numerous difficulties with this historical evidence is

---

[18] See the items cited in n. 16, above, as well as Bund, art. cit. [n. 3], pp. 419-431.

[19] See in particular Bund, art. cit. [n. 3], pp. 422-424; D'Orgeval, op. cit., [n. 3], p. 43 and n. 8.

[20] For a detailed discussion see Bund, loc. cit.

[21] D'Orgeval, op. cit. [n. 3], p. 42, gives a summary similar to the preceding one.

[22] In Jacques-Paul Migne, ed., *Patrologia Latina*, vol. 27 (Paris, 1849), pp. 617-618.

[23] For discussion see Bund, loc. cit., and Guarino, art. cit. [n. 617], pp. 70-72.

the question of the exact meaning of the term *edictum perpetuum*, which is not found, in any context related to Hadrian's reign, in any extant document of the second century. This controversy has given rise to the theory that there was in fact no "codification" of the praetor's edict, a myth to this effect having arisen in late antiquity, and that all that occurred under Hadrian was the revision, toward uniformity, of the edicts of the provincial governors, as part of that emperor's centralization of the Roman Empire. In theory at least, according to this viewpoint, little or nothing had changed regarding the legal responsibilities of magistrates until at least the third century.[24] Confusion on the part of later Roman historians and jurists may be due to the restriction of the status of the urban praetor from all of Italy to the area surrounding Rome under Hadrian, followed in 212 C.E. by the Edict of Caracalla, which, by granting citizenship to all the free inhabitants of the entire Roman Empire, rendered obsolete the provincial edicts and the original responsibility of the office of the *praetor peregrinus*, both of which dealt with law affecting exclusively non-citizens residing in the Roman provinces, i.e., the Empire excluding Italy.[25] Although modern scholars are far from unanimous about how the codification of the edict affected the provinces, the general consensus is that there was one uniform permanent unalterable (except by the emperor) praetor's edict from Hadrian's reign onward, and that the false theory that there was no codification arises from ambiguity as to the meaning of the term, since what was done under Hadrian was not codification in the fifth- or sixth-century meaning of the term but merely editing and forbidding alterations; additionally, arguably Hadrian merely wanted to forbid alterations before hitting on the idea of having Salvius Iulianus also edit the edict.[26]

The exact date of the codification of the edict, the background of its main codifier, Salvius Iulianus, and the reconstruction of the edict's contents, are matters to be dealt with before concluding with comments on the general tendencies of second-century Roman law forming the codification's context and leading toward the codes of late antiquity. Jerome's date corresponds, as has been noted, with 131 C.E. However, we know from the *History* of Dio Cassius (69.11.12)

---

[24] Guarino, art, cit. [n. 17], pp. 68-97, esp. at pp. 91-97.
[25] Cf., e.g., Schulz, op. cit. [n. 2], p. 127.
[26] Bund, art. cit. [n. 3], pp. 423-424.

that the Emperor Hadrian spent that year in Egypt (it hardly needs to be noted that ancient chroniclers writing hundreds of years after the event were frequently a few years off in dating). It is more reasonable to suppose, in the opinion of many modern scholars, that the codification took place after Hadrian's return to Rome in 134.[27] Another possibility, 125-128, has been rejected because Salvius Iulianus, on the basis of the known biographical information, would have been too young to have been entrusted with so important a project.[28] The year 138, on the other hand, is to be rejected because it was the year of the Emperor Hadrian's death, and there is ample evidence that Hadrian's health began to seriously deteriorate before the beginning of the year.[29] A strong argument in favor of the year 137 is that the twentieth anniversary of the Emperor's accession to the throne (*vicennalia*) was being celebrated: as was customary on such occasions, special coins were issued, and such a project as the codification would have been appropriate in such a year.[30]

There is a great deal of uncertainty regarding not only the exact date of the codification but other details involved with it, owing to problems with regard to the chronology of the career of Salvius Iulianus and confusion between his codification of the edict and his having written commentaries including references to it as well as citations of his works in later commentaries on the edict.[31] Neither the praetor's edict in any from, codified or otherwise, nor any second-century work on Roman law except that of Gaius, probably written under the Emperor Antoninus Pius, is extant except through extracts found in other legal works, specifically the *Code of Justinian* and certain documents attached to it, such as Gaius' elementary law textbook and the collection of extracts from legal writers called the *Digest*. Modern scholars, in the last two centuries, have undertaken the painstaking, uncertain, and often controversial work of reconstruction.[32]

---

[27] Ibid., pp. 426-427, and literature there cited; D'Orgeval, op. cit. [n. 3], pp. 46-47.

[28] Bund, loc. cit., agrees with most scholars in dating Iulianus' birth at about 100 C.E.

[29] Ibid.; see also D'Orgeval, loc. cit.

[30] D'Orgeval, op. cit. [n. 3], p. 47 and n. 20.

[31] Cf., Guarino, art. cit. [n. 17], pp. 83-97; Aldo Schiavone, "Il pensiero giuridicio fra scienza del diritto e potere imperiale," in *Storia di Roma*, op. cit. [n. 4], pp. 49-54, and material there cited.

[32] Notably Otto Lenel, *Das Edictum Perpetuum* (3rd ed; Leipzig, 1927; first ed.

Details of the career of Salvius Julianus are, fortunately, available from other sources, both literary and epigraphic, casting additional light on his juristic accomplishment.[33] The often-unreliable collection of imperial biographies known since the Renaissance as the *Historia Augusta* states at the beginning (1.1-2) of the life of the Emperor Didius Julianus, who reigned briefly in 193 C.E., that this emperor was the great-grandson of Salvius Iulianus, twice consul, urban prefect and jurisconsult, which, most of all, made him famous. Since the same biography gives Didius Iulianus' birth year as 137 C.E. (9.3) and Dio Cassius (73.17.5) gives it at 133, it is highly improbable that the jurist was the great-grandfather of the emperor. The general consensus among modern scholars is that the jurist was most probably the grandfather, grand-uncle, or uncle of the emperor.[34] Inscriptions, one on the base of a statue, found in what is now Tunisia tell us that one Lucius Cornelius, son of Publius, Salvius Iulianus Aemilianus held a number of offices, having been, among others, quaestor, when his salary was doubled on account of his distinguished erudition, tribune of the plebs, praetor, consul (in 148), and later governor of the provinces of Germania Superior and Hispania Citerior, finally holding the post of Proconsul of Africa, probably in 163/164.[35] Allegations that this individual is not the jurist simply because there is no mention of his juristic career in these inscriptions have been rightly been dismissed by scholars.[36] The remaining evidence, however, deals directly with that career. Both the *Historia Augusta* (*Vit. Hadr.* 1.18.1) and Dio Cassius (69.7.1) state that Iulianus was a member of Hadrian's council (*consilium*), the first source also noting that the famous jurists Iuventius Celsus and Neratius Priscus were also members. Iulianus himself is quoted

---

publ. in 1883); see also extensive modern literature on both the edict and second-century Roman jurists' writings, much of it recent work in Italian, cited in Schiavone, loc. cit., and in Guarino, art. cit.[n. 17], pp. 92-97 ; for works published prior to 1952, see the extensive bibliography at pp. 800-801 of Adolf Berger, *Encyclopedic Dictionary of Roman Law* (Transactions of the American Philosophical Society, new series, Vol. 45, Part 2; Philadelphia, 1953); for works published from 1940 to 1970 see Manlius Sargenti, ed., *Operum ad ius Romanum pertinentium quae ab anno MCMXL usque ad annum MCMLX edita sunt* (3 vols.; Ticino, 1978-82), which is magisterial but could be better organized.

[33] See Bund, art. cit., [n. 3], pp. 409-431.
[34] Ibid., pp. 409-10, and literature there cited.
[35] Ibid., pp. 411-16; D'Orgeval, op. cit. [n. 3], pp. 46-47.
[36] Compare Guarino, art. cit., [n. 7], pp. 92-94, with Bund, art. cit. [n. 3], pp. 422-429, and extensive literature there cited.

in *Digest* 40.2.5 to the effect that another famous jurist, Iavolenus Priscus, was his law teacher. Little else of any importance to his juristic significance is known about Iulianus' career. Scholars, on the basis of available information on the customary ages for appointment to various offices, have dated his birth as about 100 C.E. and his death before 185.[37]

His literary output, in addition to the codification of the edict, seems to have been substantial. The Greek index prefaced to the *Digest*, as ordered by Justinian, is known from the most complete extant manuscript as the *Ind ex Florentinus*.[38] This index, which lists all books from which extracts appear in the *Digest*, includes five works by Iulianus, the *Digesta*, in ninety books, of which 839 citations appear in other works, which includes commentaries on edicts and is a major source of Lenel's reconstruction of the praetor's edict, while apparently being devoted to solutions to legal problems, the *Libri ex Minicio*, of which forty fragments survive and apparently consists largely of questions and answers on contested legal points, the *Libri ad Urseium Ferocem*, a work in the same genre, the *Liber singularis de ambiguitatis*, of which few fragments survive but which seems to be a rhetorical work, perhaps influenced by the Stoic philosophy along the general lines of Cicero's *Paradoxa Stoicorum*, rather than a juristic work, and finally the *Quaestiones* of Adricanus, in nine books, of which 121 fragments survive, apparently a dialogue on legal questions between Iulianus and one of his law students.[39] At this point it is appropriate to mention that Iulianus headed a law school in Rome, supposedly one of two with differing beliefs, of which much has been made by scholars, but recent research has favored the theory that these two schools were most probably little more than legal debating societies which held mock trials.[40]

Iulianus' literary style and outlook has been characterized as conservative, opposed to abstraction, cosmopolitan, Hellenistic and anti-nationalistic in tune with his times, unadorned, humorless, and

---

[37] Bund, art. cit., pp. 409-430.
[38] See Schulz, op. cit. [n. 2], pp. 144-145.
[39] Bund, art. cit., pp. 431-440; on the last work, see generally Andreas Wacke, "Afrikans Verhältnis zu Julian und die Haftung für Höhere Gewalt," in *Aufstieg...*, op. cit. [n. 3], II, 15, pp. 456-493.
[40] See, e.g., Detlef Liebs, "Rechtsschulen und rechtsunterricht im Prinzipat," in the same volume as the preceding, pp. 215-229, and literature there cited; *idem..,* "Römische Provinziajurisprudenz," *ibid.*, p. 297; R, Jolowicz and Nicholas, op. cit. [n. 6], p. 385; Tellegen-Couperus, op. cit. [n. 10], p. 97.

uninterested in legal history, judging laws by their usefulness, not their origins.[41] Aside from revising, rewriting, pruning, eliminating repetitions, and the like, Iulianus apparently contributed only one legal point to the praetor's edict. *Digest* 37.8.3 notes that "this chapter of the edict, is that which was introduced by Iulianus." The title of the chapter indicates its subject matter, relating to a point regarding succession in certain cases of intestacy. Previously the law was unclear in cases where one of the sons of a person who had died without a will had been emancipated, i.e., freed from parental control of many aspects of his life, including career and disposition of certain types of property. Traditionally, emancipation was a public ceremony which both freed the emancipated son and allowed the father to totally cut him off in his will. The new rule added by Iulianus gave preference to the emancipated son over other, more distant, relatives, providing that the emancipated son received half of the appropriate portion of the estate, i.e., half of the portion going to children of the deceased, excluding those adopted into another family (e.g., certain married daughters); the other half of this portion, assuming that there were no unemancipated sons, as was frequently the case in the second century, went to the children of the emancipated son.[42] Iulianus seems to have made a minor grammatical correction at another point in the edict; the degree of rearrangement and rewriting is unknown and controversial.[43] Consequently, numerous scholars have asserted that the codification of the edict was of little real importance.[44] However, despite the great conservatism of the Roman lawyer, it simplified, centralized, modernized,

---

[41] Schiavone, art. cit. [n. 31], pp. 43-44; Schulz, op. cit. [n. 2], pp. 258-260; Antonio Guarino, "Gli aspetti giuridici del principato," in *Aufsteig...*, op. cit., II, vol. 13, *Recht. Normen, Verbreiten, Materien* (Berlin, 1980), p. 25.

[42] For brief discussions of the legal technicalities involved, see Berger, op. cit. [n. 32], pp. 451-452 and 376; literature is cited at both points; see also Bund, art. cit. [n. 3], pp. 423-424, noting that the evidence that this is a new clause added by Iulianus is far from conclusive; see also Tellegen-Couperus, op. cit. [n. 10], p. 89; David Johnston, *Roman Law in Context* (Key Themes in Ancient History, ed. P.A. Cartledge and P.D.A. Garnsey; Cambridge, U.K., 1999), p. 4; Jolowicz and Nicholas, op. cit. [n. 6], p. 357, and literature there cited; see also, generally, Pasquale Voci, "Linee storiche del diritto ereditario romano. I. Dalle origine ai Severi," in *Aufstieg...*, op. cit. [n. 3], pp. 433-435, esp. p. 434 and n. 236.

[43] See Lenel, op. cit. [n. 32], p. 243; Tellegen-Couperus, op. cit. [n. 10], p. 90, admits that her opinions on this matter are difficult to prove.

[44] E.g. Robinson, op. cit. [n. 10], p. 45; D'Orgeval, op. cit. [n. 3], p. 44; Schulz, op. cit. [n. 2], p. 129.

increased imperial power, set a precedent for later codification, and must be viewed in context of general second-century developments, set in motion by the emperors, in this direction.

As for the content of the codified praetor's edict as reconstructed by Otto Lenel from 1883 onward, the full text may be most conveniently found at pp. 335-389 of vol. 1 of *Fontes iuris Romani antejustiniani*, edited by Salvator Riccoboni, usually abbreviated *FIRA*. A reproduction of the table of contents and summary appears, with organization slightly different from that in *FIRA,* at e.g., pp. 149-151 of Fritz Schulz' *Roman Legal Science.* Part I, about thirteen pages long in *FIRA,* which is printed in a very small format, with pages the size of those in a mass-market paperback, deals with procedure up the beginning of the actual trial, beginning with the safeguards of the jurisdiction of the praetor and municipal officials, who were guaranteed the support of higher authorities in jurisdictional matter in addition, presumably, to having the power of command (*imperium*) dating from Roman republican times. Next come a miscellany of regulations relating to summonses and what might today be called search warrants, followed by pacts of compromise, including arbitration, which made summonses unnecessary. Then pacts in general are treated of, then other types of summonses including types in which people charged with certain offenses were released on their own recognizance (without having to provide sureties), then certain aspects of litigation involving proceedings where an official appears on behalf of an absent party. Various types of proceedings and actions before the actual trial, in many cases apparently mentioned at that point because the preceding action reminded the compiler of the current point, the two having something in common, ("attraction"),[45] are then briefly treated. Part II, following Schulz, Parts II and III, according to Riccobono, deals first (IIa Schulz) with ordinary, then summary (IIb Schulz, III Riccobono), legal remedies, the latter being outside the traditional court system and a development of the Empire.[46] Both parts deal with various kinds of property, including

---

[45] Salvator Riccobono *et al.,* , eds., *Fontes iuris Romani Anteiustiniani* (3 vols.), vol. 1, *Leges,* ed. Salvator Riccobono (Milan, 1941), pp. 335-389; the new edition of this volume cited in some works is in fact an unaltered reprint; Riccobono's preface to the edict (in Latin), at pp. 335-337, briefly summarizes a great deal of information; see also D'Orgeval, loc. cit. Robinson, op. cit. [n. 10], pp. 55, cites other editions and translations of the edict, including some (incomplete) English translations.

[46] On "extraordinary jurisdiction" and related subjects, on which much has

those consecrated for religious purposes, such as tombs, property belonging to wives, with a section on divorce, stolen property, wills, guardianship, water rights, private tax-collecting services designated by the government (*publicani.*, the "publicans" of the King James Bible), property destroyed in fires and shipwrecks, and property deliberately damaged. Part IV (III Schulz), four pages long in *FIRA,* deals with execution of judgment, including pleas of guilty and execution of judgments relating to disputed property. Part IV lists legal formulae, mentioning those related to religious property, discussed in a different context in Part III Riccobono (IIb Schulz), public places and roads, rivers, pathways, possession through use, and numerous other related topics, e.g., trees falling down, and finally exceptions. The appendix, the three-page aedile's edict, deals with lesser matters within the jurisdiction of the aedile, a lower-ranking magistrate traditionally in charge of markets and public games (the latter had been abolished by the time of the Justinianic Code). Topics include sale of goods, fairs, and the prohibition of the castration of boys (at about the same time as the codification of the edict, similar legislation, being confused with the prohibition of circumcision, resulted in the Jewish revolt of 135-138). In some cases Lenel gives the full text of the law, where this is known, in others the mere title as cited in the legal textbook of the third-century writer Ulpian. Occasionally a question mark appears, when the manuscript reading of the work in which this material is cited is uncertain.

The eminent Roman historian Theodor Mommsen understandably (and famously) called this order a disorder.[47] Such, however, was the state of the law in the second century, according to most scholars, who note that even this "disorder" constituted progress. The original praetor's edict is believed to have consisted of numerous layers of annual accretions, with repetitions and ambiguities, constituting an even worse disorder.[48] The extremely poor and inefficient condition of the Roman legal archives in this period, to the point that the law was not always known, even by lawyers and judges,

---

been written, see e.g. André Magdelain, *Auctoritas Principis* (Paris, 1947), pp. 77-110 *et passim.*; Coriat, op. cit. [n. 8], pp. 8-10 and literature there cited; Ignazio Buti, "La 'cognitio extra ordinem;' da Augusto a Diocleziano," in *Aufsteig...,* op. cit. [n. 3], I, Vol. 14, *Recht (Materien [Forts.])* (Berlin, 1982), esp. pp. 29-30, and literature there cited.

[47] Theodor Mommsen, "Über das Inhalt des rubrischen Gesetzes," in *Juristische Schriften* (= *Gesammelte Schriften,* Vol. I; Berlin, 1905), p. 164.

[48] See e.g. Jolowicz and Nicholas, op. cit. [n. 6], p. 357

must also be taken into consideration.⁴⁹ Of course, by comparison, the Theodosian and Justinianic Codes represented enormous steps forward, but by the time they were compiled the emperor was an absolute monarch in theory as well as in practice. Thus the loss of freedom was the price of order. The codification of the praetor's edict under Hadrian, then, can be seen as a sign of the times. The centralized, bureaucratic, cosmopolitan, philosophically-influenced and yet practically-oriented, humanitarian, Hellenistic, emperor-dominated legal and political system characteristic of at least the early Byzantine Empire, with its ethics at this point based on Stoicism rather than Christianity, was beginning to emerge over four hundred years before the compilation of the Justinianic Code, reminding the modern scholar that were it not for the massive disruption caused by the barbarian invasions of the West, Rome and Byzantium would be seen to a greater extent as a single continuing society.⁵⁰

To illustrate the preceding contention, several particular examples of second-century humanitarian reform, comparable in some ways to the relief given to emancipated sons of intestate fathers in Iulianus' codification, will at this point be briefly examined in chronological order, beginning with Trajan's reign. Under Trajan (98-117 C.E.), legal concessions were made by the emperor toward greater flexibility in the writing of wills.⁵¹ The *Senatusconsultus Rubrius* of 105

---

⁴⁹ On this topic, a highly complicated one, see D'Orgeval, op. cit. [n. 3], p. 63; Tellegen-Couperus, op. cit. [n. 10], pp. 97-8, and literature there cited; Spagnuolo Vigorito and Marotta, art. cit. [n. 4], pp. 109-111; Robinson, op. cit. [n. 10], p. 36. On citations in later legislation and legal writing of the praetor's edict, see Coriat, op. cit. [n. 8], p. 533, citing CJ 4. 26. 2 of 196 C.E., the only second-century citation of the edict according to Coriat, and several third-century citations; on later commentaries, see Schulz, op. cit. [n. 2], pp. 189-193; Györgi Diósdi, "Gaius, der Rechtsgelehrte," in *Aufsteig...*, op. cit. [n. 3], II, 15 , p. 613.

⁵⁰ Among the few modern works taking this viewpoint is F.W. Bussell, *The Roman Empire: Essays on the Constitutional History from the Accession of Domitian (81 A. D.) to the Retirement of Nicephorus III (1081 A.D.)* (2 vols.; London, 1910), which has since its publication been regarded by scholars with almost unanimous execration (the present writer was "warned against" it as a graduate student by several very well-known ancient historians). The praetor's edict does not appear in this work's index.

⁵¹ Compare Pliny, *Letters* 10.65.3; 3.10.66 2; *Digest* 26.7.12.1; 29.1.1, here citing respectively the third-century jurists Paulus and Ulpian; for a discussion of various reforms achieved by and attributed to Trajan, see Spagnuolo Vigorita and Marotta, art. cit. [n. 4], pp. 100-107, and literature there cited; thus reforms began before Hadrian's reign; the latter, however, achieved so great a reputation as a reformer that modern scholars have credited undatable reforms to his reign (ibid., p. 108, citing additional literature on this specific point).

C.E., *Digest 30.5.26.7*, permitted the praetor to free a slave according to a will, even if the main heir refused. A father who mistreated his son was now required to emancipate him, and, if this son died shortly thereafter, the father was excluded from the succession (*Digest* 37.12.5). Other Trajanic reforms in succession, all tending in a humanitarian direction, appear in e.g., *Digest* 5.3.7. Criminal procedure was reformed in the direction of simplification and increased efficiency (*Dig.*2.12.9; 28.18.1).

Hadrian's reforms included a reduction in the penalty against moving boundary stones (*Digest* 3.2.11.3), a reduction of the penalty for homicide if committed with a brick rather than with a weapon (*Digest* 48.8.1.3), reflecting in part the emperor's own philosophically-inspired humanitarianism, in part those of the jurists on his council, including Salvius Iulianus.[52] Other humanitarian reforms included prohibiting appeal of a decision ordering the opening of a will (*Digest* 49.5.7. prooemium), authorizing judges to pay the travel expenses of witnesses (*Digest* 22.5.3.4), improving the legal condition of illegitimate children of soldiers (*Ibid.*49.17.9.3), who, however, were still not allowed to marry, limiting the rights of real estate owners regarding architectural ornaments belonging to a former owner of a house, allowing these to be moved to the new house (31.1.41.1), requiring the reconstruction of buildings following their destruction or demolition (1.18.7), exempting certain agricultural goods from taxes, thus favoring small farmers (*Lex Hadriana*: *Digest* 48.14.3.6), dividing inherited debts in an orderly fashion (46.1.49), strengthening anti-counterfeiting laws (48.10.32), liberalizing inheritance and guardianship laws, continuing reforms under Trajan (28.1.15.17), and allowing wills to be written in Greek (the evidence in this case is from inscriptions[53]).[54] The *Senatusconsultum Iuventianum* of 129 C.E., described in the Justinianic Code 7.9.3, was an important measure against fraud in matters of inheritance. It also gave cities the right to free slaves.[55] The *Senatusconsultum Tertullianum* also

---

[52] For discussion see Franco Casavola, "Cultura e scienza giuridicia nel secondo d. C: il senso del passato," in *Aufstieg...*, op. cit. [n. 3], II, 15, pp. 147-154.

[53] *Corpus Inscriptionum Latinarum*, vol. 3, no. 12283 = *Inscriptiones Latini Selectae*, no. 7784.

[54] These and other reforms are discussed in d'Orgeval, op. cit. [n. 3], pp. 39; 86-150; 170-185.

[55] See ibid., pp. 144-46, for discussion; Hadrian's reforms improving the condition of slaves and former slaves are discussed at pp. 68-82.

reformed inheritance rights, increasing, *inter alia*, those of freedwomen (*Cod. Just.* 66.8.58).

Hadrian's successor, Antoninus Pius, relaxed the ban on circumcision in the case of Jews, while retaining it as far as other groups were concerned (*Digest* 48.8.11 prooemium). This emperor acted against the bad treatment of slaves and in effect granting the right to the equivalent of bail.[56] In criminal cases, the judge was legally obliged to consider the spirit, rather than the mere letter, of the law, and to make necessary corrections in a humane direction (*Dig.* 40.10.5.3; 4.1.7). The principle of the presumption of innocence was introduced (*Dig.* 48.3.6.1; 48.2.7.4-5; 40.2.9.1).

The philosopher-emperor Marcus Aurelius continued to reform the law of inheritance, in this case regarding intestacy, in a more humane fashion (*Dig.* 28.4.3), aided by the famous jurist Ulpius Marcellus.[57] Antoninus Pius' rescript penalizing unprovable instruments (*Dig.* 48.10.31) was modified by excluding liability in the case of mistake. The *Senatusconsultum Orfitianum*, of 178 C.E., improved the status of women regarding inheritance (*Dig.* 37.17) In *Dig.* 48.18.1.27 the emperor and his co-emperor Lucius Verus decided in favor of freeing a slave whose confession of homicide was prompted by fear of being returned to his master. In this decision, upholding that of a provincial governor, the latter is praised for acting with prudent and excellently reasoned humanitarianism. A rescript against punishing a son who killed his parents while he was temporarily insane (*Dig.* 48.9.9.2) is similar in spirit.[58] Marcus also improved the legal status of burial societies (*Dig.* 34.5.21; 40.3.1)[59] Even in the reign of Commodus there were a few humanitarian reforms on points relating to trial procedure, tax law, trusts, and the freeing of slaves.[60]

---

[56] *Dig.* 1.6.2; 48.3.3; for discussion see Richard Alexander Bauman, "The 'Leges iudicorum publicorum' and their Interpretation in the Republic, Principate, and Later Empire," in *Aufstieg...*, op. cit. [n. 3], II, 13, pp. 171-73 and literature there cited.

[57] For discussions see Casavola, art. cit. [n. 52], pp. 157-60.; Crook, op. cit. [n. 7], pp. 284-285; Another reform regarding inheritance, in effect protecting heirs, is mentioned in *Historia Augusta, Vit. Marci* 210. 11; for discussion and additional references see Jolowicz and Nicholas, op. cit. [n. 6], p. 396; among other reforms, that mentioned in *Cod. Just.* 1.3.31, simplified certain procedures regarding inheritance.

[58] For discussion see Bauman, art. cit. [n. 56], p. 174 and n.109, and Coriat, op. cit. [n. 8], pp. 2-3 and n. 6.

[59] Examples could be multiplied; cf., ibid., pp. 182-184 and literature there cited.

[60] For discussion see, e.g., Albino Garzetti, *From Tiberius to the Antonines: A History*

Finally, the tradition continued into the next century under the Severan dynasty, and tenuously through the difficult period of the "military anarchy" and into the Christian Empire. To conclude this article, there will be a brief discussion of reforms in the tradition of the codification of the praetor's edict between 193 and 200 C.E., followed by a few words on humanitarianism, modernization, and codification.

Septimius Severus, who reigned from 193 to 211 C.E., was responsible for a substantial volume of legislation.[61] Arguably the most important reform before 200 C.E. was the *oratio* of 195, improving the condition of poor children in a state of guardianship: their assets could no longer be legally alienated by the guardian (*Digest* 26.6.22, citing the jurist Modestinus).[62] Humanitarian legislation was undoubtedly in great part the work of the great jurists Paul, Ulpian, and Papinian, members of the imperial *consiiuum*. In general, the modernization, philosophically-inspired humanitarianism, and absolutism (or elitism) informing the spirit of the codified praetor's edict was an increasingly important part of Roman legislation during the principate, arguably beginning with Augustus and influencing later codifications, in turn informing much of the ethos behind the Roman law under which a majority of the non-English-speaking people of the world now live. In this country some of this attitude informed early-twentieth-century Progressivism and succeeding movements. It is perhaps not too extravagant to speculate that Theodore Roosevelt, a Harvard Law School graduate who is known to have read and admired the work of his namesake and fellow-Nobel laureate, the Roman historian Theodor Mommsen, might have called (or perhaps even did call) the spirit, if not the letter, of the codification of the praetor's edict "bully." [63]

---

of the Roman Empire A.D. 14-192, transl. J.R. Foster (London, 1974), p. 544; this is a neglected topic.

[61] For a very elaborate survey, see Coriat, op. cit. [n. 8], pp. 24-67.

[62] For discussion, cf., ibid., pp. 507-509 and literature there cited.

[63] On humanitarianism in Roman imperial legislation generally, see Bauman, art. cit. [n. 56], pp. 174-176 and primary and secondary literature there cited On codification and the *codex* (book with pages as opposed to scroll), see Coriat, pp. 632-634 and literature there cited. There is a set of Mommsen's works in the library at Theodore Roosevelt's mansion, Sagamore Hill, at Oyster Bay, Long Island.

PART TWO

THE MISHNAH IN LITERARY AND AESTHETIC CONTEXT

THE MISHNAH AND ANCIENT BOOK PRODUCTION

CATHERINE HEZSER

University of Dublin

Although much scholarship has been devoted to the study of the Mishnah, the processes of its development, redaction, publication, and usage remain largely obscure. Neither the Mishnah itself nor any other ancient source provides direct evidence of the way in which the Mishnah was created. Whereas traditional scholars have usually based their arguments on late and dubious references in the Talmud, contemporary and more critical scholars have focused on the text of the Mishnah itself in search for clues to its sources and development. In the following, an alternative approach, which supplements rather than replaces the two already mentioned ones, is suggested. An approach that has rarely been applied, with the exception of Saul Lieberman's chapter on "The Publication of the Mishnah,"[1] is to view the Mishnah in the context of ancient book production. Recent studies of the creation, propagation, and usage of books in Graeco-Roman antiquity provide the most appropriate context for understanding the development of the Mishnah.[2] Even if no final conclusions can be reached on the basis of mere analogies, one can nevertheless assume that the processes affecting the Mishnah cannot have been too different from what was commonly

---

[1] See Saul Lieberman, *Hellenism in Jewish Palestine* (2nd ed., New York, 1962), pp. 83-99.

[2] See, e.g., Frederic Kenyon, *Books and Readers in Ancient Greece and Rome* (2nd ed., Oxford, 1951; A.F. Norman, "The Book Trade in Fourth-Century Antioch," in JHS 80 (1960), pp. 122-26; B.A. Van Groningen, "ΕΚΔΟΣΙΣ," in *Mnemosyne*, series 4, vol.16 (1963), pp. 1-17; Tönnes Kleberg, *Buchhandel und Verlagswesen in der Antike* (Darmstadt, 1967); C. Roberts, "Books in the Graeco-Roman World and in the New Testament," in P.R. Ackroyd and C.T. Evans, eds., *Cambridge History of the Bible* (Cambridge, 1970), vol.1, pp. 48-66; L.D. Reynolds and N.G. Wilson, *Scribes and Scholars: A Guide to the Transmission of Greek and Latin Literature* (Oxford, 1974); Raymond J. Starr, "The Circulation of Literary Texts in the Roman World," in *The Classical Quarterly* 37 (1987), pp. 213-223; Harry Y. Gamble, *Books and Readers in the Early Church: A History of Early Christian Texts* (New Haven and London, 1995); Jocelyn Penny Small, *Wax Tablets of the Mind. Cognitive Studies of Memory and Literacy in Classical Antiquity* (London and New York, 1997); H. Gregory Snyder, *Teachers and Texts in the Ancient World. Philosophers, Jews and Christians* (London, 2000).

practiced in antiquity. In the following a number of aspects of the development and usage of the Mishnah shall be examined in this regard.

1. Composition and Redaction

One of our main questions concerns the nature of the sources the Mishnah's editors used and the ways in which they revised them. Did the editors rely on traditional material or did they "invent" the contents and forms of the discussions? If they used traditional material, was it transmitted to them in written or oral form? Did they quote their sources in the exact words in which they received them, or did they take great liberty in reformulating them? Was one (circle of) editor(s) responsible for the collection or was the editing a more complex process involving a larger network of rabbis and a longer period of time? It is already obvious at the outset that the answer to none of these questions can be reduced to a simple either/or. But it is difficult to reach more specific conclusions on the basis of a study of the Mishnah or later references to the Mishnah alone, as has been done in the past. Before we look at ancient composition techniques, it is necessary to briefly review some of the solutions and suggestions offered by scholars in the past.

According to Epstein, Judah ha-Nasi, whom he considers the editor of the Mishnah edition later considered authoritative, but not the only editor of a Mishnah collection, made use of a variety of earlier traditions, some of which were part of prior (written?) collections already.[3] These traditions, whether written or oral, differed from each other with regard to their formal styles and the views and teachings they attributed to particular earlier Rabbinic authorities. Since Rabbi is assumed to have left his sources relatively unchanged, the differences within the traditional material led to inconsistencies within the Mishnah itself. Whereas Epstein's hypothesis that the Mishnah is based on a very diverse body of earlier teachings is undisputed by most scholars and almost self-evident, as Bokser has pointed out,[4] the assumption that the nature of the earlier material

---

[3] See Jacob N. Epstein, *Introduction to the Text of the Mishnah* [Hebr.], 2 vols. (2nd ed. Jerusalem, 1964), and Baruch M. Bokser, "Jacob N. Epstein's *Introduction to the Text of the Mishnah*," in Jacob Neusner, ed., *The Modern Study of the Mishnah* (Leiden, 1973), pp. 14-19.

[4] See Bokser, "Epstein's *Introduction*," p. 16.

can be deduced from the text of the Mishnah as it came down to us is more difficult to substantiate. Chanoch Albeck seems to agree with Epstein both on the diverse nature of the earlier traditions and on the truthful transmission of that material in Rabbi's Mishnah.[5] This theory leaves many questions open, however. The role of the editor is reduced to the mere ordering and reproduction of a centuries-old tradition. This tradition is viewed as diverse but basically unchanged over centuries. The purpose of the Mishnah collection is the mere preservation of tradition rather than a creative adaptation of it.

Later scholars have, to varying degrees, emphasized the changes the traditions underwent in the processes of transmission and redaction. David Weiss Halivni assumes that some sources originally created in the context of scriptural exegesis (Midrash) were later abbreviated and separated from their scriptural basis to be transmitted as legal statements (Mishnah), allegedly "to facilitate memory."[6] He suggests that the writing down of traditions that had previously been transmitted orally served the same purpose and "was based on the realization that oral literature could not survive."[7] Although Halivni reckons with certain formal changes to at least some of the sources during the process of transmission, he believes that the editors of the Mishnah were "quoting them [i.e., their sources] verbatim."[8] It seems that, according to Halivni, the Mishnah should not be seen as an original composition but as a scrapbook of quoted, excerpted, recorded, and partly abbreviated earlier material, some of which stems from halakhic midrashim.[9] Like Epstein and Albeck, he holds Judah ha-Nasi responsible for the redaction.[10] The mishnaic form was not invented by Rabbi, though,

---

[5] See Chanoch Albeck, *Einführung in die Mischna* (Berlin and New York, 1971), p. 149: "... dass der Redaktor der Mischna keine Änderungen, keine Umstellungen und keine Kürzungen an dem Stoff vornahm, der ihm vorlag, sondern ihn in unserer Mischna so festlegte, wie er ihn empfangen hatte." See also pp. 154-155: "All dies zeugt für verschiedene Quellen sowie für den typischen Charakter der Redigierung, deren kennzeichnende Eigenart es war, zu sammeln und zusammenzufassen, niemals aber zu ändern, zu streichen oder hinzuzufügen." Albeck assumes that even the original connections between halakhot were maintained by the editor.

[6] See David Weiss Halivni, *Midrash, Mishnah, and Gemara. The Jewish Predilection for Justified Law* (Cambridge, MA and London, 1986), p. 40.

[7] Ibid.

[8] Ibid., p. 48.

[9] See ibid., p. 53.

[10] See ibid., p. 59.

but developed after 70 C.E., as a means to facilitate the preservation of teachings.[11]

In his study of the relationship between the Mishnah and Sifra, Ronen Reichman tries to concretize Halivni's suggestion that midrashic sources formed the basis of the Mishnah.[12] He argues that Mishnah parallels to Sifra texts are directly dependent on the latter, that is, revised versions of them.[13] In addition to the material from Sifra, the Mishnah's editors adapted other traditions of various forms, some of which may have already existed as disputes or larger literary complexes at the pre-redactional stage.[14] The integration of this diverse material into a new literary entity may be considered a "substantial transformation," even if the redactional additions and changes to individual prior texts were limited in nature.[15]

Another, similar argument for the Mishnah's usage of a particular body of earlier material has been made by Alberdina Houtman.[16] Even though the Tosefta as it came down to us seems to have been composed after the Mishnah,[17] the Tosefta allegedly preserves "more original formulations of the traditional material (...) and a more original arrangement."[18] According to Houtman, the editor/s of the Mishnah probably abridged material the Tosefta preserved in a more elaborate form.[19] Both seem to have drawn from earlier collections or compositions that already possessed some of the structural features shared by the later documents.[20] When the editors of the Mishnah had selected, abridged, and rearranged the material of these earlier collections into a new whole, the editors of the Tosefta "decided to assemble an alternative collection of material that had been eliminated, abbreviated or reformulated by the editor(s) of the Mishnah."[21] They represented a more conservative standpoint,

---

[11] See ibid., p. 40.

[12] See Ronen Reichman, *Mishnah and Sifra. Ein literarkritischer Vergleich paralleler Überlieferungen*, in TSAJ 68 (Tübingen, 1998).

[13] See ibid., p. 238.

[14] See ibid., p. 239.

[15] See ibid., p. 241.

[16] See Alberdina Houtman, *Mishnah and Tosefta. A Synoptic Comparison of the Tractates Berakhot and Shebiit*, in TSAJ 59 (Tübingen, 1996).

[17] See ibid., p. 225. Houtman assumes "that the Tosefta was composed shortly after the Mishnah."

[18] Ibid., p. 226.

[19] See ibid., p. 227.

[20] See ibid., p. 235.

[21] Ibid.

rejecting the idea that the Mishnah contained the entire Oral Torah.[22]

The Mishnah editors' usage of heterogeneous earlier material has also been stressed by Hayim Lapin.[23] Lapin points to literary indications of the usage of sources such as contradictions, parallels within the Mishnah itself or with other documents, stylistic anomalies, and the usage of different terminology.[24] The phenomenon that such traces exist leads him to assume that the editors were rather conservative in their attitude towards earlier material: "Whatever revision and adaptation of material occurred in the process of redaction, a deep conservatism towards utilized material is in evidence. This conservatism allows us to see the traces of various alternative strategies for presenting material and for organizing it."[25] Some of the Mishnah's pericopae show signs of "secondary redaction," that is, the traditions seem to have been available to the "final" editors in an edited form already.[26] Such earlier redactions of traditional material may have taken place within the various Rabbinic schools and circles which annotated and collected traditions. The Mishnah's tractates would then consist of "several such clusters, from different 'schools.'"[27] The Mishnah editor/s would have revised, glossed, corrected, and added to these pre-redacted clusters and combined them to a new whole, whereas the basic forms and stylized language were a feature of the school traditions already.[28]

All of the scholars discussed so far seem to assume that the Mishnah's editor/s generally preserved the sources in (almost) the same form in which they received them. The Mishnah's redaction is seen as the final fixation of a centuries-long process of Rabbinic transmission. Whereas the more traditional scholars assumed that the traditions were transmitted basically unchanged during that period of time, the more critical scholars allow for revisions and additions during transmission and reckon with possible pre-redactional stages. What they share is the assumption that the "final" editors' impact on the formulation and (in the case of pre-

---
[22] See ibid., p. 237.
[23] Hayim Lapin., *Early Rabbinic Civil Law and the Social History of Roman Galilee. A Study of Mishnah Tractate Baba' Mesia'* (Atlanta, 1995), p. 50.
[24] See ibid., pp. 40-50.
[25] Ibid., p. 59.
[26] See ibid., p. 67.
[27] Ibid.
[28] See ibid., p. 86.

redacted clusters of tradition) on the arrangement of the material was rather limited.

A radically different standpoint has been taken by Jacob Neusner. Whereas Reichman, Houtman, and Lapin seem to claim largely written pre-redactional (clusters of) traditions, Neusner has pointed to the "mnemonic system" of the Mishnah, which seems to indicate a largely "oral formulation and oral transmission by means of memorization."[29] The so-called "syllogistic patterns" of logic, topic, and rhetoric reflect an oral stage before and after the redaction of the Mishnah: at both stages syllogisms "serve by definition to facilitate the easy memorization of the text."[30] Neusner nevertheless hesitates to draw far-ranging conclusions from this literary pattern to the oral or written nature of the traditions which the Mishnah editors used: "Clearly many traditions before us were formulated so as to facilitate their memorization. But whether or not the redacted pericopae derive from originally oral materials is a question that obviously cannot be settled one way or the other by the character of the materials which we have only in written form."[31]

Neusner seems to share Lieberman's theory of an "oral publication"—which was probably preceded by an oral composition—of the Mishnah, though.[32] Lieberman has argued that the Mishnah did not exist in writing throughout the Talmudic period.[33] The written notes with legal decisions and comments some rabbis may have possessed had a private and inofficial character only. They resembled the *hypomnemata* used by Graeco-Roman writers in the preliminary stages of literary composition.[34] These notes served the private purposes of their owners but were not suitable for "official" publication. Lieberman assumes that an earlier form of the Mishnah was compiled and systematized orally by Aqiba, on the basis of both oral traditions and students' notes, and taught and transmitted by Tannaim.[35] In the process of oral transmission "the old *Mishnah* was

---

[29] See Jacob Neusner, *The Memorized Torah. The Mnemonic System of the Mishnah* (Chico, 1985), p. 1.
[30] Ibid.
[31] Ibid., p. 27.
[32] See ibid. 28: "The materials which we have catalogued provide evidence in favor of the theory of the publication of the Mishnah advanced by Lieberman."
[33] See Lieberman, *Hellenism*, p. 87.
[34] See ibid.
[35] See ibid., pp. 92-93.

augmented by a new stratum formed of the later interpretations,"[36] until Judah ha-Nasi's revision "was virtually canonized."[37] It was "committed to memory by the *Tannaim* of the colleges" and allegedly existed in this oral form only.[38]

Neusner reckons with a much larger impact of the "final" editors on the formulation of the Mishnah text and the formation of the intermediate units than the above-mentioned scholars do. Whereas the latter draw a sharp distinction between tradition and redaction and reckon with a more or less truthful preservation of the (oral and/or written) tradition on the part of the editors, Neusner assumes that the Mishnah "is the work of tradent-redactors,"[39] that is, the "traditions" are formulated by the redactors, so that their pre-redactional form and content is not recognizable anymore. The Mishnah's editors stylized the text so much that any search for the sources underlying their (re)formulation becomes futile. In direct contradiction to the source-historical theories outlined above Neusner writes: "If there are traces of diverse theories of formulation and redaction in our division, which would reflect the individual preferences and styles of diverse circles over two hundred years, we have not found them."[40] Not the language but only the general views and ideas of earlier generations of rabbis are preserved in the text. The text of the Mishnah itself, both with regard to its formulation and content, must be seen as the work of its anonymous editors, though.

A review of ancient book composition techniques may elucidate some of the issues at hand. The central question in this regard concerns the nature of the sources and the ways in which the authors and editors made use of them. The intertextuality that Daniel Boyarin has stressed in connection with Rabbinic midrash was not only a feature of midrash or Rabbinic literature in general but of all ancient literary creations.[41] Like modern literary works, ancient works were always based on a whole body of prior texts and ideas whose origins cannot always be identified anymore. The usage of such material by ancient literary writers has been the sub-

---

[36] Ibid., p. 93.
[37] See ibid., p. 96.
[38] Ibid., p. 97.
[39] Neusner, *Memorized Torah*, p. 109.
[40] Ibid., p. 113.
[41] See Daniel Boyarin, *Intertextuality and the Reading of Midrash* (Bloomington and Indianapolis, 1990), pp. 22-38.

ject of a number of scholarly studies, some of which shall be introduced here.

Even when written literary sources existed, they were rarely checked and quoted verbatim. Papyrus rolls were cumbersome to handle, and to find a particular passage in a large roll was an almost impossible and at least time-consuming process.[42] Therefore authors/editors who wanted to quote a particular passage from a prior literary work would most often rely on their memory rather than go and check the text to represent it verbatim.[43] The reliance on memory was inevitable in a case where one did not own a copy of the work. One may have borrowed and read the text from a friend's copy once, but would have to get in contact with that more or less distant friend again in order to gain direct access to the text.[44]

Sometimes a reader, especially one who was an author himself, may have taken notes when reading a text. Frederic Kenyon writes:

> There is frequent reference to the use of notebooks *(tabellae, pugillares)*, which could be carried on the person and used for casual annotation or for rough copies of the poems. Normally these were of wood, coated with wax, on which writing was inscribed with a stylus, or covered with whitewash on which ink could be used.[45]

The notes of the text itself and of one's own comments on it will often have become blurred, so that a distinction between the two would become difficult if not impossible later on. Even when (re)presented without one's own annotations, the text may have been paraphrased or abridged rather than quoted verbatim and at full length.

---

[42] See Kenyon, *Books*, p. 67: "The lack of assistance to readers, or of aids to facilitate reference, in ancient books is very remarkable," and ibid., p. 69: "It must also have been very difficult to find a given passage when required, and impossible to give a reference to it which could be generally applied." See also Small, *Wax Tablets*, p. 16: "It was not until after antiquity, especially from the Renaissance, that readers felt a need for precise citation that never seemed to arise in their ancient counterparts." Sometimes cross-references to particular books are given, but never to chapters or pages: "A concept of the page simply did not exist" in antiquity, since pagination differed in each individual copy (see ibid.).

[43] See Small, *Wax Tablets*, p. 71.

[44] On the exchange of books among friends, see Starr, *Circulation*, p. 213: "Romans circulated texts in a series of widening concentric circles determined primarily by friendship." See also Small, *Wax Tablets*, p. 44: A private library would be "used by its owner and his friends only", and even when trying to gain access to the books of public libraries "it was very probably a matter of whom you knew."

[45] Kenyon, *Books*, p. 92.

It is important to note in this connection that the notion of an original text was absent in antiquity. Since no copyright laws existed, hardly two identical copies of a work would circulate.[46] When the written versions of a literary work would already differ from each other to a certain extent, one may assume that the writer who represented a passage from such a work in his own writing would feel even less need to quote it verbatim. Accordingly, Small has pointed out: "The entire gamut of errors occur in ancient quotations. The words are wrong. The author cited is wrong. The speakers are incorrect."[47]

Notes did not only consist of paraphrases of and comments on prior literary works but also of records of one's own or someone else's thoughts and ideas expressed instantaneously, in conversations, discussions or speeches, which had never been formulated in writing. Pliny the Elder, for example, is said to have been accompanied by his secretary wherever he went, whether traveling on the road or visiting a bathhouse, in order to be able to take note of whatever came to his mind.[48] Similarly, students of philosophical schools are likely to have taken occasional notes of their teachers' views and deliberations.[49] Cicero's son allegedly asked his father to provide him with a secretary who could accompany him to class sessions and write down lecture notes for him.[50] Such notes may sometimes have consisted of citations or paraphrases of earlier literary texts, read out or quoted from memory by their teacher, together with the latter's comments on these texts.[51] Both in the case of quotations from literary works and orally uttered opinions or comments by the teacher's own teachers or philosophical colleagues the above-mentioned reservations concerning verbatim quotation apply. The teacher's representation of prior texts, teachings, and opinions would always be colored by his own perception and point-of-view. Synder writes:

> As a delivery vehicle for the text, as its articulator and exegete, the teacher exercises a high degree of authority vis-à-vis the text. It is no

---

[46] See Small, Wax Tablets, p. 28.
[47] Ibid. p. 220 and 318 n. 80 for examples.
[48] See Randolf E. Richards, *The Secretary in the Letters of Paul*, WUNT 2.42, (Tübingen, 1991), pp. 64-65.
[49] See Snyder, *Teachers*, p. 22 with reference to Epictetus, who recommended his students to take notes during his lectures to have his thoughts "ready at hand by night and by day, write them, read them." Other philosophical teachers seem to have held different views on the advantages of note-taking, however.
[50] Cicero, Ad Fam. 16.21.8, referred to by Snyder, *Teachers*, p. 25.
[51] See ibid., pp. 23-24.

exaggeration to describe a teacher in this position both as a text provider and as a text-broker.[52]

The knowledge of the text or tradition which the students gained through the intermediacy of their teachers was already a secondary knowledge and the version which they themselves put down in writing would be distanced from the author of the text or saying by another degree. One could imagine that theoretically the student would (at least sometimes) have been able to consult the quoted text directly or to contact and ask the authority to whom his teacher had attributed a teaching. But out of reverence for and trust in his own teacher, because of lack of access to the "original" text and author, and a general lack of concern for verbatim quotation in antiquity the student will have felt little need to check his teacher's words.

The social context of the philosophical teaching session points to another phenomenon relevant in this regard. During such teaching sessions prior texts and opinions were, of course, not only represented by the teacher but also discussed, analyzed, applied, and expanded. On the basis of prior teachings, new hypotheses were drawn:

> It may have involved fashioning one's own premises and arguments, based on the model provided by the text, perhaps formulating premises under which a fallacious argument might become true, or extending an argument by adding a premise.[53]

One may assume that in the students' notes distinctions between the "quoted" texts and arguments attributed to prior authorities and their own teacher's newly devised hypothetical statements and expansions will often not have been indicated as such. Accordingly, it would later be impossible to distinguish between these authorities' "actual" views and sayings, even in the secondary form in which they were represented by one's teacher, and arguments which were hypothetically constructed during the study sessions.

Notes would usually be written on wax tablets or individual pieces of papyrus. Wax tablets were used as a writing surface for all types of writing that were not meant to be permanent and lasting.[54] As far as wax-covered wooden tablets are concerned, the writing was

---

[52] Ibid., p. 25.
[53] Ibid., p. 27 with reference to Epictetus. See ibid., p. 235, n .63 and 64 for examples.
[54] See Colin H. Roberts and T.C. Skeat, *The Birth of the Codex* (London, 1983), p. 11.

scratched into the wax with a stylus and could easily be erased. A number of tablets could be connected to form a notebook which could accommodate a relatively larger but still small amount of text. Such tablets and notebooks were used in schools, as well as for occasional letters, notes, and drafts.[55] Pieces of papyrus were probably lighter to carry, but they could not be reinscribed a number of times. They were used for more permanent types of record keeping such as bills and receipts.[56] Depending on the number of notes taken and the quantity of papyrus needed, one may assume that papyrus would be a more expensive writing surface than the wax tablets, which were also quite expensive themselves.[57] The least expensive note-writing material were ostraca, that is, small pieces of broken clay vessels which could probably be found everywhere, but depending on their size only a few letters, words or sentences would fit on them. Other materials are rarely mentioned in ancient sources in this regard.[58]

Notes *(hypomnemata)* would always have an informal nature only, whether as temporary reminders of matters read, heard or thought or as rough drafts and outlines of literary works. In some philosophical schools special efforts were made to preserve and collect such notes but in others not.[59] The notes were meant to serve the personal purposes of their writers only or the internal needs of study circles such as review and memorization.[60]

Small has argued that the usage of written notes within the processes of literary composition was rather limited in antiquity. Whereas some scholars believe that Pliny used "a pile of little tablets, of scraps of papyrus" when composing his Natural History, Small stresses that "the idea of an ancient equivalent of modern note cards is totally misguided."[61] The reasons for the limited use of notes are mostly practical-pragmatic in nature: neither sherds of papyrus nor ostraca can be easily sorted into stacks; notes written on papyrus rolls could not be properly separated and organized; comments written in the

---

[55] See Kenyon, *Books*, p. 92. See also Catherine Hezser, *Jewish Literacy in Roman Palestine*, TSAJ 81 (Tübingen, 2001), pp. 127-130.
[56] See Hezser, *Literacy*, p. 131.
[57] On the prices of papyrus, see ibid., pp. 132-133.
[58] See Kenyon, *Books*, p. 92.
[59] See Snyder, *Teachers*, p. 50 with reference to the circulation of informal "literature" among the Epicureans.
[60] See ibid., p. 54.
[61] Small, *Wax Tablets*, p. 188.

margins of rolls were difficult to find.⁶² In addition, as already pointed out above, many notes will simply have been lost over time, especially if no special efforts at preserving them were made.

Small therefore suggests that ancient writers would mostly rely on their memory in order to recall earlier ideas, texts, and teachings: "Because of the classical training in mnemotechnics, Greeks and Romans trusted their memories to an extent that we would never trust ours today."⁶³ The consequence of ancient writers' reliance on their memory would be that "quotes" consisted of the general "gist" of earlier statements rather than being verbatim reproductions of speeches and texts: "The entire gamut of errors occurs in ancient quotations. The words are wrong. The author cited is wrong. The speakers are incorrect."⁶⁴ This phenomenon is, for example, evident in Plutarch's usage of earlier traditions: he streamlined earlier material, conflated similar items, changed the times and places, expanded traditions, and fabricated entirely new items which are often indistinguishable from the transmitted ones.⁶⁵ Plutarch and other authors like him "would make inferences based on 'gist,' on what should have happened, even if it did not,"⁶⁶ and similar stories would easily "get mixed up with each other."⁶⁷ Since the ancients had a notion of "truth" that differed from ours today,⁶⁸ and since texts were difficult to check anyway, the reliance on one's memory when reproducing earlier texts and traditions was a common and perfectly legitimate practice.⁶⁹

These considerations should make anyone suspicious of the assumption of a trustworthy adaptation of earlier written (or oral) traditions by the editors of the Mishnah. In fact, references to notebooks or the taking of notes never appear in the Mishnah itself but only in the Tosefta and the Yerushalmi, and they are never asso-

---

⁶² See ibid., pp. 188-189.
⁶³ Ibid., p. 189.
⁶⁴ Ibid., p. 220. See 318, n. 80, for examples.
⁶⁵ See ibid., p. 193.
⁶⁶ Ibid., p. 195.
⁶⁷ Ibid., p. 200.
⁶⁸ See ibid., p. 192: "the ancient standard of accuracy is 'gist.'"
⁶⁹ See also William Chase Greene, "The Spoken and the Written Word," in *Harvard Studies in Classical Philology* 60 (1951), p. 24: "But the occasional graffito on pottery or on a statue, and the utilitarian use of inscriptions for records, as reminders (ὑπομνήματα, *aides-mémoire*), or even the reduction to writing and the circulation of Delphic oracles, do not of themselves prove that writing was used in the recording, still less in the composition, of literature. Indeed even in the classical period written laws were regarded as inferior to 'unwritten laws'...."

ciated with student notes. They rather seem to have been taken by particular rabbis during or after discussions and served as personal memos of particular practices, rulings, or items to which rulings applied.[70] There are few references to such notes, and we do not know whether the editors actually had such texts available in written form. It is interesting, however, that alleged quotations from written notes are indicated as such by a particular formula by the editors.[71] This may imply that the existence of written notes of halakhic content was exceptional for them. If they had received most of their traditional material in this form, that is, as collections of written notes of various rabbis, transmitted by their students, such references, even if formulaic in nature, would have been redundant. One might argue that this was the case with the Mishnah, which therefore lacks such references, but such an argument is not very convincing.

Unless parallel texts in other Rabbinic documents exist as, for example, in Sifra examined by Reichman and in the Tosefta examined by Houtman (see above), the sources available to the editors of the Mishnah cannot be determined. Even if parallels point to a common source, this source may not have existed in written form. If informal and private written notes existed, the language of these notes may have been Aramaic rather than Hebrew. This phenomenon may be indicated by Y. Kil. 1:1, 27a, where an Aramaic list of various kinds of produce allegedly written "on the wall" (of the house or study room?) of Hillel b. Alem is quoted, which appears in Hebrew in M. Kil. 1:1.[72] Although this Aramaic graffiti can, of course, not be considered the source of the mishnaic ruling but is probably a later Amoraic adaptation of it, the possibility that in Amoraic times mishnaic rulings would be circulated and discussed in Aramaic rather than in Hebrew may suggest that the sources of the Mishnah, whether written or oral, were at least sometimes formulated in Aramaic rather than in Hebrew as well.[73]

The emphasis on oral memorization in ancient philosophical schools and other settings of higher education (e.g., rhetorics and law)[74] and the general lack of concern for accurate verbatim quo-

---

[70] See Hezser, *Literacy*, pp. 96-97, for a discussion of these references.
[71] See the references ibid.
[72] See Hezser, *Literacy*, pp. 96-97, on this text.
[73] See also ibid., p. 246.
[74] See, e.g., Loveday Alexander, "The Living Voice: Scepticism towards the Written Word in Early Christian and in Graeco-Roman Texts," in JSOT.S 87 (1990) pp. 221-247.

tations in antiquity suggest that the majority of sources available to the Mishnah's editors were transmitted orally and that even in the case of written sources neither the original authors nor the original contents and forms of the traditions can be extracted from the text in its edited form. The circle of editors of the Mishnah, whether or not assembled by Judah ha-Nasi, is likely to have contacted Rabbinic colleagues at various places in Roman Palestine and asked them to collect and submit (orally or in writing) all of the traditions of teachings, stories, rulings they possessed as notes or—more likely— had memorized, so that the whole gamut of sources that the editors amalgamated will have been very variegated indeed. Since there is no evidence that particular efforts were made throughout the first two centuries C.E. to record Rabbinic teachings in writing and to collect these written records at Rabbinic schools or central archival places, it is very unlikely that many such written collections of notes existed, and even where they existed once, they may have been lost in the course of time. Therefore one has to assume that most of the traditions the Mishnah's editors received from their Rabbinic contemporaries were memorized teachings and rulings of these colleagues' teachers and teachers' teachers, which probably circulated in variant forms and had been subjected to considerable changes in the process of transmission.

Scholars have repeatedly emphasized the important role of orality in Rabbinic culture, irrespective of whether the notion of the "Oral Torah" was developed early or late.[75] This emphasis on the oral discussion and transmission of teachings does not imply, however, that traditions were not allowed to be written down[76] or that they were transmitted verbatim, as Zlotnick seems to assume.[77] The

---

[75] See, e.g., Philip S. Alexander, "Orality in Pharisaic-Rabbinic Judaism at the Turn of the Eras," in Henry Wansbrough, ed., *Jesus and the Oral Gospel Tradition* (Sheffield, 1991), pp. 159-184. On the distinction between the concept of Oral Torah and the practice of oral discussion and transmission, see Martin S. Jaffee, "How Much 'Orality' in Oral Torah? New Perspectives on the Composition and Transmission of Early Rabbinic Tradition," in Shofar 10 (1992), pp. 60-61.

[76] See Jacob Neusner, "The Rabbinic Traditions About the Pharisees Before AD 70: The Problem of Oral Transmission," in JJS 22 (1971), pp. 5-6: It is methodologically illegitimate to take Babylonian Talmudic references to the prohibition of writing literally and assume that therefore Tannaim refrained from writing down traditions altogether. But there is also no real evidence that written traditions existed; see idem, "The Written Tradition in the Pre-Rabbinic Period," in JSJ 4 (1973), pp. 56-65.

[77] See Dov Zlotnick, "Memory and the Integrity of the Oral Tradition," in

highly patterned structure of the Mishnah clearly indicates that the traditions the editors used were subjected to a thorough recasting to fit the Mishnah's formulaic character. Neusner is certainly right in assuming that the imposition of this formulaic pattern must be seen as the work of the editors rather than the form in which the traditional material was transmitted to them: "... the text is so formulated as to be relatively easy to memorize. But the mode of formulating a text for future preservation tells us nothing at all about the origins of the contents of that text."[78] It is impossible "to uncover the point of origin of the materials at hand.... The Mishnah was formulated pretty much all at once, in a single process and through a sustained and incremental history of conglomeration and aggregation."[79]

Going back to the above-mentioned model of the editorial process, one may hypothesize that the circle of mishnaic editors, once they had contacted their network of colleague-friends and received an amorphous body of traditional teachings and rulings, would, on their basis, construct something entirely new and unprecedented. Whether they would first record the orally received traditions in a preliminary written form or whether they would rely on their memory completely when reformulating traditions and presenting them in the Mishnah's characteristic formulaic patterns cannot be determined. What is certain, however, is that the traditional material that was eventually integrated into the Mishnah was removed from its "origin" by a number of steps and will have represented the "gist" of a teaching or ruling rather than the actual teaching or ruling itself. As in the case of other ancient writers' and editors' usage of earlier material, attributions will have been confused, teachings expanded to be applicable to other situations and combined with newly formulated rulings which were formally indistinguishable from the traditional ones. Since the purpose of the Mishnah's redaction was not the historiographically accurate and chronologically organized recording of the "history of halakhah" but the thematic presentation of halakhic problems and issues, the question whether or

---

JANES 16-17 (1984-85) p. 234: "Painstaking exactness was a matter of necessity.... The links between ministering to the master, memorization, study, and the transmission of an accurate text of the Mishnah had to be firm."

[78] Jacob Neusner, *Oral Tradition in Judaism. The Case of the Mishnah* (New York and London, 1987), p. 74.

[79] Ibid., p. 75.

not an earlier authority's words were preserved verbatim will not have interested anyone.

2. Publication and Circulation

One may assume that once mishnaic tractates were compiled and edited, this body of work will have been made available to at least some people. Yet the form of the publication and circulation of the Mishnah in Amoraic times is highly disputed among scholars and far from clear. Lieberman's theory of "oral publication" has already been mentioned.[80] This theory was also promulgated by Rashi on the basis of a literal understanding of later Rabbinic texts prohibiting the writing down of the oral tradition. Albeck, on the other hand, postulates a written fixation of the Mishnah, which was subsequently transmitted orally in the schools by Tannaim who possessed an exceptionally good memory.[81] Supplementing Albeck's negative argument in favor of a written version of the Mishnah (no conclusive evidence against the writing down of the Mishnah exists), Weiss Halivni provides a positive reason for the existence of a written version: "The dispensation for the change from the oral to the written was based on the realization that oral literature could not survive...."[82] If the Mishnah had not been written down, it would hardly have survived throughout Amoraic times, at least not in the highly formulaic and concise form in which it came down to us. Ronen Reichman and Alberdina Houtman, who see a large scale adaptation of written sources by the Mishnah's editors,[83] accordingly assume that the redactional process produced a written text.

The question whether the Mishnah was "published" orally or in writing cannot be ultimately decided, but the existence and circulation of at least a few written versions of the Mishnah seems more likely than a centuries-long oral transmission of the text. Despite the possibility that the ancients' memories were far superior to our own,

---

[80] See Lieberman, *Hellenism*, p. 87. See also Yaakov Elman, *Authority and Tradition: Toseftan Baraitot in Talmudic Babylonia* (Hoboken, 1994), p. 48.

[81] See Albeck, *Einführung*, p. 167, and ibid., p. 169: "...dass es keinen Beweis von irgendeiner Seite her dafür gibt, dass die Mischna nicht schriftlich redigiert worden ist." Therefore one has to assume "dass die Mischna in schriftlicher Form geordnet worden ist, damit sie nicht vergessen werde."

[82] Weiss Halivni, *Midrash*, p. 40.

[83] See the discussion in section 1, above.

it seems hardly plausible that a text of the size of the Mishnah would be transmitted in fairly the same form by different individuals and different generations for hundreds of years. A characteristic of oral transmission is its great flexibility and constant adaptation to varying new circumstances rather than the preservation of a fixed text formulated in the past.[84] The fact that the Mishnah contains Tannaitic traditions only and does not show much evidence of Amoraic additions and revisions mitigates against the oral transmission theory.

There is also no analogy for the oral transmission of a literary corpus as large as the Mishnah in late antique Graeco-Roman society.[85] In Roman times, a multitude of written literary texts were circulating, despite the great role oral performance and communication continued to play. Rosalind Thomas has suggested seeing Roman society "as a society in which the spoken word, though important, was increasingly dominated and influenced by written texts,"[86] that is, written texts formed the basis of oral discussions and argumentations and performances on stage. Written texts were also "used extensively for teaching purposes..., and many official or unofficial texts of a speech were in circulation, once it had been delivered."[87] Accordingly, the main question is "what the precise significance of memorization is in such a literary context: whether or how far these orators' ability to memorize was altered by the fact that they could use a written text to memorize from."[88] It seems,

---

[84] See also Werner H. Kelber, *The Oral and the Written Gospel. The Hermeneutics of Speaking and Writing in the Synoptic Tradition, Mark, Paul, and Q* (Philadelphia, 1983), p. 27: "Verbatim memorization as a key factor in oral transmission has been abandoned by the majority of experts, who now admit the inevitability of change, flexibility, and degrees of improvisation." In oral transmission statements were constantly "adjusted to prevailing social expectations" to which they had to conform, a process which Kelber calls "preventive censorship" (see ibid., p. 29).

[85] See also Jaffee, "How Much 'Orality,'" p. 63. An example for the oral transmission and fixation of a relatively large corpus of traditions outside of the Graeco-Roman realm is the Vedic tradition, referred to by David R. Olson, "Literacy as Metalinguistic Activity," in David R. Olson and Nancy Torrance, eds., *Literacy and Orality* (Cambridge, 1991), p. 253. Olson stresses, however, that "such texts have an accumulative, archival function. New information can be added and old superseded and abandoned"(ibid.), that is, in oral transmission the text is subject to constant changes and adaptations to varying circumstances.

[86] See Rosalind Thomas, *Literacy and Orality in Ancient Greece* (Cambridge, 1992), p. 159.

[87] See ibid., p. 160.

[88] Ibid., p. 161.

then, that even in societies in which orality was important, this was a "secondary orality" based on written texts in the form of speeches, tragedies and comedies, poetic works, historical, philosophical, and legal texts.

In antiquity "publication" simply meant the release of a text for recopying.[89] This recopying would usually be carried out on an individual basis by all those who wanted to own a copy of the text, that is, primarily by friends and students of the authors and editors.[90] The large-scale production of manuscript copies by book sellers concerned the most popular classical texts only. Once the text was "abandoned" and made available to others, the authors/editors had lost all control over it.[91] They could neither determine the number of copies made, nor the form in which the text was copied, since no copyright laws existed. Therefore a number of copies with more or less different versions of a text would circulate: "chacque copie manuscrite est unique, présentant ses propres caractéristiques, ses propres écarts de l'original, intentionnels ou accidentels, et qu'elle n'est pas le représentant d'un groupe d'exemplaires identiques."[92]

Accordingly, one has to reckon with the circulation of a number of different versions of the Mishnah, or individual mishnaic tractates, recopied by individual sages, their scribes and their students. How many copies of the Mishnah were made immediately after its release or circulated in Amoraic times is impossible to determine. Perhaps many rabbis did not possess a copy of the Mishnah at all, some rabbis had only a written copy of a particular tractate, and the complete written work could be accessed by rabbis who lived in the major cities only. Most rabbis would therefore have to rely on the oral transmission of the Mishnah enacted by colleagues who had memorized (particular parts of) the (written) text. Following Lieberman, these memorizers can be called "living books,"[93] but only in so far as they represented existing written books. They were not the sole incorporations of the text.

The memorization and oral transmission of the probably written Mishnah can perhaps be compared to the transmission of the Twelve Tables in Roman society. Walter Eder has pointed out that "Ro-

---

[89] See van Groningen, pp. 2-3.
[90] See Starr, *Circulation*, p. 213: "Romans circulated texts in a series of widening concentric circles determined primarily by friendship."
[91] See van Groningen, p. 5.
[92] Ibid., pp. 7-8.
[93] See Lieberman, *Hellenism*, p. 90.

man pupils were obliged to memorize the text of the Twelve Tables,"[94] which formed the basis of Roman civil law, although these laws existed in codified written form and could theoretically be read from a scroll at that time.[95] According to Schwind, the written publication of the law had a control function, that is, the text could be checked in case of doubts and disputes.[96] But the populace would primarily learn about these laws by oral transmission and memorization. In a society in which literacy was limited to relatively small and circumscribed circles of the population the oral transmission of written texts is likely to have played a significant role.[97]

Since the written versions that formed the basis of the memorization will already have differed from each other to a certain extent, the memorized versions recited by Tannaim would have varied as well, and perhaps even more so, since they may have been further transformed in the process of oral transmission. The orally recited passages would have formed the basis of Rabbinic discussions and teachings, and it is unlikely that the Amoraim would have regularly checked the written versions of the text.[98] Whether or not such written versions were available, rabbis may have considered the Tanna's oral version as reliable and authoritative as the written text.[99]

One can imagine that each Tanna had only memorized particular parts of the Mishnah. Consequently, the choice of the Mishnah texts that formed the basis of Rabbinic discussions would not so much depend on a specific rabbi's predilections and interests but rather

---

[94] See Walter Eder, "The Political Significance of the Codification of Law in Archaic Societies: An Unconventional Hypothesis," in Kurt A. Raaflaub, ed., *Social Struggles in Archaic Rome. New Perspectives on the Conflict of the Orders* (Berkeley, 1986), p. 267.

[95] See Fritz Freiherr von Schwind, *Zur Frage der Publikation im römischen Recht, mit Ausblicken in das altgriechische und ptolemäische Rechtsgebiet* (Munich, 1940), p. 18.

[96] See ibid., pp. 18-19.

[97] See also C.G. Thomas, "Literacy and the Codification of Law," in *Studia et Documenta Historiae et Iuris* 43 (1977), p. 457.

[98] See also Elman, *Authority*, p. 48: "Whether or not it [the Mishnah] was so available [i.e., in written form], it is clear that the Amoraim did not resort to such a written text." Cf., Lieberman, *Hellenism*, p. 87: "In the entire Talmudic literature we do not find that a book of the Mishnah was ever consulted in case of controversies or doubt concerning a particular reading." That there is no evidence for rabbis consulting a written version of the Mishnah is no conclusive argument against the existence of such a version.

[99] See also Martin S. Jaffee, "A Rabbinic Ontology of the Written and Spoken Word: On Discipleship, Transformative Knowledge, and the Living Texts of Oral Torah," in JAAR 65 (1997), p. 528.

on the Tannaim who were available at a certain time and place. These Tannaim may have moved from disciple-circle to disciple-circle and from place to place to provide rabbis with a wider variety of traditional material than an individual Tanna could. Nevertheless Elman seems to be correct in pointing out that familiarity with all mishnayot cannot be assumed to have been universal among Amoraim.[100] Rabbis' access only to particular tractates (whether in written or oral form) may be indicated by talmudic references, e.g., "[the tractate] Ketubot of the house of the teacher" (Y. Ket. 2:4, 26c) and to tractates Neziqin and Nedarim as rabbis' study base (cf., Y. B.Q. 9:14, 7a).

Halivni has argued that the Mishnah's success was "short-lived" and that it was accepted by some schools only.[101] He assumes that it obtained "undisputed supremacy" at the time of Judah ha-Nasi only.[102] Since it is commonly assumed that the Mishnah associated with Judah ha-Nasi favors the material of particular schools (e.g., the school of Aqiba) while neglecting, downgrading, and excluding the traditions of other circles (e.g., the school of Ishmael), i.e., that the choice and presentation of the material is partial to some extent, one may assume that not all rabbis were satisfied with this version. These scholars would probably try to obtain copies of the written text, dispute orally transmitted mishnayot, and perhaps circulate alternative collections. Whether the Tosefta originated from some rabbis' discontent with the Mishnah, as Alberdina Houtman has argued,[103] and whether alternative Mishnah-collections besides the extant one existed, is possible but cannot be ascertained.

Only those who could read literary texts, were sufficiently wealthy to afford the "luxury" of purchasing book scrolls, and had a scholarly interest in the material can be considered potential private owners of a Mishnah text.[104] Accordingly, the private ownership of Mishnah texts may, by and large, have been restricted to a few highly literate and well-off rabbis. Since each tractate will have been copied on a separate papyrus roll,[105] a rabbi may have owned one or

---

[100] See Elman, *Authority*, p. 48.
[101] See Halivni, *Midrash*, p. 59.
[102] See ibid.
[103] See Houtman, *Mishnah*, pp. 234-235.
[104] See also Norman, *Book Trade*, p. 126 who emphasizes that in Graeco-Roman society, too, scholars were the ones who were most interested in owning books.
[105] See Kenyon, *Books*, p. 65: "Two or three books of the Iliade were as much as an ordinary roll could contain."

several individual tractates only. Where local study houses existed, these study houses may have had a partial or full set of tractates that could be consulted by resident scholars if necessary. Since the verbatim citation from a written text was not valued more highly than the citation from memory,[106] and since the handling and checking of passages in papyrus rolls was very cumbersome,[107] one may assume that the use of written versions of the Mishnah was limited and that, accordingly, the re-copying and circulation of the text would have been limited as well.

3. Purpose and Usage

A number of possible purposes of the creation of the Mishnah have been suggested in the past. The Mishnah may have been compiled as a text book for rabbinical students, a legal compendium for Rabbinic judges, or simply a collection of highly valued school material that might otherwise have disappeared over time. What is clear, though, is that the editors were not interested in deciding halakhic matters, in presenting a systematic and homogeneous outline of authoritatively fixed and finally determined halakhah.[108] They rather seem to present the traditional material in such a way that it would easily lead to further discussion. Whether this was the real intention of the editors we do not know, but the fact that such further discussion actually took place is evidenced by the Amoraic discussions of and comments on the Mishnah transmitted in the Talmud Yerushalmi and Bavli.

It seems that at the end of Tannaitic times, that is, at the turn from the second to the third century C.E., some rabbis felt that it was necessary to collect their predecessors', teachers', and colleagues' traditions and to subsequently transmit them to future generations in a specific format and form. This determination to create a more or less permanent and structured body of traditional material out of an abundant and very diverse stock of teachings, stories, sayings, rumors, notes, and hear-say must be considered a major new de-

---

[106] See Small, *Wax Tablets*, p. 16: "It was not until after antiquity, especially from the Renaissance on, that readers felt a need for precise citation that never seemed to arise in their ancient counterparts."

[107] See ibid., p. 14.

[108] See also Albeck, *Einführung*, pp. 155-156.

velopment rather than the end of a long process of gradual amalgamation.[109]

One may adduce various reasons for explaining why the Mishnah was created at that time. The high profile, influence, and connections of Judah ha-Nasi may have played a decisive role. For the first time, a rabbi may have found himself at the center of an extensive network of like-minded Torah scholars whose support and cooperation he could generate. As I have argued elsewhere, Judah seems to have stood out among his Rabbinic colleagues because of his great Torah knowledge and personal charisma, exceptional wealth, distinguished family heritage, and connections to high-standing Romans.[110] The combination of these criteria led to his exceptionally high status as patriarch and *primus inter pares*. It seems that no patriarch after Judah was able to achieve an equal recognition and prominence.[111]

His central position and significant connections among the rabbis, the Jewish populace, and the Romans will have allowed Judah ha-Nasi to exert exceptional control and authority, notwithstanding the fact that some rabbis will have rejected his claims and remained independent of or even hostile towards him. He would have been able to get into contact with rabbis at many different places and win them for his Mishnah project. Through direct and indirect connections to a large number of Rabbinic colleagues all over Palestine, he could collect a large number of school traditions, whether in oral or (preliminarily) written form. One may assume that he had a number of close collaborators, messengers, and scribes, whom he could send out to collect material from various locales, or that rabbis at other places would send material to his place of residence.

The reasons why Judah would initiate such a vast editorial project are more difficult to determine. An important reason why ancient legal scholars felt a need to compile traditional material was the vast diffusion and inaccessibility of the traditional material before its compilation took place. At the time of Judah ha-Nasi rabbis will have been aware of the vast amount of school traditions that had accu-

---

[109] See the considerations in section 1 above.

[110] See Catherine Hezser, *The Social Structure of the Rabbinic Movement in Roman Palestine*, TSAJ 66 (Tübingen, 1997), pp. 411-412.

[111] See also Martin Jacobs, *Die Institution des jüdischen Patriarchen. Eine quellen- und traditionskritische Studie zur Geschichte der Juden in der Spätantike*, TSAJ 52 (Tübingen, 1995), pp. 122-123.

mulated over centuries and were transmitted from one generation of students to the next. One may assume that, before the creation of the Mishnah, the traditions of a particular earlier rabbi such as, e.g., Aqiba, would have been available to this rabbi's immediate friends and to a circumscribed circle of students and students' students only, but not to (later generations of) rabbis at distant places who had no immediate contacts or connections to his school. At the end of the second century, rabbis may have felt the need to collect and access the great variety of teachings of various disciple circles that circulated in Palestine and to preserve and transmit this material in a form in which it would be useful to their contemporaries and future scholars.

Analogies from Roman legal compilations may be helpful in this regard. Walter Eder has pointed out that the "codification of customary law" should be "regarded as a measure to ensure aristocratic predominence; it was an attempt to stabilize the political and economic status quo, which was being seriously threatened by social unrest."[112] This hypothesis, which refers to the laws of Solon and the Twelve Tables, which were allegedly "prompted by strong political pressures,"[113] cannot be directly applied to the redaction of the Mishnah, since neither the rabbis nor the patriarch possessed political power and authority in Roman Palestine. Nevertheless, the general consideration that legal codification helps consolidate the influence of those who stand behind the laws, that is, the (political or) intellectual elites, and that it tries to create a certain common denominator in the midst of (political unrest or) great diversity seems plausible.

At the end of the second century C.E. and especially at the time of Judah ha-Nasi the Rabbinic movement seems to have been well-established throughout Palestine. Rabbis seem to have considered themselves the scholarly and spiritual elite of Jewish society.[114] They claimed a monopoly on the interpretation of the Torah and its application to various everyday-life situations. On the other hand, the Rabbinic movement was not institutionalized or centralized, but a diffuse network of Torah scholars at many different locales, who shared their basic interest in Torah study and its transmission to close

---

[112] Eder, *Political Significance*, p. 263.
[113] See ibid.
[114] On rabbis' self-consciousness as sages see Hezser, *Social Structure*, 130-37.

circles of students but differed amongst themselves with regard to almost any halakhic detail.[115] The compilation of the Mishnah, which included a wide variety of different opinions rather than presenting clear-cut decisions, would serve as an integrative device and as the basis of further discussion that, it was probably hoped, almost all rabbis could accept. The very fact that Rabbinic teachings would henceforth exist in a structured written form would lend credence to rabbis' claims to be Torah teachers and religious authorities.[116]

Eder has stressed that "codification of law is at the same time creation of law because customary and new regulations are inseparably intertwined in it: in its written form, customary law acquires a new quality...."[117] This consideration also applies to the Mishnah, since, as pointed out above, the editors seem to have (re-)formulated most of the received traditions and combined them with contemporary views and concerns. Accordingly, the Mishnah is not merely a collection of prior teachings but the creation of its editors, whose opinions and world-views determined the selection, formulation, and arrangement of the material at hand. The specific selection and formulation of the material and its (likely) fixation in written form would lend authority and future prominence to those Rabbinic circles represented in it while others would fall into oblivion.

If Judah ha-Nasi actually initiated the redaction of the Mishnah, why would he and his editorial staff remain anonymous rather than identify themselves within the text?[118] Perhaps the integrative function of the Mishnah necessitated the anonymity of the editors and the "pluralistic" presentation of the material. The editors may have reckoned that the Mishnah would be accepted by a wider variety of rabbis if it did not bear the marks of one particular circle only. They may have thought that an explicit association with Judah ha-Nasi and his Rabbinic friends would lead those of his colleagues who

---

[115] See ibid., pp. 228-239.

[116] Lapin's claim in idem, *Civil Law*, p. 116, that "the redaction of the Mishnah was, at least in part, an effort to increase the centralization and institutionalization of the Rabbinic movement" goes much further. See below.

[117] Eder, *Political Significance*, p. 274.

[118] On the formal and substantial anonymity of the Mishnah, see Neusner, *Memorized Torah*, p. 115: the Mishnah is "formally anonymous, in that it does not bear a signature or a single first-person identification." It is also "substantively anonymous, in that it does not permit variation of patterns of formulation to accord with the traits of individuals or even to suggest that individuals who do occur have distinctive traits of speech, word-choice, or, in the final analysis, even generative conception."

were not sympathetic with them to reject the text.[119]

David Kraemer has convincingly argued for a scholarly readership of the Bavli.[120] His arguments can be applied to the Mishnah as well. A broad knowledge of Scripture and the understanding of certain key concepts and issues that are discussed in detail are presupposed. The reader or listener must be able to follow the inner logic of the arguments, to make connections between them, and to draw his or her own conclusions with regard to the issues at hand: "This means that the Mishnah assumes an active intellect, capable of perceiving inferred convention, and a vividly participating audience, capable of following what was said with intense concentration."[121] The internal structure of the Mishnah, which presents different and partly contradictory opinions side by side, and the fact that matters are left undecided, would motivate the audience and readers to engage in and continue the discussion themselves. Therefore one may assume that rabbis and their students were the intended audience and readership of the text. The Mishnah would provide them with a firm basis for further discussion of a wide variety of halakhic issues encountered in daily life and theoretical debate.

The editors' probable intention, to create a body of traditional material that would be widely accepted among rabbis and play an integrative and stabilizing role within the Rabbinic movement, seems to have been achieved only partially. As already pointed out, some rabbis may have used alternative collections of mishnayot and baraitot. Amoraic traditions indicate that even those rabbis who used the Mishnah as the basis of their discussions would sometimes reinterpret, contradict, or outright reject its rulings and opinions. The reception of the Mishnah by the various Amoraic Rabbinic circles remains unclear.[122] What is clear, though, is that the Amoraim engaged in various other intellectual activities besides the interpretation of the Mishnah. Direct comments on the Mishnah constitute

---

[119] Ibid., p. 122 Neusner suggests an alternative but complimentary reason for the editors' anonymity: "The people who made the Mishnah do not want us to know them, because, I should imagine, nothing about them was deemed important in the understanding of what they did." Neither Judah ha-Nasi nor his editorial circle tried to present their halakhic views as the only valid ones by dismissing other views and teachings.

[120] See David Kraemer, "The Intended Reader As a Key to Interpreting the Bavli," in *Prooftexts* 13 (1993), pp. 125-140.

[121] See Neusner, *Memorized Torah*, p. 123.

[122] See also Halivni, *Midrash*, p. 59.

only a relatively small portion of the Amoraic material transmitted by the Talmudim.

In connection with Roman legal codes Eder has pointed out that "there is a tendency to overestimate the effectiveness of a written code in creating legal certainty."[123] The high-minded intentions of the editors of such codes are usually not fulfilled in actual practice. The authority and bindingness of legal corpora is basically dependent on people's willingness (or refusal) to accept them for themselves and on the existence of external powers to reinforce their legitimacy. If such external powers are absent, unity, homogeneity, and stability cannot be achieved.

Both the nature of the Mishnah itself, which cannot be considered a lawcode in the strict sense of the word, and later patriarchs' disinterest in enforcing its acceptance among rabbis may explain why the "publication" of the Mishnah did not lead to a unification and institutionalization of the Rabbinic movement in Amoraic times.[124] In Amoraic times, the Rabbinic movement does not seem to have been more centralized and institutionalized than in Tannaitic times. and the patriarch's general influence on Palestinian rabbis seems to have been rather limited.[125] Talmudic discussions show that the Amoraim disagreed amongst themselves as much or even more so that the Tannaim did. In Amoraic times, the Mishnah served as rabbis' basis of discussion but not as a legally binding document. The fact that the editors of the Yerushalmi adopted the basic formal structure of the Mishnah and arranged their material accordingly indicates that they valued the Mishnah as the most important Rabbinic document of the past. The fact that the Talmud is much more than a commentary on the Mishnah, that it integrates material that was not, in the first place, formulated in connection with the Mishnah, and that Talmudic *sugyot* develop their own subject matter and logic of argumentation shows that the Mishnah is made subservient to rabbis' new concerns and perspectives. In so far as the Mishnah was meant to generate discussions and debates, the Talmud is evidence for the achieving of this goal.

---

[123] Eder, *Political Significance*, p. 287.

[124] Against Lapin, *Civil Law*, p. 116. For the argument that the Rabbinic movement became institutionalized in the third century see also Lee I. Levine, *The Rabbinic Class of Roman Palestine in Late Antiquity* (Jerusalem, 1989), pp. 77-78.

[125] See Hezser, *Social Structure*, pp. 185ff.

THE MISHNAH IN THE LATER MIDRASHIM

RIVKA ULMER

University of Pennsylvania

The citation from one body of literature within another is one of the key characteristics of Rabbinic literature, which is, is to a certain extent, a literature of citations.[1] Many of these quotations are from the Tannaitic stratum of Rabbinic literature, either the identifiable works "Mishnah" and "Tosefta" or the statements of the non-canonized Baraitot. In addition to the early midrashim and the Talmudim, the so called "later midrashim" incorporate quotations from the Mishnah, although in an uneven distribution.[2] Midrash in general,[3] and in particular the homiletic later midrashim contain numerous quotations, whereas the purely aggadic later midrashim have very few Mishnah quotations. Therefore, for the purposes of this article, I divide the "later midrashim" into two very fluid and often overlapping categories: (I) The later midrashim that display the discernible forms of Rabbinic midrash or the Rabbinic homily,[4]

---

[1] See A. Goldberg, "Zitat und Citem. Vorschläge für die descriptive Terminologie der Formanalyse rabbinischer Texte," in *Frankfurter Judaistische Beiträge* 6 (1978) pp. 23-26.

[2] The meaning of the term "later midrashim" depends upon the particular method applied to the analysis of midrash. M.D. Herr (*Encyclopaedia Judaica*, Jerusalem, 1972, vol. 11, cols. 1510-1514, s.v. "Midrash") divides this literature into early midrashim (or "classical amoraic midrashim"), midrashim of the middle period, and the late period. Here I exclude midrashic works that are mainly comprised of "halakhic midrashim" and that are companions to the Mishnah. I investigate those later midrashim that are "companions to the Talmudim" according to Neusner and some of the "later midrashim" according to Herr's categories. Some of the later midrashim are possibly pseudepigraphic, as mentioned by Herr (ibid., col. 1513). The inclusion of midrashic works such as Gen. Rabbah, Lev. Rabbah, and Pesikta de-rav Kahana is based upon the analysis of Jacob Neusner, "Rabbinic Judaism, Formative Canon of (4): The Aggadic Documents. Midrash: The Later Compilations," in J. Neusner, A.J. Avery-Peck, and W.S. Green, eds., *The Encyclopaedia of Judaism* (Leiden, Boston, Köln, 2000), vol. III, pp. 1176-1206.

[3] J.N. Epstein, *Mavo le-Nusah Ha-Mishnah* (Jerusalem, 2000), pp. 759f.

[4] In this group, I looked at Gen. Rabbah, Midrash Tanhuma, ed. Buber and printed edition, Pesikta de-rav Kahana, Pesikta Rabbati, Lev. Rabbah, Deut. Rabbah, Song of Songs Rabbah, Ruth Rabbah, Eccl. Rabbah, Ruth Zutta, Lam. Zutta, Eccl. Zutta, Song of Songs Zutta, Aggadat Bereshit, Midrash Tehillim, Pirke

which are often referred to as the "classical midrashim;" (II) the later, usually medieval, midrashim that are somewhat reminiscent of the previously mentioned homiletic or exegetical midrashim but show few formal characteristics and that rarely cite the Mishnah.[5] In the later midrashim of the homiletic genre (I), we find interactions between different textual "canons" as well as different levels of texts interpreting each other. First there is an interaction between *two* "canonical" traditions, the bible and the Mishnah/Tosefta stratum. The next interaction is between these "canonical" texts and the midrash. However, the ultimate interaction in the later midrashim is with propositions raised from biblical lemmata and the homiletic agenda. In addition, the midrash accomplishes the exegetical procedure that is often missing in the Mishnah. Usually the Mishnah states halakhic statements without displaying an involvement in the exegetical process that is underlying these statements. In their utilization of the Mishnah the later midrashic texts provide an exegetical framework for the Mishnah statements.

---

de-R. Eliezer, and Num. Rabbah. The editions and translations of midrashic texts cited in this article are the following: L.M. Barth, *Pirqé Rabbi Eliezer*. [Under construction] (http://www.usc.edu/dept/huc-la/pre-project); W. Braude, trans., *Pesikta Rabbati. Discourses for Feasts, Fasts, and Special Sabbaths* (New Haven and London, 1968, 2 vols.); S. Buber, ed., *Midrash Mishle* (Vilna, 1883); id., *Midrash Shmu'el*. (Cracow, 1883); id., *Midrash Zutta 'al Shir Ha-Shirim, Rut, Ekhah Ve-Kohelet*. (Berlin, 1884; repr. Tel-Aviv, 1971); idem., *Midrash Tanhuma Ha-Kadum Ve-Ha-Yashan*. (Vilna, 1885; repr. Jerusalem, 1964); idem, *Midrash Shoher Tov 'al Tehillim*. (Vilna, 1890; repr. Jerusalem 1967); M. Cohen, ed., *Midrash Bereshit Zutta* (Jerusalem, 1962); J.D. Eisenstein, ed., *Otzar Midrashim. A Library of Two Hundred Minor Midrashim, I-II* (New York, 1915; repr. 1969); G. Friedlander, trans., *Pirke De Rabbi Eliezer. The Chapters of Rabbi Eliezer the Great* (New York, 1981); A. Jellinek, comp. and ed., *Bet Ha-Midrasch. Sammlung Kleiner Midraschim und Vermischter Abhandlungen aus der Ältern Jüdischen Literatur*, 6 Vols. in 2 Pts. (Jerusalem, 1967); S. Lieberman, ed., *Midrash Devarim Rabbah, Ed. from the Oxford Ms. No. 147*. (Jerusalem, 1974); B. Mandelbaum, *Pesikta de-Rav Kahana* (New York, 1962); M. Margulies, ed., *Midrash Vayyikra Rabbah* (New York and Jerusalem, 1993); *Midrash Rabbah* (Vilna, 1887; repr. Jerusalem, 1961); Y. Theodor and H. Albeck, *Midrash Bereshit Rabba mit kritischem Apparat und Kommentar* (Jerusalem, 1962); R. Ulmer, *A Synoptic Edition of Pesiqta Rabbati Based Upon All Extant Manuscripts and the Editio Princeps* (Atlanta, 1997-1999); H. Zundel, ed., *Midrash Tanhuma*. [Tanhuma, Printed Ed.] (Jerusalem, repr. 1973/74). Pesikta Rabbati serves as the matrix for my inquiry.

[5] In this group I have checked the following Rabbinic works: Midrash Jonah, Midreshe Yehudit, Midrash Haserot Viyterot; Midrash Va-yosha'; Midrash 'Eser Galuyot, Megillat Antiochus, Midrash Hallel, Petirat Aharon, Aggadat Bereshit, Pesikta Hadta, Midrash Konen, Petirat Moshe, Midrash Temurah, Divrei ha-yamim shel Moshe, Midrash Tadshe, Midrash Va-yisa'u, Gen. Zutta, Midrash Proverbs, Midrash Samuel.

This article is not a source-critical study but is based upon the premise that the sources that are quoted are an essential part of the midrashic homiletic agenda. Therefore the quotations have to be studied from the perspective of a text at hand that is only complete with the quotation of other textual sources. The texts of the midrashic works do not consist of unrelated Rabbinic dicta but instead establish a textual discourse that contains among other strata some opinions attributed to Tannaitic rabbis. These opinions are often presented in a certain discernible sequence. One pattern of dicta is that the first generation of Tannaim is followed by the second generation and then by the third generation. Immediately thereafter the pattern is reversed: citations from the third generation are followed by quotations from the second and then the first generation of Tannaim. This compositional configuration of Mishnaic traditions as an ordered structure could relate a message that is not immediately discernible.[6] We can assume from this pattern of citations in the homiletic midrashim that the midrashic text followed a higher order of arrangement that was carefully crafted to present a well-reasoned argument. With the phrase "higher order of arrangement," I am suggesting that the *darshanim* were not quoting citations at random but rather chose a particular structure to most effectively advance their arguments. The *darshan* speaks with the voice of the Mishnah, and the Mishnah becomes part of his own voice and mode of speech. Furthermore, the comparison of Mishnah quotations in the later midrashim to the Mishnah itself may demonstrate a certain limit to a historical-critical comparative method. Under the historical-critical method, if the textual passages in the later midrashim and the Mishnah are identical, they are considered to be interdependent. This interrelationship and the identity of certain passages as Mishnah quotations in the later midrashim raises the issue of which methods homiletic and aggadic texts employed when utilizing an established body of text. My analysis of the midrashic texts here involves a dialectic between the so called "atomistic" and "holistic" approaches.[7] In order to find traces of the methods of

---

[6] As an aside, this pattern of Tannaitic authorities in the order of 1, 2, 3, 3, 2, 1 is also found in some exegetical material such as Gen. Rabbah. An interesting study would explore this pattern and its significance.

[7] P.S. Alexander, "Midrash," in R.J. Loggins, J.L. Houlden, and P.S. Alexander, eds., *A Dictionary of Biblical Interpretation* (London and Philadelphia, 1999), p. 455.

citation, my inquiry into the Mishnah in the later midrashim is guided by the following considerations and questions:

(1) The Mishnah in a "non-Talmudic" environment; (2) Why is a "halakhic" text cited in aggadic material? (3) What happens if one Rabbinic document, the Mishnah, is cited in another Rabbinic document? (4) Are the quotations from the Mishnah used as a commentary on the propositions of the midrash or in the alternative is the midrash to be viewed as a commentary on the Mishnah? (5) Which passages of the Mishnah are cited and are these citations merely allusions to the Mishnah material? (6) Which version of the Mishnah is cited in the later midrashim and (7) what can we learn about the transmission of documents such as the Mishnah from the quotations in the later midrash?

(1) The quotations[8] from the Mishnah in the later midrashim appear in a "non-talmudic" environment, i.e., the Mishnah quotations are usually cited without further talmudic commentaries or reflections. Even if the continued discussion of Mishnaic lemmata in a talmudic sugya is reflected in a midrashic text the quotation is lifted out of one context and inserted into another. The Mishnah quotation and its attachments become an insert within the surrounding frame of the midrashic context and a "recontextualization" takes place. The phrase "non-talmudic" in this article refers to the creative use of Tannaitic sources in the midrash. In a limited sense, the midrashim in the homiletic works could be regarded as "school texts" since they, like other Rabbinic works, represent the accumulation of textual traditions studied within the Rabbinic schools over a long period of time in order to instruct the reader/recipient. Rabbinic homilies generally take shape around a didactic purpose. In this manner of study, former texts had to be reviewed and cited. Mishnah quotations play a central role in this type of preservation and transmission of texts. It is safe to assume in the case of the later midrashic works that they cite the Mishnah and not vice versa. Mishnaic text quotations are immediately discernible in these texts, since these

---

[8] For example, there are approximately sixty quotations in Pesikta Rabbati: 2.1; 5.1; 5.28; 7.1; 8.1; 9.3; 10.1; 11.1; 14.34; 14.38; 14.40; 14.43; 15.8; 15.49; 16.5; 16.7; 16.10; 17.8; 17.12; 18. 3; 18.14; 19.1; 20.11; 21.1; 21.31; 22.12; 22.19; 23.13; 23.14; 23/24.4; 23/24.5; 23/24.10; 25.1; 31.1; 51.2; 33.1; 3 3.49; 36.9; 38.1; 39.1; 39.4; 42.1; 42.9; 43.10; 44.1; 45.1; 48.1; 49.1; 50.6; 50.18; 51.6; 51.7; 51.25; 52.1; 52.17

quotations are usually introduced by stereotypical *formulae quotationis*, such as *shanu raboteinu, taman taninan, tanu rabbanan, hatanei*, etc. The sequence of Mishnaic quotations presented in the midrashic texts takes up and develops ideas formulated in the period before the year 200.[9] Any further contextualization is impossible, since we do not know which group wrote the first cluster of the later midrashim and why.

First, I want to offer a definition of some of the texts in which the Mishnaic quotations appear. The homilies of the later midrashim are collections of individual propositions that on the whole add up to a sustained and coherent argument that attempts to discover manifest as well as hidden textual data in its midrashic enterprise. Even if a work such as Pesikta Rabbati is to a large extent a duplicate or imitation of the other Pesikta,[10] it is nevertheless a tightly shaped composition and overall a work that has its own identity. Pesikta Rabbati has a rhetorical and logical plan in which it presents its theological perspective. Almost every single chapter deals with Israel's dilemma of self-reproach and introspection including a response to some alleged different heirs of the oral tradition; this response possibly referred to adherents of Christianity. The theological perspective of Pesikta Rabbati maintained that Israel could continue to exist through the ongoing study of the tradition relating to the festivals and special *Shabbatot*. Israel can prevail as a people and in the perception of Pesikta Rabbati the people of Israel will be redeemed. A critical part of the Rabbinic tradition is studying the Mishnah.[11] This necessity of studying texts related to the festivals is a potential source of answers and comfort to the Jewish people.

---

[9] A.J. Avery-Peck, "The Mishnah, Tosefta, and the Talmuds. The Problem of Text and Context," in J. Neusner, ed., *Judaism in Late Antiquity. Part 1: The Literary and Archaeological Sources* (Leiden, 1995), pp. 173-216; I.M. Gafni, "The Historical Background," in S. Safrai, ed., *The Literature of the Sages. First Part: Oral Tora, Halakha, Mishna, Tosefta, Talmud, External Tractates 1* (Assen and Philadelphia, 1987), pp. 1-34; J. Neusner, "The Use of the Mishnah for the History of Judaism Prior to the Time of the Mishnah," in *Journal for the Study of Judaism in the Persian, Hellenistic and Roman Period* 11 (1980), pp. 177-185.

[10] Utilizing textual units that appear in another body of text, for example in Pesikta de-rav Kahana, is an indirect type of quotation that possibly reworks passages from another text without referring to this primary text.

[11] Compare A. Goldberg, "The Mishna. A Study Book of Halakha," in Safrai, op. cit., p. 214, who calls the Mishnah a "text-book" for halakhah. In the preparation of this article, I consulted and frequently adopted Jacob Neusner's Mishnah translations and commentaries, listed in the bibliography

This study of texts relating to the Jewish festivals supports the essential argument of Pesikta Rabbati of observing the *mitzvot*. This homiletic agenda entails an overall theme of continuity and future redemption. This is true for the core material of Pesikta Rabbati notwithstanding the differences in the manuscripts and the medieval and early modern supplements to the text. Within the Rabbinic argumentation in the homiletic midrashim we find long as well as short quotations of the Mishnah that are part of this overall discourse. The quotations in the later midrash have to be read under this aspect.

A citation of a Tannaitic text is usually taken from recognizable texts such as the Tosefta and the Mishnah and only to a lesser degree from Beraitot that are not included in extant versions of the Tosefta, Mishnah, or Talmud. The Tannaitic stratum in the homiletic midrashim is much more solid than the Amoraic material. The question of textual boundaries in homiletic midrashim during a period when midrash in general and Pesikta Rabbati in particular embraced many texts is extremely complex. Did the creators of the homilies shape the citations in order to blend the texts or did they leave the borders intact? In citing the Mishnah were the creators just focusing upon that very passage itself or were the creators implying the extended context of the original Mishnah passage? If a midrashic text goes beyond the citation to the context of the citation in the Mishnah we can assume that the perceived audience of the text was familiar with the original section containing this Mishnah. In other words: the study of the Rabbinic texts was still active and there seems to have been some agreement between the implied recipients of the midrashic texts and the creators as to what kind of information this "audience/readership" anticipated and hoped to receive.

For example, a textual unit in Pesikta Rabbati 39 (*Harninu*) contains a non-halakhic question, a quotation from the M. Sot 1:7, a *mashal*, a midrashic sentence, and an answer to the initial question. The larger units within this text mark significant boundaries. In this text there is a question focusing upon a lemma of the '*inyan* verse of the homily. The midrashic question in Pesikta Rabbati 39 is posed as to why only Jacob was mentioned in Ps. 81:2 and no mention was made of Abraham or Isaac. This text contains a brief excerpt from M. Sot. 1:7. The redactor elected not to include the entire Mishnah text, probably concluding that the brief reference was sufficient for the reader to understand that the phrase "to measure"

referred to the implementation of divine justice by God.
The question that addresses the issue why Jacob instead of the other patriarchs was mentioned in Ps. 81:2 is part of a typical midrashic procedure. The patriarchs are portrayed as the friends of God in a *mashal*. The question delineates already the *nimshal* of the subsequent *mashal*. The *nimshal* relates that Jacob was different than the other friends of God. Although the answer to the initial question pertaining to Jacob's difference cites a very general statement that is found throughout Rabbinic literature, "measure for measure," the unusual feature of this type of general answer is that it contains an introductory formula referring to the Mishnah. The context of the Mishnah speaks about the punishment of the *Sotah*, which is administered according to the general statement "measure for measure." The Mishnah describes in detail the measures that are meted out by God. The Mishnah quotation in Pesikta Rabbati thus points to its context in the Mishnah. The point is that God is involved in the punishment of sinners in the Mishnah as well as in the homiletic text. The Mishnah quotation raises the general statement and we can presume that the Mishnah was cited on purpose. The *darshan* and his audience were familiar with the idea that the Mishnah in this section spoke about God's actions. Within a homily, God's intervention in human affairs is a rhetorical topic. The Mishnah and the midrash thus share the same perspective. This example presents the Mishnah in a "non-talmudic" environment, since the Mishnaic text is used to respond to the midrashic question, to introduce the *mashal* and to serve as a foreshadowing of the concluding sentence of the unit which says, "Asaph also, in speaking of the blowing of the shofar, took special care to mention only Jacob, *Blow the shofar unto the God of Jacob*." Jacob recognized God in his special way and he is therefore recognized by God in a special way. This mirror image of a parallel expression is concentrated in the Mishnah quotation.

Pesikta Rabbati 39 § 4
Another note: [*Sing aloud unto God ... blow the shofar] unto the God of Jacob* (Ps. 81:2) Why does it mention Jacob rather than any of the other Patriarchs? Our Rabbis taught the following [at M. Sotah 1:7]: *In the measure a man measures out—in the very same measure it is measured out to him.* This is like a king who had three friends. When he wanted to build a palace, he brought the first [friend] and said: Look at this place where I will build a palace. His friend replied: Ever since I can remember, I have thought of it as a mountain. [The king] brought the second [friend], who said to him: Ever since I can remember, I have thought

of it as a field. The king dismissed them and brought his third [friend].
§ 5
He said: Ever since I can remember, I have thought of it as a palace.
The King said to him: By Jove! When I build that palace I will name
it after you.
The friends were Abraham, Isaac, and Jacob, friends of the Holy One,
Blessed be He ....
§ 7
Asaph also, in speaking of the blowing of the shofar, took special care
to mention only Jacob, *Sing aloud unto God ... blow the shofar unto the God
of Jacob* (Ps. 81:2).[12]

The citation of M. Sotah 1:7 appears in a different context in Pesikta Hadta, Pesah.[13] This text compares the treatment that the children of the Israelites experienced at the hands of the Egyptians to the punishment meted out by God to the children of the Egyptians during the Exodus. It is possible that this Mishnaic statement was used as a cliché in multiple contexts without referring back to the Mishnah as a document in each and every case.

(2) Why is a halakhic text cited in aggadic material?
The juxtaposition of aggadah and halakhah within one coherent text can be found in many variations throughout midrashic literature. Approaches to the interplay between halakhah and aggadah always separated the two and focused upon their differences in content and message. A content analysis would address the rules of the "Law" in halakhic texts and the descriptions of events in aggadic texts. A genre analysis would define halakhah as apodictic or commentary and aggadah as containing smaller units of folk literature and story telling literature. A literary description would describe halakhah as legalistic and aggadah as narrative. A linguistic description would view halakhah as operating on the object-linguistic level of language, instructing people to act or specify their actions according to certain norms, and aggadah on the meta-linguistic level describing fictitious events or speaking in fictitious language. A completely innovative approach has recently been taken by Neusner[14] in a philosophically

---

[12] Braude, op. cit., pp. 696f.
[13] Jellinek, op. cit., vol. 6, p. 38.
[14] J. Neusner, *Dual Discourse, Single Judaism. The Category-Formations of the Halakhah and of the Aggadah Defined, Compared, and Contrasted* (Lanham, New York, and Oxford, 2001), p. 175.

inspired work of pure textual conception utilizing deductive and inductive approaches: "If the Aggadah organizes large components of its entire system within such categories as Eden/Land of Israel or Adam/Israel or fall/exile, the Halakhah responds with large categories that deal with Kilayim, mixed seeds, Shebiit, the Sabbatical year, and Orlah, produce of a tree in the first years after its planting ..." Thus, halakhah does not intersect categorically with aggadah. Neusner accomplishes the overwhelming task of transforming aggadic material into a set of generalizations and into systematic statements.[15] However, Neusner goes beyond the initial definitions; he applies the newly defined categories to a large body of text, operating from one matrix—aggadah in the halakhah—and the second matrix—halakhah in the aggadah.[16]

A very difficult question that I wish to pose is why is a halakhic text cited in aggadic passages in later midrash?[17] Although I maintain that the Mishnah in the later midrashim is presented in a "non-talmudic" environment, nevertheless, in some respects, the usage of the Mishnah in Pesikta Rabbati seems to be remotely comparable to the interpretation of the Mishnah found in the Yerushalmi.[18] Mishnaic quotations in some homilies tend to develop around the interplay between a halakhic topic and a homiletic topic. Only through a discussion of the Mishnah do we recognize the topic of the homily that the *darshan* attempts to negotiate but that he rarely spells out.[19] For example, in Pesikta Rabbati 52 *Beyom Ha-Shemini* the discussion within the Mishnah quotation (M. Suk. 4:8) is con-

---

[15] On the interplay of aggadah and halakhah, see also J. Neusner, "Aggadah in the Halakhah," in J. Neusner, A. Avery-Peck, and W. S. Green, eds., *The Encyclopaedia of Judaism*, Suppl. 2 (Leiden, 2002, in preparation). I am grateful to Prof. Neusner for a copy of this article.

[16] See J. Neusner, *The Unity of Rabbinic Discourse. Volume One* (Lanham, 2000, 3 vols.); Neusner addresses such questions as: How do the Rabbinic documents work together? How do the documents make a statement in common? And: Why is aggadah necessary to Halakhic discourse? (vol. 1, p. 263).

[17] J. Neusner, *The Aggadic Role in Halakhic Discourse* (Lanham, 2000), vol. III, p. xviii, observes that the halakhah "announces its category-formations" and that aggadah is approached with "*a priori* expectation" in respect to the aggadic topics; in regard to Gen. Rabbah, Lev. Rabbah, Pesikta de-rav Kahana, Song of Songs Rabbah and Lam. Rabbah, he remarks: "Then the lines of definition of the Aggadic category-formations do not coincide with the documentary limits that present the Aggadah...." (ibid.). See also the analysis in Neusner, *Dual Discourse*, op. cit.

[18] J. Neusner, "Redaction and Formulation. The Talmud of the Land of Israel and the Mishnah," in *Semeia* 27 (1983) pp. 117-145.

[19] Exceptions are the "creation" midrashim or the "*teshuvah*" homilies.

tinued in the midrashic text. This supplemental midrashic discussion does not constitute a revision of the halakhah. Rather, it concentrates on subtleties of the halakhah of Sukkot that are critical for the purposes of the homily. These interpretations of the halakhah cited by Pesikta Rabbati are also found in Pesikta de-rav Kahana 28 and Y. Suk. 5:4. The purpose of these continued discussions of the *sukkah* and its new significance within the homily is to differentiate the observance of Shemini Atzeret from the festival of Sukkot. This purpose is emphatically stated in an initial contention in the midrash, which reads, "Though Shemini Atzeret comes right after the seven days of Sukkot, it is a festival in its own right." As one example of the differentiation between the two festivals, the homiletic midrash concentrates on the *sukkah*, which is not used for ritual purposes on Shemini Atzeret.

> Pesikta Rabbati 52 § 17
> R. Yohanan said, [Although Shemini Atzeret comes right after the seven days of Sukkot], it is a festival in its own right. It has its own benediction, its own sacrifice, its own Psalm. Its own benediction: R. Avin said, With regard to all [the other days of Sukkot] Scripture says, *And on the day* (Num. 29:17, 20, 23, 26, 29, 32), but here [in regard to Shemini Atzeret] Scripture says, *On the ... [Eighth]*[20] *day* (Num. 29:35). From here we [learn] that Shemini Atzeret is a festival in its own right. As to the lots, R. Yose said, We are taught the following there [in M. Suk. 5:6]: *On the Eighth Day they cast lots as they do at the other festivals*. As to its proper sacrifice: Scripture says, *one bullock, one ram* (Num. 29:36). Its own benediction: R. Illa said, From here that [it is required that on Shemini Atzeret the blessing] "You have enabled us to reach this season" be said. We are taught there [in a M. Suk. 4:8]: *It is required that the sukkah continue for a full seven days. Thus after one has finished eating, one should not pull down the sukkah, but should bring down its furnishings in the afternoon, or even later, because of the honor due to the last day [of Sukkot]*. R. Abba bar Kahana said, R. Hiyya bar Rav Ashi said in the name of Rav, One is required to invalidate the *sukkah* sometime during the [seventh] day. R. Joshua ben Levi said, One is required to say the kiddush on the eve of the Eighth Day in one's house....

As can be seen from this text, one reason the Mishnah was inserted into this text was to enable the *darshan* to extend the discussion from the Festival of Sukkot to the Festival of Shemini Atzeret within the

---

[20] Or any other particular day.

homily. The dialectic of the discourse surrounding the Mishnah quotation does not contribute to the halakhah through scriptural exegesis. The framers of Pesikta Rabbati do not create new halakhot. Rather, they analyze existing Mishnaic halakhah and reenact established usage. Only the expectations of an "audience/readership" might be changed whenever the Mishnah is quoted in a new discourse. The message of the Mishnaic quotation in the new compound text might lead to expectations of learning something different or additional than in the original Mishnah text. A comparison of halakhic analysis and its placement in homiletic midrash and in the Talmud indicates that in the homiletic midrash the exegetical analysis of the Mishnah takes place in the *yelammedenu* part, while in the Talmud the exegesis of the Mishnah transpires in a *sugya*. The halakhic discussion in a homily inevitably leads to the aggadic format. The midrash is merely looking for supporting points in the earlier halakhic literature to relate to the homiletic theme of the midrash.

The crucial question in regard to this preference for citing halakhah concerns from which perspective or with what pre-understanding the composers of the midrashic homilies read the Mishnah as an authoritative text. The Mishnah most likely provides a didactic authority perceived to be closer to the source of revelation, and the later midrashim thus give access to knowledge of the revealed Torah that could be learned through these homilies. The main focus of the quotations is how that tradition could attain authoritative expression for the reader. The authoritative foundation of a Mishnah quotation is based upon the perceived validity and credibility of the Mishnah itself.[21] This latter thesis is relevant in the literary analysis of Pesikta de-rav Kahana 4 *Parah adumah*,[22] which cites the same Mishnah passage twice: *R. Eliezer taught: The heifer whose neck is to be broken must be one year old; and the Red Heifer must be two years old* (M. Par. 1:1). The identical form of the quotation serves to underline the authority of the Mishnah through midrashic contexts: Thus,

---

[21] For a thorough discussion of the nature of quotations and the discussion of evidence, testimony and credibility, see C.D. Stanley, "The Rhetoric of Quotations: An Essay on Method," in C.A. Evans and J.A. Sanders, eds., *Early Christian Interpretation of the Scriptures of Israel. Investigations and Proposals. Journal for the New Testament, Suppl. 148 (1997)*, p. 45; Stanley refers the reader to Quintilian, *Inst. Orat.* 5.36ff.

[22] Compare Pesikta Rabbati 14:15.

Moses hears God recite a Mishnah that was taught by Eliezer; upon the question why God recites a law ascribed to humans, God repeats the same Mishnah and instructs Moses by reciting a short chain of tradition. This homily deals with the Red Heifer, and the *darshan* seems to impress upon his audience the unceasing validity of a Mishnah and the authority of Rabbinic Judaism.

The ensuing dialectic discourse in the late midrash does not contribute to the halakhah through scriptural exegesis but is more like a contemplation of already established exegetical results. If we are to be pressed for a comparison, the Talmudic unit of exegetical Mishnah discourse is a *sugya* whereas in the homiletic midrashim it is the *yelammedenu* part. There are really no corresponding forms. The major difference between the *sugya* and the *yelammedenu* is the more exegetical, programmatic use of the Mishnah in the former whereas the latter leads to a creative use of the Mishnah quotation.

Another aspect of the citation of the Mishnah in the later midrashim are choices made by the *darshan*. In some cases there are longer reviews of the halakhic material relating to the homily although there are no disputes between the Rabbinic authorities. Thus, these lengthy halakhic compilations are not framed within a controversy between the Rabbinic authorities cited in the midrash. Rather, the cited sources are juxtaposed and speak to one another. An example of this is found in Pesikta Rabbati 8 *Ve-haya Ba'et Hahi*, a homily for Hanukkah that was probably incorporated into Pesikta Rabbati at some later stage of redaction than the core material of Pesikta Rabbati. This passage entails an explicit answer that one is not permitted to kindle a lamp for profane purposes from a Hanukkah lamp. However, a Hanukkah lamp may be kindled from another Hanukkah lamp.

> Pesikta Rabbati 8 § 1
> *At that time I will search Jerusalem with lamps* (Zeph. 1:12). Let our rabbi instruct us: Is a man permitted to kindle from a Hanukkah lamp a lamp which is to be used [for a secular purpose]? [Relying upon] the tradition [of the Amoraim] our rabbis instructed us: "R. Aha said in the name of Rav, From a Hanukkah lamp it is forbidden to kindle a lamp which will be used for a secular purpose; but to kindle one Hanukkah lamp from another Hanukkah lamp is permitted." [Bavli] R. Jacob ben Abba said in the name of R. Aha, From the menorah in the Holy of Holies, it was taught that our Rabbis taught [in M. Tam. 3:9]: *Whenever the priest found that the lamp stand's* [*two eastern most*

lamps had gone out, he would clear away their ashes, then] rekindle them from the lamps which were still burning. Now, if "WHENEVER HE FOUND THAT ONE OF THE LAMPS ON THE MENORAH which was IN THE INNERMOST PART [OF THE TEMPLE] HAD GONE OUT"... HE REKINDLED IT FROM A COMPANION, all the more it follows that it is permitted to kindle one Hanukkah lamp from another Hanukkah lamp. The Holy One, Blessed be He, said, Similarly, as these seven lamps are kindled in my holy abode, so I am going to act in the future when I will build Jerusalem. From where [do we derive this?] From that which is concluded with [the reading from] the prophet: *At that time I will search Jerusalem with lamps* (ibid.).

The passage from Pesikta Rabbati 8 § 1 is an assortment or combination of Amoraic and Tannaitic strata. The *darshan* of the passage pushes hard to cite halakhic proof for his proposition. However, only the Tannaitic stratum follows the identifiable order of one textual document, i.e., M. Tam. 3:9, whereas the Amoraic stratum of the citation was not taken directly from another text.[23]

Pesikta Rabbati 8 § 1 "Structure"
[1] Scriptural citation
[2] Formula: *Yelammedenu* "Let our rabbi instruct us..."
[3] Formula (Amoraic statements): *Talmud limdunu* "[Relying upon] the tradition [of the Amoraim] our Rabbis instructed us..."
[4] Authorities: "R. Aha said in the name of Rav..." (Somewhat similar to B. Shab. 22a)
"R. Jacob ben Abba said in the name of R. Aha..."
[5] Formula (Tannaitic): "our rabbis taught as follows:" From a Hanukkah lamp .... for our Rabbis taught as follows: *Whenever the priest found that the ... lamps had gone out, he would clear away their ashes, then rekindle them from the lamps which were still burning.* (M. Tam. 3:9)
[6] Now if, "WHENEVER HE FOUND THAT ONE OF THE LAMPS ON THE MENORAH IN THE INNERMOST PART [OF THE TEMPLE] HAD GONE OUT"...HE REKINDLED IT FROM A COMPANION, all the more it follows....
[7] Decision: "it is permitted to kindle one Hanukkah lamp from another Hanukkah lamp."
[8] Scriptural citation.

The typical *yelammedenu* question in the above passage [2] is followed

---

[23] See J. Neusner, "Dating the Mishnah-Tractates: The Case of Tamid," in his *Method and Meaning in Ancient Judaism. Third Series* (Chico, 1981), pp. 103-115

by *talmud limdunu* [3], which is a halakhic answer based on Amoraic reasoning. This passage in Pesikta Rabbati is somewhat similar to B. Shab. 22a ("Rav said, One does not kindle from another lamp; Samuel said, One does"); there is only one short string of words that is actually identical with a partial sentence from the Bavli. Part of the answer from the Amoraic stratum raises a new issue, "it is permitted to kindle a Hanukkah lamp from another Hanukkah lamp." This new issue leads to the Tannaitic stratum that is the following Mishnah quotation. "*Whenever the priest found that ... the lamps had gone out, he would clear away their ashes, then rekindle them from the lamps which were still burning.*" This secondary halakhic citation is used to draw an inference from the custom of kindling one Temple lamp from another Temple lamp and thus implying that it is permissible to kindle a Hanukkah lamp from another Hanukkah lamp. Thus the Mishnaic citation is in the position of a secondary proof-text. It could be argued that in this homily the Mishnaic source is sufficient to address the halakhic issue concerning the lighting of the lamps used during the festival of Hanukkah. However, the homiletic agenda additionally relies upon Amoraic sources to progress from a question dealing with secular lamps to the issue of festival lamps. This relationship between secular and festival is applied to the `*inyan* verse of the homily, Zeph 1:12. The implication of this textual unit is that kindling lamps by humans will be replicated by God in the future.

In summary, the *darshan* of this passage moves between different sources to make his point. In sentence no. 3, a halakhic statement is brought from Amoraic sources, introduced by *talmud limdunu rabboteinu*; the passage has some resemblance to B. Shab. 22a.[24] In sentence no. 5 the quote is from M. Tam. 3:9 and is introduced by *limdu she-shanu raboteinu*. Sentence no. 6 proceeds to an elaboration of this source. This procedure results in a Talmud-like review of halakhah; however, it is important to emphasize that the quoted halakhah is consecutively listed and not questioned. This method of citing cumulative halakhic authority is presented in order to add further corroboration to the initial halakhic point. Furthermore, this initial point of view is expanded and clarified. This approach of relying upon "case precedents" is a critical dynamic in the persuasive character of the homily. One view-point is expanded and made clear; and this halakhic view-point fits into the persuasive structure

---

[24] *Tur Shulhan Arukh* 674.

of the homily. The quoted halakhah is serialized but not questioned. The only variant would be to quote a different halakhic view point in the first place.

So far I have mainly focused upon the fragmentation of one text, Pesikta Rabbati 8 § 1, into its components; now I want to precede to the larger homiletic agenda of the *darshan*. The *darshan* of Pesikta Rabbati in this case could assume that the recipient of the homily was familiar with the idea that the combination of an Amoraic and a Tannaitic stratum spoke about a past and a future Hanukkah in this homily and in particular about God's actions in a future Jerusalem as related to the biblical passage "*And it shall come to pass at that time that I will search Jerusalem with lamps*" (Zeph. 1:12). The arrangement of the text creates a dynamic and meaningful progressive reading, from the secular Menorah to the Menorah of a particular festival. We gain this understanding not by merely looking at the fragmentary sources but by trying to comprehend the meaning of Pesikta Rabbati at the level of the final composition we have at hand. Within the larger context of Hanukkah homilies in Pesikta Rabbati, this last homily, No. 8, reaches a climax in that Hanukkah foreshadows a future completion of Hanukkah not by humans nor by secular means but by the kindling of the Hanukkah flame by divine hands. This text is not only a scriptural based midrash but uses other authoritative texts, including Mishnaic sources, as its basis for interpretation.

> Tanhuma, printed edition, *Va-era'* 4
> *When Pharaoh shall speak unto you, saying* (Exod. 7:9). May our rabbi instruct us: May someone who is bitten by a snake during the *tefillah* stop praying? Our rabbis taught [M. Ber. 5:1]: *Even if the king salutes, one may not return his greeting, and even if a snake is twisted around one's heel one may not interrupt the tefillah.*

The citation of a Mishnaic statement[25] in a *yelammedenu* passage establishes the two propositions that prohibit the interruption of prayer; later in this passage from Midrash Tanhuma *Va-era'* 4 these two propositions are assigned to the scriptural passage (*'Inyan*) of the homiletic discourse by means of a question "why did the sages

---

[25] The conceptual order and the resulting peculiarities of Mishnah Berakhot are discussed in A. Vivian, "Il Lessico Concettuale del Trattato Mishnico Berakhot (MBer)," in A. Vivian, ed., *Biblische und Judaistische Studien. Festschrift Paolo Sacchi* (Frankfurt am Main, 1990), pp. 383-534.

compare a serpent that is twisted around someone's heel with the kingdom of Egypt?" The answer: "just as the snake hisses and kills, so the kingdom of Egypt hisses and kills..." This midrash is, like other midrashim, bi-directional; the argument flows in one direction and then turns around to the opposite direction. The Mishnah occupies the pivotal position in this turn. It interprets scripture, and the lemma "Egypt" interprets the Mishnah. In object language, we learn that the attack of the snake that represents Egypt does not interrupt compliance with God.

> Tanhuma, printed edition, *Yitro* 16
> *I am the Lord your God* (Exod. 20:1). Let our rabbi instruct us: If a fire breaks out in a house in which there is a Torah scroll, may their owner save them from the fire on the Sabbath? Thus do our rabbis teach us [M. Shab. 16:1]: *Any of the Holy Scriptures may be saved from burning whether they are read or not.* Why did they decree that they must be saved? Because of the honor [due to them].... You find that when the Holy One, blessed be he, gave the Torah, it was entirely of fire, as it is said, *At his right hand was a fiery law unto them* (Deut. 33:1).

The combination of two scriptural passages is made possible by a Mishnah quotation. A halakhic text is cited in aggadic material to support the flow of the argument in the midrash.

(3) Another aspect of the citation of the Mishnah in Pesikta Rabbati is the methodology employed by each *darshan*. The case of the later midrashic works is in this respect especially interesting, because the encounter between earlier and later texts demands special solutions to the question of textual boundaries. In light of the Mishnaic quotations, a further question that could be raised concerns what happens if one Rabbinic document is cited in another Rabbinic document. Are we to imagine a kind of textual amalgamation, in which scriptural, halakhic, and aggadic boundaries recede to the extent that a new compositional text replaces separate textual boundaries? In discussing this issue, I would like to address general questions concerning citations.

The quotation of text into text is aptly discussed in a subfield of linguistics, in the field of text linguistics. Text linguistics for our purposes is the study of the production of new meanings in texts, i.e., a certain amount of linguistic creativity in respect to a received body of text such as the Mishnah and the received ways or devices of formulating texts as established in later midrashic texts such as "our rabbis taught." Hypothetically one would expect the descriptive semantics of a text whereby the text in this area of Rabbinic literature is disassembled and then reconstructed from the pieces by applying rules and receiving the same text as previously existent. However, only coherent information of texts can be handled efficiently by formulating rules of a Rabbinic text in some meta-language or the other. This procedure applies to the coreference between single sentences and would be a very limited, locally restricted, transformation.[26] However, one could posit a coreference between the topic of the midrashic text and the quotation in its new context. The text is not transformed on the surface—rather, a faithfulness to the quoted medium is noteworthy in Rabbinic texts—but in the reception of the text.

Does the theory of text transformation assist us in understanding the Mishnah in the later midrash? In response to this question it could be argued that actual contact between different texts diminishes the boundaries between them and the dominant text tends to provide an integrating framework for a variety of other texts. The Mishnah is cited within well-defined borders. Again, in text linguistic terms, this may be described as a peculiar case of coreference between sentences, i.e., the sentence in the Mishnah as a work and the Mishnaic sentence in a quote. Direct quotations of the Mishnah lead to the question of whether these are an attempt to avoid interpretation. The "surface structure" of these quotations does not seem to have changed. However, in order to accommodate the notion of a possible change of meaning of the Mishnah quotations, it should be mentioned that in text linguistics it has been noted that certain verbs have an extended range. The citation formula *tanu, shanu* could also have a certain range that goes beyond the original text and that is extended in the new text.[27] Some limits are imposed upon the

---

[26] In a summary of the text linguistic theories of Teun van Dijk, *Zur Bestimmung Narrativer Strukturen auf der Grundlage von Textgrammatiken* (Hamburg, 1972), in H. Rieser, "On the Development of Text Grammar," in W.U. Dressler, ed., *Current Trends in Linguistics. Research in Text Theory 2* (Berlin and New York, 1978), pp. 11f., these limited successes are called "micro-restrictions;" Rieser continues: "Microrestrictions or micro-structures such as e.g. the restrictions on pronouns, proadverbs, and connectives are examples of such local restrictions. Apart from these microrestrictions there are more global restrictions which are determined by the primary and secondary topics of the discourse, they are called 'macro-restriction'...."

[27] R.E. Longacre, *The Grammar of Discourse. Second Edition. Topics in Language and Linguistics* (New York and London,1996), p. 86, wites: "... there are speech verbs

exegesis of the Mishnah, the text of the midrash does not seem to change the text of the Mishnah in its quotations but rather works around it. This is in opposition to quotations or references to the Hebrew bible that are often totally integrated into their midrashic reading. The textual transformation of a Mishnaic quotation can be accomplished by copying it into different types of discourse. An almost comical use of the Mishnah in Pesikta Rabbati is found in a passage in which a rabbi is accused by a non-Jew of breeding pigs. The rabbi obviously denies this and cites a passage that states that Jews are forbidden to breed pigs. In this case, M. B.Q. 7:7 is cited as a proof-text in respect to the rabbi's behavior. The extended passage contains a dialogue between a gentile and rabbi. Within this hypothetical context we find that the Mishnah is part of a procedure in which three separate sources are utilized for proof texts: Scripture, the Mishnah and a *minhag*. This passage could be understood within the larger historical context of fourth-fifth century Christian preaching.[28] The Christian approach to teaching and exegetical scholarship of this era has some parallels within later midrash. In this case, the Mishnah serves as a rebuttal to Christian polemics. The Mishnah provides a didactic authority in this dialogue within this homily since a representative of the Rabbinic class can rely upon the statements of Mishnah, he lives according to them and can cite them.

> Pesikta de-rav Kahana 4 (*parah adumah*)[29]
> Another topic: *Who is a wise man* (Eccl. 8:1)—that is the student of the wise. *Who knows the interpretation of a thing* (ibid.)—that is someone who can interpret his Mishnah (lection). *A person's wisdom makes his face shine* (ibid.)—when he is asked and is able to answer. Rabbi sat and taught: From where can we bring proof that a negative command is violated when a substitute is designated for a firstling? The face of Bar Pedaiah lighted up. Rabbi said, this one knows what I am teaching. A gentile saw R. Judah bar Ilai—saw him with his face shining—and said: One of the following applies to this man: Either he is drunk with wine, or he lends money upon interest, or he raises swine. R. Judah bar Ilai, overhearing the remark, said to him, May the soul of this man ex-

---

which occur with surface structure complements which are prolongations of the meaning of the verb itself , i.e., range in the notional structure."

[28] P. Brown, *Power and Persuasion in Late Antiquity: Towards a Christian Empire* (Madison, 1992), p. 36.

[29] Compare Pesikta Rabbati 14 § 34.

pire, for not one of these things is true. I do not raise swine, since it is forbidden for a Jew to raise swine [M. B.Q. 7:7]: *A person may not raise swine anywhere.* Nor do I lend money upon interest, for it is written: *You shalt not lend upon interest to they brother* (Deut. 23:20).

Whereas a rabbi follows Mishnaic law, the oppressor Pharaoh transgresses Mishnaic law according to the following passage:

> Pesikta Rabbati 19 § 1
> *And it came to pass, when Pharaoh had let [the people] go* (Exod. 13:17). Let our rabbi instruct us: If a person unlawfully put to his own use something which another left in his keeping, how is he to repay? Our rabbis taught as follows [M. B.M. 3:12]: *If a man unlawfully put to his own use what had been left in his keeping, then, according to the School of Shammai, whether its value had fallen in the meantime or risen in the meantime, the man is penalized by having to repay at the higher value. According to the School of Hillel, [he has to repay at the value it had]* when he unlawfully[30] put it to his own use. *According to R. Aqiba at its value when claimed*[31] *by its owner.* Our rabbis taught further: Indeed, whenever a man unlawfully puts to his own use something left in his keeping by his fellow, he deserves to have his arm broken. From where do you learn this? From [the example of] Pharaoh, when Israel was left in his keeping, [and he put them to his own use, the Holy One, blessed be He, broke his arm], it says, *I have surely left you in keeping* (Exod. 3:16).

The meaning of the cited Mishnah is dependent upon its present rhetorical context and does not reflect upon the context of the cited source. The quotation is fully integrated into its new context in the later midrash. In general text linguistic theory, text transformation operates under the assumption that the dominant text diminishes textual boundaries of citations and, as a result, the ideas in the citations are subsumed under the agenda of the dominant text. This is certainly the case when the midrash cites short, cursory Mishnaic statements without further developing the arguments in a halakhic discourse. In these cases the meanings of the Mishnah quotations derive from their present context in the midrash with all its rhetorical implications. The Mishnaic quotations in midrashic homilies tend to develop around the interplay between a halakhic topic and a homiletic topic. Usually through a midrashic discussion of the

---

[30] The wording in the Mishnah is slightly different (this was also noticed by Epstein, op. cit., p. 760). The string as it reads here is also found at B. B.M. 43a.
[31] The Mishnah and *editio princeps* of Pesikta Rabbati have a slightly different reading.

Mishnaic text do we realize the theme of the homily. In Pesikta
Rabbati 45, the quote from the Mishnah makes the sermon relevant.
From the theory of text transformations one might further argue that
as soon as a canonical text was available it was transformed and
further developed through the process of the study of that text. In
the process of studying a text redactions and emendations were
frequently made because the material that was quoted from the
Mishnah had to be relevant to its new context.

In short, the self-contained Mishnaic text is transformed into a
series of proof-points in the text of the later midrash. However,
overall there is no constant interaction with the homiletic discussion; rather one point in the homily uses the Mishnah to elucidate
a midrashic point; thus the Mishnah quotations are superficially
subjected to midrashic study. This becomes evident in Pesikta de-
rav Kahana 27 in which M. Suk. 4:5 is quoted. This passage states
that the altar is circled on Sukkot. The quotation is a secondary proof,
following the scriptural text (Ps. 26:6) that contains the proposition
of circling the altar. A reversal of the joint reading of biblical and
Mishnaic propositions is found in Pesikta Rabbati 39, in which the
formula *mah ta'meh* combines M. R.H. 3:6 with a scriptural verse.
The resulting textual unit is truly introductory to this homily, which
has been assigned to Rosh Ha-Shanah. The *darshan* embeds the
quotation in an interpretative unit (the *yelammedenu*) that predisposes the questionable object toward a particular response that is found
in the Mishnah for the festival. The question surrounding a hole in
a shofar leads to the festival during which a perfect shofar is blown;
underlying this line of questioning is the suggestion that only God's
shofar is truly complete.

> Pesikta Rabbati 39 § 1
> *Sing aloud to God our strength* (Ps. 81:2). Let our rabbi instruct us: Is a
> shofar which had a perforation in it that was patched up, regarded as
> fit to blow? Our rabbis taught as follows [M. R.H. 3:6]: *If the patch
> hinders the blowing, the shofar is regarded as unfit; but if the patch does not hinder
> the blowing, the shofar is regarded as fit*. And the proof? *And the Lord shall
> blow the trumpet [shofar]* (Zech. 9:14), as the shofar of the Holy One,
> blessed be He, is all of a piece, so the shofar for New Year's Day must
> be all of a piece. Why? Because on New Year's Day they [Israel] are
> redeemed from the angel of death.

The next question I wish to address is related to the previous one:

(4) Another issue is whether quotations from Mishnaic texts are used as a commentary on the propositions of the midrash or, in the alternative, is the midrash to be viewed as a commentary on Mishnaic dicta? As we have seen before, the Mishnah quotations are intended to substantiate the homiletic proclamations by virtue of their authority. Yet in most instances the authority structure is only marginally the object of homiletic analysis. The interrelationship of the two texts, the Mishnaic and the midrashic, is hermeneutically presupposed rather than delineated. The later midrash gives the impression of a fundamental continuity of Rabbinic teachings and Rabbinic culture due to the frequent reliance of the composer of the homilies upon another established textual stratum, namely Tannaitic sources or, at least the appearance of the text could convince the recipient of this continuity by imitating previous structures. This is the case in the following later midrash in which the law in the Mishnah quotation is superficially derived from scripture. The claim of Revealed Law is thus followed by this midrash: (1) the written medium: scripture; (2) the oral medium: Mishnah. The Mishnaic statement has to explain a verse from Genesis because the midrashic collection Gen. Zutta topically arranges midrashic sentences on Genesis. If read as a strict midrashic sentence on the metalevel this would spell out as "Mishnaic lemma" derived from "midrashic operation" : "scriptural lemma." Overall Bereshit Zutta rarely cites the Mishnah.

> Gen. Zutta on Gen. 1:4
> And our rabbis taught [M. Ber. 3:1]: *One says the blessing over the candle only when the light goes forth.* From where do we know this? From the Holy One, blessed be he, *God saw the light that it was good* (Gen. 1:4).

The interrelationship of the two strata, biblical and Mishnaic, can reach a certain balance in order to sustain a reasoned argument in the midrash. In Gen. Rabbah 57:2 a quotation from M. Ber. 9:2 is utilized to interpret scripture. The time-gap between the scriptural lemma and the Mishnaic statement is removed; the only relevant fact in this text is that "signs" are utilized and that the meaning of these signs is uncovered. The biblical text and the Mishnaic text have reached an equilibrium in the midrash. In the later midrash the label "Mishnaic" is important; it is almost a political statement. Citing the Mishnah demonstrates that the creator of the midrashic text is part of the Rabbinic discourse and minimalistic in his expression and fully immersed in a previously existing, now vanished world.

> Genesis Rabbah 57:2
> *As cold waters to a faint soul, so is good news from a far country* (Prov. 25:25). We learned there [M. Ber. 9:2]: *For rain and good news one recites, "Blessed be He who is good and does good."* What did they notice that they juxtaposed "good news" to "rainfalls"? R. Berekhiah in the name of R. Levi said, because of *As cold waters to a faint soul, so is good news from a far country* (ibid.). As for good news one recites, "Blessed be He who is good and does good," so for cold water one recites, "Blessed is He who is good and does good." *As cold waters to a faint soul, so is good news from a far country* (ibid.)—refers to Abraham. When he was still on Mount Moriah he received news that his son's mate was born, as it is written, *Behold, Milkah has also given birth* (Gen. 22:20).

The purpose of the Mishnah quotation in the above passage is to enable a *gezerah shavah* operation in the midrash; the Mishnah states that the same blessing is appropriate for two seemingly unrelated events, rain and good news. These two dimensions are derived from a scriptural verse which is applied to Abraham during the Akedah. In Bereshit Rabbah the complete narrative of Abraham is implied; by means of quoting the Mishnah, the scriptural verse is explained and expanded to include other instances of "good news" in the past and in the future. For both, "good news" and "rain," the same benediction is recited.

The Mishnah explains scripture and is found in the position of the midrashic explanatory sentence:

> Midrash Psalms 7:9
> *God judges the righteous and God is angry with the wicked every day* (Ps. 7:12). We learnt there [M. Sot. 9:12]: *Rabban Simeon b. Gamaliel says in the name of R. Joshua, Since the day that the Temple was destroyed there has been no day without its curse, and the dew has not fallen in blessing and the fruits have lost their flavor [R. Yose says, The fruits have lost] their richness. R. Simeon [b. Eleazar] says, When purity ceased it took away the flavor and the fragrance; when the tithes [ceased] they took away the fatness of the corn; and the Sages say, Fornication and sorcery have made an end of all of these.* All these [came about] since the Temple was destroyed, as it says *and God is angry with the wicked every day* (Ps. 7:12).

The explanations in the above text move to a certain level of historicity—since the Temple has been destroyed many terrible things have occurred that are described in M. Sot. 9:12. This is the result of God's anger, as mentioned in a proposition from Ps. 7:12. In Pesikta Rabbati 33 *Anokhi* a quote from M. San. 4:3 serves as a prooftext for a midrashic proposition. The use of the roots 'GL, "round," and GRN, "neck," in the scriptural quotations from Ez. 16:11-12. "And a chain on your neck and roundels [earrings] in your ears." and in the Mishnah are compared in order to elucidate the midrashic reading of a scriptural lemma. The skill of the *darshan* is evident in the fact that he found a Mishnah passage that had both of these roots in conjunction. The continuation of the Mishnah that states that the Sanhedrin sat in a semi-circle so that they might see one another is irrelevant for Pesikta Rabbati. The same procedure is extant in Pesikta Rabbati 14 § 11, in which the use of a term in the Mishnah is called upon to explain a biblical term. In these cases a lemma from the Mishnah is treated in the same way as a lemma from scripture. Both texts, the bible and the Mishnah, are in a balanced relationship of similar authority and previous existence.

> Pesikta Rabbati 33 § 49
> *And a chain on your neck [garon]* (Ez. 16:11)—this is the Torah scroll [as it says,] *this book of law shall [not depart] out of your mouth* [Jos. 1:8]. *I decked you with ornaments!* [Ez. 16:12]—this is the bet midrash. *And roundels ['agilim] in your ears* (Ez. 16:12)—this is the Sanhedrin because our Rabbis taught [in M. San. 4:3]: *The Sanhedrin sat in a semicircle [ka-hatzi goren 'agulah] the way people sit half way around a threshing floor.*

Another example of how a Mishnah citation served the purposes of the *darshan* of a later midrash is found in the homily entitled *Be-hatzi ha-lailah* in Pesikta Rabbati. The question is asked until what time the evening *tefillah* may be recited. M. Ber. 4:1 states that there is no set time for the evening *tefillah*; however, the midrash supplements this response. The commentary in Pesikta Rabbati says, "at any time that someone wishes to recite the *tefillah*, he may recite it." This supplemental comment is different from other sources, such as T. Ber. 3. By focusing upon the unrestricted time for the evening *tefillah* the Mishnah quotation serves as a transition to the homiletic argument. Thus the homiletic text unit ends with, "Therefore David said: *But as for me, let my prayer be unto Thee, O Lord, in an acceptable time* (Ps. 69:14), at a time, that is, when the gates of Prayer are open." The argument in regard to the time of prayer in the midrash is a combination of the following two propositions which are to be read in conjunction: one may recite the Tefillah when the gates of prayer are open. This midrashic passage (Pesikta Rabbati 49) demonstrates that there are some halakhic commentaries upon Mishnah quotations that consider implications not explicitly addressed in the original Mishnah.

Pesikta Rabbati 49 § 1
And it came to pass that at midnight the Lord smote all the first born in the land of Egypt (Exod. 12:29). Let our rabbi instruct us: Until when may the evening Tefillah be recited? Our rabbis taught [in M. Ber. 4:1]: *There is no set time for the evening Tefillah but at any time, when a person wishes to recite the Tefillah, he may recite it.* Why [is this question raised]? Because [the times for reciting] the Tefillah are set times. R. Hanina bar Pappa asked R. Samuel bar Isaac, What is implied by the words *You have covered Yourself with a cloud* (Lam. 3:44)? R. Samuel bar Nahman said to him, the times for the Tefillah are set times! Therefore David said: *But as for me, let my prayer be unto You, O Lord, in an acceptable time* (Ps. 69:14), at a time, when the gates of Prayer are open...

In other cases the Mishnah quotation also focuses upon the time concept that is mentioned in a biblical quotation; e.g., in Gen. Rabbah 72:4 there is a quotation of M. B.M. 7:1, introduced by "we learned there:" *If someone hired laborers and arranged with them to work early or to work late, he has no right to compel them to do so where the custom is not to work early or not to work late.* Scripture limits the work-day to the evening, not to the night, but the Mishnaic quotation is used to define the time of the evening when Jacob returned from the field (*And Jacob came from the field in the evening,* Gen. 30:16). In Pesikta Rabbati 14 § 43 there is a quote from M. Sheq. 4:2 within the sermon entitled *Parah [adumah]:*[32] "We are taught there [M. Sheq. 4:2]: *Abba Saul said: The High Priests built the runway for the Red Heifer at their own expense.*"[33] This quote is followed by a commentary on the Mishnaic proposition "For not one of them would lead his Red Heifer out on the runway built by his predecessor. Each one demolished his predecessor's runway, then rebuilt it at his own expense." This text presents another argument in the name of R. Aha and questions the proposition of this argument by quoting a Baraita: "*Simeon Ha-tzadik, who led out two Red Heifers, deemed it unnecessary to lead out the second Red Heifer on the runway, upon which he led out the first ....*" This Baraita is reminiscent of M. Par. 3:5.[34] The lemma from the Mishnah serves as a "proof-text" and is treated in a similar manner as a lemma the bible.

In order to respond to the question of whether or not the midrash in the later midrashim is a commentary upon the Tannaitic

---
[32] Compare Tanhuma, ed. Buber, *Hukkat* 25.
[33] Compare Pesikta de-rav Kahana 4.
[34] Y. Sheq. 4:5.

sources or vice-versa, we should take a glimpse into the transmission or redactional history of one document, Pesikta Rabbati, which may help us to understand the extensive reliance upon Tannaitic sources as a means of advancing the homiletic agenda. The bulk of Pesikta Rabbati is from fifth century land of Israel and contains much older material. The rest of the Pesikta Rabbati homilies were added early in the diaspora; the redaction of Pesikta Rabbati was probably completed in Ashkenaz. Palestinian material was transmitted, preserved, and studied to a large extent in Ashkenaz. Thus, by relying upon Tannaitic sources and at the same time discounting the traditions from Babylonia, an enormous effort was made by the *darshan* of Pesikta Rabbati to keep alive the Palestinian liturgical calendar. This method of preservation gives an illusion of uninterrupted study of ancient sources. Thus, Pesikta Rabbati presents a narrative for the diaspora to study and reenact the Palestinian rites. This narrative is also present in other late midrashim of the homiletic genre of midrash.

One of the topics addressed in this narrative of the diaspora is the rite of *parah adumah*, the Red Heifer, that is made relevant to Jews in the larger context of the homily *parah adumah* in Pesikta Rabbati. In a story in Pesikta Rabbati 14 § 6 and in Midrash Aseret ha-diberot[35] we are told that a gentile is persuaded by a "Jewish" cow to convert and join the Jewish people. A simple cow that is God-fearing and observes the Sabbath laws is sold by Jews to a gentile to work his fields.[36] This simple "Jewish" cow can be viewed as a metaphor for Jews in the diaspora or for Jews experiencing dire circumstances. By utilizing the deictic properties of the homiletic work of Pesikta Rabbati which is instructive one may suggest that the text and its *darshan* are attempting to include the recipients of the homily in the study of revered texts and practices. The lesson from the text in Pesikta Rabbati 14 § 43 may be that the ritual of the Red Heifer was taken very seriously and has something to teach diaspora Jews. Invariably, as mentioned before, the halakhic discussion in a homily leads to a homiletic format. The midrash seeks supporting points in the early halakhic literature to relate to the homiletic theme of the midrash. Therefore, I conclude that in the

---

[35] Jellinek, op. cit., vol. 1, p. 74, on the fourth commandment. Pesikta Rabbati and Midrash Aseret ha-diberot are interrelated to a limited extent.

[36] The behavior of this midrashic cow is almost an inversion of the calf in the desert that led Israel astray.

homiletic later midrash citations from Mishnaic texts are often used as a commentary on the propositions of the midrash.

In terms of text linguistics, the quotation becomes embedded in the interpretative and rhetorical discourse of the later midrash. In Lev. Rabbah 27:3, the text superficially interprets the Mishnah by reaching back to scripture, however, in the rhetoric strategy of the *darshan*, the Mishnaic statement is a far reaching implication of a biblical event. The sin of the golden calf stretches into the time of the Mishnah and beyond, cow horns are not fit to be used as a shofar. The passage singles out the following lemma: *And the soles of their [the seraphim's] feet were like the sole of a calf's foot* (Ez. 1:6). This is explained further: the seraphim covered their feet so as not to be seen by the face of the *shekhinah*.

> Leviticus Rabbah 27:3[37]
> There we have learnt [M. R.H. 3:2]: *All the shofars are suitable except that of a cow.* And why *except for a cow*? Because it is the horn of a calf. And it is written: *They made for themselves a molten calf* (Exod. 32:8). So *And it shall never again be the reliance of the house of Israel, recalling their iniquity* (Ez. 29:16)[38]

The Mishnah supports propositions of the midrash and sometimes a Mishnah is proof for a proposition in a statement of a rabbi. In Pesikta Rabbati 18, the Mishnah is cited as the proof for the statement of Avin that Israel obeys the commandment of the *omer*. This Mishnaic quotation can also be viewed as a source of law that should be of concern to the audience.

> Pesikta Rabbati 18 § 3
> R. Avin said, Come and see, what care Israel exercised in regard to the mitzvah of the *omer* [sheaf of barley]! As we learn there [in M. Men. 10:4]: *They reaped it, put it into baskets, and brought it to the Temple court. They used to expose it to fire to fulfill the ordinance that it should be parched with fire (Lev. 2:14). So R. Meir. But the sages say: They used to beat it with reeds and with the stems of plants so that the grains should not be crushed. Then they put it into a pipe and the pipe was perforated so that the fire might get at all of the grains... They spread it out in the Temple courtyard so that the wind blew over it. Then they put it into a grist mill and took therefrom a tenth [of an epah of flour] which was then sifted through thirteen sieves.* R. Levi said, Behold,

---

[37] See Tanhuma, ed. Buber, *Emor* 11.
[38] Compare J. Neusner, *Judaism and Scripture. The Evidence of Leviticus Rabbah* (Chicago, 1986), p. 469.

you have labored, ploughed, sown, weeded, cropped, hoed and reaped, bound the sheaves, threshed and piled the sheaves, but if he does not cause a breeze to winnow [the barley], how can this person stay alive, and you give only the wage for the wind to him, *what profit would there be if he were to labor to make the wind blow?* (Eccl. 5:15).

(5) Which passages of the Mishnah are cited? If we look at how the Mishnah is cited, we often find a certain lemmatization or fragmentation of the text; by and in themselves many of the Mishnah quotations are unintelligible. This mode of procedure that is the manner of all exegesis in Rabbinic texts is similar to the so-called "destruction of context."[39] Only a few Mishnaic quotations in later midrash are made up of units that are more or less self-contained; rather, most passages in the later midrashim refer to the Mishnah in a brief manner. In Pesikta Rabbati 6 § 7, M. San. 10:2 is paraphrased: "Solomon...deserved no more than to be counted with *the three kings and the four commoners*, who the Sages teach us, *have no portion in the world-to-come.*" The midrash utilizes this passage several times in order to illustrate the value of Solomon as king. Or, as has been expressed by Neusner, especially in regard to halakhic midrash, scriptural midrash is a model for constructing a literary companion to the Mishnah[40] and the later midrashim accompany the Talmud. Again, to argue from theories of text linguistics, one can differentiate between "paraphrastic" text transformations and "increments"[41] in regard to the Mishnah quotations. Sometimes not only the Mishnah but also the Tosefta is quoted; the formula *taman taninan* refers to the Tannaitic stratum as a whole; this would be an "incremental" quotation.

---

[39] A. Goldberg, "Die Zerstörung von Kontext als Voraussetzung für die Kanonisierung religiöser Texte im rabbinischen Judentum," in A.J. Assmann, ed., *Kanon und Zensur. Archäologie der Literarischen Kommunikation II* (München, 1987), p. 203; M.S. Jaffee, "Oral Tradition in Theory and Practice. Aspects of Mishnah-Exegesis in the Palestinian Talmud," in *Religion* 15 (1985), p. 389, mentions the "atomization of the Mishnah."

[40] J. Neusner, *Midrash in Context. Exegesis in Formative Judaism* (Atlanta, 1988), pp. 53, 110; J. Neusner, "Form-Analysis and Exegesis: The Case of Mishnah Parah Chapter Three," in G. Vermes and J. Neusner, eds., *Essays in Honour of Yigael Yadin. Festschrift Yigael Yadin (The Journal of Jewish Studies 33)* (Totowa, 1983), pp. 537-546.

[41] The term "paraphrastic" refers to two sets of sentences, one from the Mishnah and the other in the midrash, each set composed of sentences of a particular sentence form but containing the same word-choices, display identical relative acceptability .

Ruth Rabbah 3:3
It is written, *For to him that is joined to all living there is hope, for a living dog is better than a dead lion* (Eccl. 9:4). We have learnt there [T. Ber. 6:4]: *If one sees idolatry what should one recite? Blessed be He who is patient with those who transgress His will.* [M. Ber. 9:1]: *If one sees a place from which idolatry has been uprooted what should one recite? Blessed be He who has uprooted idolatry from our land.* [T., ibid.] *And may it be Your will, o Lord our God, to uproot it from all places and turn the heart of those who worship it to serve you with the heart.*

After the Tannaitic stratum, this passage in Ruth Rabbah enumerates those individuals who will not be resurrected. Aggadat Bereshit[42] has an allusion to the Mishnaic teaching about those that are excluded from the world-to-come (M. San. 10:2); this is introduced by the formula *our rabbis taught thus*: "Come and learn from Doeg. Even though he is dead, our rabbis taught that he has no part in the world-to-come...." If this quotation is a planned combination of the Mishnah and Tosefta or merely an unspecified quotation from "Tannaitic" sources is irrelevant to the authority structure that is accomplished by appealing to established traditions of learning, as in the following text:

Leviticus Rabbah 20:4
The first sanctuary: *on the rock [the eagle] dwells and makes its home* (Job 38:28)—one night's stay. The second sanctuary *in the fastness of the rocky crag* (ibid.)—many nights' stay. For we learnt there [M. Yoma 5:2]: *Once the ark was taken away [there remained a stone from the days of the earlier prophets, called shetiyah...].*

This Mishnaic quotation is supplemented by a question and the subsequent reply from the Tosefta "And why was the rock called *shetiyah*? "(T. Yoma 3:2). This midrashic passage is found within the sermon for Yom Kippur and it seems appropriate to cite from the teachings for this day. A certain distance from the Mishnaic teachings is expressed in the following text from the homily entitled *Yehudah Ve-yisra'el*; in this case the distance to the Mishnah is not presented in a paraphrase of a Mishnaic statement but in a sincere manner of questioning pertaining to factual issues that are raised by a Mishnaic quote. The Mishnah in this midrash is questioned and not utilized as a reply to a halakhic question.

---

[42] Jellinek, op. cit., vol. 1, p. 6.

Pesikta Rabbati 11 § 1:
Judah and Israel were many (1 Kgs. 4:20). Let our rabbi instruct us: From when on is public announcement made as to what plants must not be grown together in the same field? Our rabbis taught [in M. Sheq. 1:1]: *Public announcement as to what plants must not be grown together in the same field is made on the first of Adar.* And why was this announcement made on the first of Adar? Because during the preceding months the sprouts are so tiny they cannot be distinguished but on the first of Adar the sprouts are large and one can distinguish between wheat and barley, therefore, public announcement was made on the first of Adar....

The reason of the time for the public announcement of *kilayim* is questioned by "why." The answer explains the Mishnah statement in regard to the date with practical considerations. The topic is that the different plants have to be distinguishable. This remoteness of a Mishnaic law addresses one of the topics of the midrashic homily which is another narrative for the diaspora. One of the messages communicates that Israel should not mingle and be recognizable, similar to the plants that fall into the category of *kilayim*, plants that are not to be grown together in one field.

On the other hand, there are lengthy quotations of the Mishnah.

Song of Songs Rabbah 1, 1:4[43]
We will be glad and rejoice in you (Cant. 1:4) We have learnt there [M. Yeb. 6:6]: *If a man takes a wife and lives with her for ten years and she bears him no child, he is no longer permitted to nullify the obligation to be fruitful and multiply. [After he divorces her, she maybe married to another man, and the second husband may also live with her for ten years. If she miscarries, the period of ten years is counted from the time of her miscarriage. A man is under obligation to fulfill the commandment, be fruitful and multiply, but a woman is not under such an obligation. R. Yohanan b. Beroka taught, Of both man and woman scripture says, God blessed them; and God said to them: Be fruitful and multiply* (Gen. 1:28).] R. Idi said, In Sidon it happened that a man took a wife and he lived with her for ten years, and she did not bear children. When they came to R. Simeon b. Yohai to get a divorce, the man said to his wife, Take any precious object that I have in my house, take it and return to your father's house. R. Simeon b. Yohai said, In the same manner that you were married with food and drink so you are not to separate without food and drink. What did the wife do? She prepared a great party, gave her husband too much to drink, then signaled her female and male servants and said, Take him to my father's

---

[43] Compare Pesikta Rabbati 30 *Nahamu nahamu* and Pesikta de-rav Kahana 22 *Sos asis*.

house. At midnight [the husband] woke up and said, Where am I? She said, Did you not say, Whatever precious object I have in my house, take it and return to your father's house? I have no object more precious than you ...

The Mishnah quotation and the narrative about the husband and the wife (either as a *Maaseh* or in another text construed as a *mashal*) appear together in the homiletic texts. This is an example of the application of a case to a Mishnah passage that removes the harsh edges of the sharp Mishnaic formulation. The homilies seem to say that the application of the divorce pleadings as demanded by the Mishnaic statements can be mitigated. The Mishnah and the narrative are used in conjunction to define different types of emotional or legal attachments as raised from the propositions of different scriptural verses. Generally, the exegetical purpose of the Mishnah citation differs from Rabbinic document to Rabbinic document.

(6) In respect to the transmission of the Mishnah we can assume from the quotations in the later midrash that the Mishnah was certainly presupposed and that the approach was to read Mishnaic halakhah into the bible and to teach the Mishnah. Why the halakhah was studied within the framework of homilies was addressed above. There is certainly evidence in Rabbinic texts that the study of the Mishnah could be accompanied by the study of midrash.[44] Sometimes a later midrash is seeking an available formulation of ethical principles that can be copied from older, authoritative sources.

> Pesikta Rabbati 44 § 1
> *Return, o Israel, to the Lord, your God* (Hos. 14:2). Let our rabbi instruct us: If one is committing sins and says that he will be forgiven through repentance, what is to be said about this? Our rabbis taught [in M. Yoma 8:9]: *One who keeps saying, I will sin, and [then] I will repent, I will sin and [then] I will repent, will never have strength enough to repent.* Why [not]? Because if someone repents but then returns to transgressions, his repentance is not true repentance. When someone immerses himself in the ritual bath with a reptile in his hand, he has not obtained purification. What should he do? He should first throw away what is in his hand and after this he should immerse himself in the ritual bath, and he will be purified. Scripture says, *Let the wicked forsake his way, and*

---

[44] J. Goldin, "Freedom and Restraint of Haggadah," in G.H. Hartman and S. Budick, eds., *Midrash and Literature* (New Haven, 1986), p. 53, claims that aggadah and halakhah are corollaries that interact.

the man of iniquity his thoughts; and let him return repentant unto the Lord, and He will have compassion upon him (Is. 55:7).

The inquiry into the general topic of *teshuvah* is guided by several questions in this passage, in the *yelammedenu* format. The ethical problem concerns a person who keeps committing sins, confident that they will be forgiven. The textual unit establishes a relationship between two verses dealing with repentance. If the passage is read starting at the bottom, with the verse from Isaiah, *Let the wicked forsake his way, and the man of iniquity his thoughts; and let him return repentant unto the Lord, and He will have compassion upon him*, followed by the Mishnaic quotation, a tension develops between the biblical premise and the Mishnaic statement. This tension between the passages is diminished by the midrash. The midrash explains the Mishnah: only after casting away the sins at hand, cleansing oneself, and asking for forgiveness will true repentance be obtained. This midrash does not display a halakhic interest in the Mishnah. The Mishnah citations in Midrash Proverbs mainly refer to ethical teachings; there are numerous citations and allusions to M. Avot.[45] This is almost comparable to a list of aphorisms or maxims; one document—the Book of Proverbs—is juxtaposed to sayings from another document—Avot. The main topic of interest is wisdom.[46] These stereotypical juxtapositions, quote explaining quote, are rarely part of a discourse that includes a Rabbinic dictum on the level of this midrash.

Midrash Proverbs 1:1
To know wisdom and instruction (Prov 1:2). We learnt there [M. Av. 3:18]: *R. Eleazar b. Azariah said, If there is no Torah learning there is no derekh eretz.*

Midrash Proverbs 1:7
The fear of the Lord is the beginning of knowledge, but fools despise wisdom and instruction (Prov. 1:7). We learnt there [M. Av. 4:6]: *R. Yose said, The person who knows the Torah is himself honored by humankind and whoever dishonors the Torah will be dishonored by humankind.*

---

[45] Some further examples may suffice: Midrash Prov. 2:4 quotes M. Av. 4:18; Midrash Prov. 9:10 quotes M. Av. 2:4; Midrash Prov. 9:12 and 28:19 quote M. Av. 4:11; Midrash Prov. 15:18 quotes M. Av. 4:1.

[46] For wisdom as one of the guiding principles in the formulation of Mishnaic law see E.J. Schnabel, "Law and Wisdom in the Mishnaic System," in *Biblical Theology Bulletin* 17 (1987), p. 105.

Midrash Proverbs 27:18
The keeper of the fig tree will eat its fruit (Prov. 27:18). R. Levi said, If someone has merit in the Torah in this world he will eat its fruit in the next world. We have learnt there [M. Peah 1:1]: *These are the things that have no measure, Peah, Bikkurim, Festal Offering, kindness, study of Torah.*

In one passage, Pesikta Rabbati 14 § 35, the text mentions a *tosefta atiqta* that serves as a source of Torah interpretation:

> R. Abbahu went to Caesarea and returned from there and his face was shining. The students saw him and said to R. Yohanan: Imagine, R. Abbahu found a treasure. R. Yohanan said: Why? They said: Because his face is shining. He said to them: May it not be that he heard a new interpretation of Torah? [R. Abbahu said]: An ancient Tosefta. And he recited it. R. Yohanan applied to him the verse: *A man's wisdom makes his face shine* (Eccl.. 8:1).

Unfortunately, the wording of this "ancient Tosefta" or teaching is not found in the text. Referring to or actually using "ancient" sources demonstrates how revered the texts and authorities of the land of Israel were to the *darshan* of Pesikta Rabbati. The Tannaitic sources are viewed as an extension of scripture; the Mishnaic citations were deemed to be the revered sources of Oral Torah.

(7) Within this particular mode of text transmission it is necessary to ask which version of the Mishnah was cited in the later midrash. One might suppose that the later midrash, precisely because of its presumed later date, is more likely to preserve quotations of a fully redacted Mishnah. However, in one homily we find an unusual introductory formula: *kakh shanu rabotenu lashon mishnah*, translated by Braude: "Our Masters, using the style and the language of the Mishnah."[47] This formula introduces a halakhic answer to a halakhic question in the so called *yelammedenu* part. The question addresses the following: "If there has been a quarrel between a human being and his fellow human being, how may he obtain forgiveness on Yom Kippur?" The Mishnah quotation constitutes the answer to this inquiry.

> Pesikta Rabbati 38 § 1
> Let our rabbi instruct us: If there has been a quarrel between a person and his fellow, how may he obtain forgiveness on the Day of

---

[47] Braude, op. cit., ad loc.

Atonement? Our rabbis taught, using the style of the Mishnah [M. Yoma 8:9]: *The Day of Atonement atones for transgression of those things that are between a human being and God. And for transgression of things between a person and his fellow, the Day of Atonement does not bring atonement to a man unless he makes peace with his fellow.*

The Mishnaic passage in this text was not included in the early versions of the Mishnah. A short survey of the text transmission shows that this passage in Pesikta Rabbati is probably a later addition to the Mishnah. According to Epstein,[48] this passage is neither found in early Mishnah manuscript evidence nor in the commentaries. It may have circulated as a Baraita, as pointed out by Braude.[49] The passage is certainly found in the Tanhuma, ed. Buber (*vayar'* 30); Buber suspected that Pesikta Rabbati copied it from the Tanhuma.[50] However, the Tanhuma, ed. Buber, does not have the peculiar introductory formula linking it to some version of the Mishnah, but does have the usual introductory phrase, *shanu rabboteinu*, which indicates a definite quotation. The entire *yelammedenu* in Pesikta Rabbati 38 as well as the parallel passage in the Tanhuma, ed. Buber, supposedly derived from *midrash harninu*. The Tanhuma might have had a more "fully redacted" Mishnah at hand. However, the Rokeah refers to the *yelammedenu* passage as deriving from Pesikta Rabbati. The textual evidence therefore suggests that this unusual type of introductory formula points to a different *Vorlage* of this section of Pesikta Rabbati than the comparable section in Tanhuma, ed. Buber, or the familiar version of the Mishnah we have presently at hand. When this passage was cited in Pesikta Rabbati it probably was not yet part of the standard Mishnah of that era. The *darshan* of Pesikta Rabbati could have cited the Mishnah-like sentence that we find in the above text, and this sentence was later incorporated into the Mishnah by secondary redactors of manuscripts and printed editions of the Mishnah. One may surmise that the reason the *darshan* of Pesikta Rabbati used such a strange introductory formula was because he did not have the same Mishnah that we presently have and that Pesikta Rabbati preserved a different version of the Mishnah.

M Yoma 8:9 is also utilized in Pesikta Hadta:

---

[48] Epstein, op. cit., vol. II, p. 1306, n. 1.
[49] Braude, op. cit., ad loc.
[50] Tanhuma, ed. Buber, ad loc.

Pesikta Hadta, Yom Kippur[51]

It is written, *Blessed is he whose transgression is forgiven [whose sin is covered]* (Ps. 32:1), and it is written, *he that covers his sin shall not prosper* (Prov. 28:13). This is not a contradiction; one verse refers to the overt sinner and the other to the covert sinner, and there are those who say that one verse refers to [M. Yoma 8:9]: *transgressions that are between a person and his fellow* and the other verse refers *to transgressions that are between a human being and God.*

A Mishnah quotation that resembles the type found in the Yerushalmi, as noted by Theodor/Albeck (p. 66),[52] is found in Gen. Rabbah 8:28 (ed. Theodor/Albeck):

"*And God blessed them* (Gen. 1:28). We have learned there [M. Ket. 1:1]: *A virgin is married on Wednesday and a widow on Thursday.* Why? Because in reference to them a blessing is found in scripture...."

This could be based upon some knowledge of a version of the Mishnah that could have circled independently before being added to the Mishnah. Is this a case of *mishnayot gedolot* (fuller mishnahs) containing excluded and supplemental material to Meir's Mishnah collection? Or is it a relatively independent interpretation of the Mishnah? Another type of rendering a more complete halakhic answer than contained in the Mishnah is found in Pesikta Rabbati 33. In this case, a series of answers as to where one should fix one's heart when praying is given. In this case there is a combination of the Mishnah and T. Ber. 3:15-16, which is different from the Mishnah.[53] This procedure is also reminiscent of the Yerushalmi which usually explains the Mishnah by first reverting to the Tosefta. The extension of the answer is given in the name of Eliezer b. Jacob. There are no text-signals between these two quotations. It is important to note that the same passage with the twofold answer is found in Tanhuma, Buber ed. (*Va-yishlah* 21), in a different context; Pesikta Rabbati and Tanhuma could possibly derive it from the *yelammedenu*

---

[51] Jellinek, op. cit., vol. 6, p. 70.

[52] The difference in the Mishnah versions lies in the particle "Be-yom," which is used here as opposed to "Le-yom," which is used in the Bavli and the present Mishnah editions (see also H. Albeck, *Shishah Sidre Mishnah* (Jerusalem and Tel-Aviv, 1959, repr., 1973), ad loc.) and the explicatory sentence that is also found at Y. Ket. 1:4.

[53] Y. Ber. 4:5; B. Ber. 30a. M. Friedmann, *Midrash Pesikta Rabbati (Midrasch für den Fest-Cyclus* (Vienna, 1880), ad loc., calls this an "old Tosefta." The *editio princeps* of Pesikta Rabbati has a longer citation of the Tosefta.

genre of midrash. The question could be raised if the *darshan* of this passage saw the halakhic tradition as one continuous receptacle that could be mined for answers. It is interesting to note that the abbreviated version of the Tosefta cited here in Pesikta Rabbati is closest to the *editio princeps* of the Tosefta from Venice, 1521, which is later than the date of this Pesikta Rabbati MS; the *editio princeps* of the Tosefta in turn is based upon an unknown MS. The simple serialization of Mishnah and Tosefta quotations as they appear in Pesikta Rabbati and in related documents expand the halakhic answer and provide a synopsis of the received halakhah. As to the textual units without quotation formula, I suppose that these were omitted purposely in order to combine the different levels of text into one cohesive unit.

> Leviticus Rabbah 32:3
> *An Israelite woman's son went out* (Lev. 24:10): R. Levi said, He went out of his world (dying). That is in line with the following verse: *And a champion went out* (1 Sam. 17:4). R. Berekhiah said, *He went out* (ibid.)—from the preceding passage, for it is written, *You shall take fine flour* (Lev. 24:5). Does a king eat hot bread or cold bread? For we have learnt there [M. Men. 11:9]: *The show bread is consumed never earlier than the ninth and never later than the eleventh day [if it was baked on the day before the Sabbath and consumed on the Sabbath, that would be the ninth day; if a festival day fell on the day before the Sabbath, it is consumed on the tenth day; if the two festival days of Rosh Ha-shanah [fell before the Sabbath] it is consumed on the eleventh day]*.

This passage from the Mishnah is shorter in Leviticus Rabbah than in Tanhuma, ed. Buber, *Emor* 23. It is possible that Leviticus Rabbah copied an "incomplete" Mishnah.[54] Midrash Samuel 23:9 cites M. Erub. 1:9: "*Four things have they permitted to people that are in a camp: they may fetch wood from any place; they are exempt from the washing of hands, from the laws of demai and from building an eruv.*" Here, according to Buber, *ad loc.*, the text is closer to the version of the Yerushalmi.

> Pesikta Rabbati 33 § 1
> *I, even I, am the one who comforts you* (Is. 51:12). Let our rabbi instruct us: One who recites the Tefillah—upon what should one fix one's heart? Our rabbis taught as follows [in M. Ber. 4:5]: *A person should fix his heart upon that which is within the Holy of Holies*. R. Eliezer ben Jacob said,

---

[54] See Margulies, op. cit., p. 742, who mentions that the manuscript evidence of the Mishnah shows that most of the MSS ended here.

> If he recites the Tefillah outside the Land, he is to recite in the direction of the Land of Israel; [if he recites it in the land of Israel, he is to recite it in the direction of Jerusalem;] if he recites it in Jerusalem, he is to recite it in the direction of the Temple; [if he is reciting it in the Temple, he is to recite it towards that which is within] the Holy of Holies.[55]

This passage demonstrates that there are sometimes halakhic commentaries upon Mishnah quotations that clarify Mishnah sentences that do address every permutation of a halakhah. In terms of the transmission of a tradition in Rabbinic literature we can state that any reuse of an earlier statement in a quotation displays a development of the established tradition. The Mishnaic "canonical" tradition serves as a fixed point and the midrash interacts with the former text.[56]

Other short additions are explanations, as in Pesikta Rabbati 7:1, which cites M. Zeb. 6:3: *All the priests in going up to the altar used the right side; then, moving all around, they came down on the left side*; the addition says, "which had a ramp." This explanation shows knowledge of the Mishnah; it reflects a passage in M. Zeb. 5:3. The *darshan* of Pesikta Rabbati saw it necessary to add some information about the ramp in the sanctuary. Pesikta Rabbati analyzes the Mishnah from the perspective of its own legal theme within the text unit of the homily. Other Mishnah citations in later midrash are not particularly close to the Mishnah. Song of Songs Zutta 1 contains a paraphrase of a statement by Eleazar b. Azariah in M. Av. 3:21: "If there is no wisdom there is no Torah," which is utilized to comment upon Ps. 111:10 (*the fear of the Lord is the beginning of wisdom*). In Pesikta Rabbati 19, the midrash explains the Mishnah, and the Mishnah is part of the argumentation of the homily. The citation of the Mishnah is only partially close to the Mishnah, and the midrash also compounds passages from Amoraic literature. From the theory of text transformation, one could argue that if the original text of the Mishnah is flexible enough and has the characteristic of many tokens that can be legitimately realized, a new text can be produced, as is the case in midrash and its Mishnah quotations. To sustain this argument we have to take into consideration that

---

[55] Tanhuma, ed. Buber, *Va-yishlah* 21.
[56] A.J. Saldarini, "Reconstructions of Rabbinic Judaism," in R. Kraft and G.W.E. Nickelsburg, eds., *Early Judaism and Its Modern Interpreters* (Philadelphia, 1986), p. 446.

the Mishnah was in a state of fluidity, notwithstanding that it had been turned into a canon and was preserved in writing. Quotations had to be quoted accurately and on cue in order to appropriately set off a particular turn of thought. One can assume that these allusions to the Mishnah were not intended as citing ancient sources but rather to gain retrospection of a former situation and of an idealized ancient time when things were perceived to be holy, reliable, authentic. A Mishnaic quotation is usually verbatim; only occasionally we find extensions inserted by the creator of the midrash although the later midrash shows a relative independence in its interpretation of the Mishnah.

> Midrash Psalms 5:11
> God not only blessed the righteous but also protects him, as it is written *with favor You will compass him* (Ps 5:13) ...

This midrash contains explications of Psalms in the order of the Book of Psalms, which are broken down into lemmata; some of these scriptural lemmata are juxtaposed with statements from the Mishnah, as for example: "*For you, Lord, will bless the righteous with favor, you will encompass him as with a shield* (Ps 5:13). We learned there [M. Shab. 5:4]: *A man may not go out with a sword or with a bow or with a shield [...]*." Only certain propositions of the Mishnah and the midrash are tangential; no total message is attained which is partially due to the structure of this midrashic work. The only commonality is the word "shield," which prompts a Mishnah quotation. In the case of the Mishnah quotations in Midrash Psalms, we may assume that the study of Psalms and the study of the Mishnah can be combined. One lesson of the future merit is derived from Psalms, and the Mishnah is quoted to show how this may be achieved. In text linguistic terms, the Mishnah in Midrash Psalms shows a "global structure," which means that the Mishnah can be studied in different textual environments.

> Pirke de-rabbi Eliezer 16 (p. 106)
> [M. Avot 1:2]: *The world rests upon three things: upon the Torah, upon divine worship, and upon the service of loving-kindness.*
> [1] *Upon the Torah*, from which passage do we know this? Because it is written, *If my covenant of day and night stand not* (Jer. 33:25) and it says, *this book of the Torah shall not depart from your mouth but you shall meditate in it day and night* (Josh. 1:8).
> [2] From which passage do we know that the world rests *Upon the service*

of loving-kindness [M. Avot 1:2]? Because it is written, *For I desired love and not sacrifice* (Hos. 6:6).
[3] From which passage do we know that the world rests *Upon Divine worship* [M. Av. 1:2]? Because it is written, *And the prayer of the upright is his delight* (Prov. 25:8).

The Mishnah quotation is broken down into three propositions; each proposition is connected to a scriptural lemma. This results in a tripartite midrash with biblical lemmata. M. Av. 1:12 has proverbial character, and we can therefore assume that this not a genuine Mishnah quotation but rather the reference to a common saying. Num. Rabbah 12:5 uses the same passage from M. Av. 1:2, although the explication is different:

> We learnt there: *The world rests upon three things: upon the Torah, upon Divine worship, and upon the service of loving-kindness* [M. Av. 1:2]—and Moses remembered all three of them in one verse [when he constructed the mishkan] *You in Your mercy have led forth the people which You redeemed, You have guided them in strength to your holy habitation* (Exod. 15:13)....

Conclusion

The Midrashic enterprise in the later homiletic midrashim rests upon the bible and some Rabbinic traditions and creativity. The Mishnah quotations in later midrash, with few exceptions, show a sincere interaction with the Oral Torah. The creators of the midrashic texts wanted to be acceptable to their audience/readership and adhered to certain conventional methods of text transmission when producing their new messages. Within the greater context of my inquiry, it may be stated that this transmission of the Mishnaic texts falls into the transfer of authoritative, ancient, holy texts in antiquity and the early middle ages. The underlying reason for this continued study of Mishnaic halakhah might have been to cultivate the memory of the Jerusalem Temple and its sanctity as well as legitimizing the teachers of the laws pertaining to it and its cultural atmosphere.

In conclusion, the Mishnah quotations in the later midrashim are part of the greater context of inquiry into the Torah. The citation of the Mishnah in later midrash constitutes a transmission and an acceptance of authoritative texts and represent the study of traditional text and the creation of new texts. One would assume that the Mishnah quotations retain their original meaning. However, in many cases in homiletic midrash this is not correct.⁵⁷ When the quotations are lifted from the Tannaitic text, they are frequently adapted into a homiletic discourse and acquire a new and perhaps more expansive reading. This new reading extends into the narrative of the whole midrash. The reason for this new reading is that the midrash as a whole contains larger units of thought that present a coherent and prolonged argument that dominates the Mishnaic citation. The creators of the later midrashim embrace theological positions and select passages from Tannaitic sources to advance these positions. The *darshan* then reshapes the Tannaitic material according to his own theological and didactic purposes. Quoting the Mishnah in later midrash is part of a larger narrative that is the interpretation and transmission of ancient learning whereby the citation and the commentary often become indistinguishable. The later midrash was part of this ongoing interpretative and creative effort of transmitting ancient learning. The Mishnaic stratum in the later midrash thus evolves into an integral part of the concept of the dual Torah. The creators of the later midrashic works attempted to repeat text-based teachings in the traditional manner; they quoted and repeated the Mishnah in order to connect it to the ongoing effort of spiritual survival in the diaspora or being under rhetorical siege in the land of Israel.⁵⁸

BIBLIOGRAPHY

Albeck, H., *Shishah Sidre Mishnah* (Jerusalem and Tel-Aviv, 1959, repr. 1973).
Alexander, P.S., "Midrash," in Loggins, R.J., J.L. Houlden, and P.S. Alexander, eds., *A Dictionary of Biblical Interpretation* (London and Philadelphia, 1990), pp. 452-459.
Avery-Peck, A.J., "The Mishnah, Tosefta, and the Talmuds. The Problem of Text and Context," in Neusner, J., ed., *Judaism in Late Antiquity. Part 1: The Literary and Archaeological Sources* (Leiden, 1995), pp. 173-216.
Barth, L.M., *Pirqé Rabbi Eliezer*. http://www.usc.edu/dept/huc-la/pre-project [Under construction].
Braude, W., trans., *Pesikta Rabbati. Discourses for Feasts, Fasts, and Special Sabbaths* (New Haven and London, 1968).

---

⁵⁷ J. Neusner, *Judaism. The Evidence of the Mishnah* (Atlanta, 1988), p. 454, writes "the Mishnah as read later on is not the document as written."
⁵⁸ This article is partially based upon my "Aggadah and Mishnah: The Mishnah in Pesiqta Rabbati" (Society of Biblical Literature Annual Meeting, Boston, 1999) and "The Tannaitic Stratum in Pesiqta Rabbati" (Association for Jewish Studies Conference, Boston, 2000).

Brown, P., *Power and Persuasion in Late Antiquity: Towards a Christian Empire* (Madison, 1992).
Buber, S., ed., *Midrash Mishle* (Vilna, 1883).
Buber, S., ed., *Midrash Samuel* (Cracow, 1883).
Buber, S., ed., *Midrash Zutta' 'al Shir Ha-Shirim, Rut, Ekhah Ve-Kohelet* (Berlin, 1884; repr. Tel-Aviv, 1971).
Buber, S., ed., *Midrash Tanhuma Ha-Kadum Ve-Ha-Yashan* (Vilna, 1885; repr. Jerusalem, 1964).
Buber, S., ed., *Midrash Shoher Tov 'al Tehillim* (Vilna, 1890; repr. Jerusalem, 1967).
Cohen, M., ed., *Midrash Bereshit Zutta* (Jerusalem, 1962).
Eisenstein, J.D., ed., *Otzar Midrashim. A Library of Two Hundred Minor Midrashim. I-II* (New York, 1915; repr. 1969).
Epstein, J.N., *Mavo le-Nusah Ha-Mishnah: Nusah Ha-Mishnah Ve-Gilgulav Lemi-Yeme Ha-Amora'im Ha-Rishonim Ve-'Ad Defuse R.Y.T. Lipman Heler* (Jerusalem, 2000).
Friedlander, G., trans., *Pirke De Rabbi Eliezer. The Chapters of Rabbi Eliezer the Great* (New York, 1981).
Friedmann, M., *Midrash Pesikta Rabbati (Midrasch für den Fest-Cyclus)* (Vienna, 1880).
Gafni, I.M., "The Historical Background," in Safrai, S., ed., *The Literature of the Sages. First Part: Oral Tora, Halakha, Mishna, Tosefta, Talmud, External Tractates 1* (Assen and Philadelphia, 1987), pp. 1-34.
Goldberg, Abr., "The Mishna. A Study Book of Halakha," in Safrai, ed., *The Literature of the Sages*, pp. 211-251.
Goldberg, Arn., "Zitat und Citem. Vorschläge für die descriptive Terminologie der Formanalyse rabbinischer Texte," in *Frankfurter Judaistische Beiträge* 6 (1978), pp. 23-26.
Goldberg, Arn., "Die Zerstörung von Kontext als Voraussetzung für die Kanonisierung religiöser Texte im rabbinischen Judentum," in Assmann, A. and J., eds., *Kanon und Zensur. Archäologie der Literarischen Kommunikation II* (München, 1987), pp. 201-211.
Goldin, J., "Freedom and Restraint of Haggadah," in Hartman, G.H., and S. Budick, eds., *Midrash and Literature* (New Haven, 1986), pp. 51-76.
Herr, M.D., "Midrash," in *Encyclopaedia Judaica* (Jerusalem, 1972), vol. 11, cols. 1510-1514.
Jaffee, M.S., "Oral Tradition in Theory and Practice. Aspects of Mishnah-Exegesis in the Palestinian Talmud," in *Religion* 15 (1985), pp. 387-410.
Jellinek, A., ed., *Bet Ha-Midrasch. Sammlung Kleiner Midraschim und Vermischter Abhandlungen aus der Ältern Jüdischen Literatur*, 6 Vols. in 2 Pts. (Jerusalem, 1967).
Lieberman, S., ed., *Midrash Devarim Rabbah, Ed. from the Oxford Ms. No. 147* (Jerusalem, 1974).
Longacre, R.E., *The Grammar of Discourse. Second Edition. Topics in Language and Linguistics* (New York and London, 1996).
Mandelbaum, B. [Dov], ed., *Pesikta de-Rav Kahana* (New York, 1962).
Margulies (Margaliot), M., *Midrash Vayiqra Rabbah* (New York and Jerusalem, 1993).
Midrash Rabbah (Vilna, 1887).
Neusner, J., "Aggadah in the Halakhah," in Neusner, J., A.J. Avery-Peck, and W.S. Green, eds., *The Encyclopaedia of Judaism*, Suppl. 2 (Leiden, Boston, Köln, forthcoming, 2002).
Neusner, J., *The Aggadic Role in Halakhic Discourse* (Lanham, 2000).
Neusner, J., *Dual Discourse, Single Judaism. The Category-Formations of the Halakhah and of the Aggadah Defined, Compared, and Contrasted* (Lanham, New York, Oxford, 2001).
Neusner, J., "Form-Analysis and Exegesis: The Case of Mishnah Parah Chapter

Three," in Vermes, G., and J. Neusner, eds., *Essays in Honour of Yigael Yadin. Festschrift Yigael Yadin (The Journal of Jewish Studies 33)* (Totowa, 1983), pp. 537-546.
Neusner, J., *A History of the Mishnaic Law of Appointed Times* (Leiden, 1981-1983).
Neusner, J., *A History of the Mishnaic Law of Damages* (Leiden, 1983-1985).
Neusner, J., *A History of the Mishnaic Law of Holy Things* (Leiden, 1978-1980).
Neusner, J., *A History of the Mishnaic Law of Women* (Leiden, 1980).
Neusner, J., *Judaism. The Evidence of the Mishnah* (Atlanta, 1988).
Neusner, J., *Judaism and Scripture. The Evidence of Leviticus Rabbah* (Chicago, 1986).
Neusner, J., *Method and Meaning in Ancient Judaism. Third Series* (Chico, 1981).
Neusner, J., *Midrash in Context. Exegesis in Formative Judaism* (Atlanta, 1988).
Neusner, J., *The Mishnah. A New Translation* (New Haven, 1988).
Neusner, J., "Rabbinic Judaism, Formative Canon of (4): The Aggadic Documents. Midrash: The Later Compilations," in Neusner, J., A.J. Avery-Peck, and W.S Green, eds., *The Encyclopaedia of Judaism* (Leiden, Boston, Köln, 2000), vol. 3, pp. 1176-1206.
Neusner, J., "Redaction and Formulation. The Talmud of the Land of Israel and the Mishnah," in *Semeia* 27 (1983), pp. 117-145.
Neusner, J., *The Unity of Rabbinic Discourse* (Lanham, 2000).
Neusner, J., "The Use of the Mishnah for the History of Judaism Prior to the Time of the Mishnah," in *Journal for the Study of Judaism in the Persian, Hellenistic and Roman Period* 11 (1980), pp. 177-185.
Rieser, H., "On the Development of Text Grammar," in Dressler, W.U., ed., *Current Trends in Linguistics. Research in Text Theory 2* (Berlin and New York, 1978), pp. 6-20.
Saldarini, A.J., "Reconstructions of Rabbinic Judaism," in Kraft, R., and G.W.E. Nickelsburg, eds., *Early Judaism and Its Modern Interpreters* (Philadelphia, 1986), pp. 437-477.
Schnabel, E.J., "Law and Wisdom in the Mishnaic System," in *Biblical Theology Bulletin* 17 (1987), pp. 104-111.
Stanley, C.D., "The Rhetoric of Quotations: An Essay on Method," in Evans, C.A., and J.A. Sanders, eds., *Early Christian Interpretation of the Scriptures of Israel. Investigations and Proposals. Journal for the New Testament, Suppl. 148* (1997), pp. 44-58.
Theodor, Y., and Albeck, H., *Midrash Bereshit Rabba mit kritischem Apparat und Kommentar.* (Jerusalem, 1962).
Ulmer, R., *A Synoptic Edition of Pesiqta Rabbati Based Upon All Extant Manuscripts and the Editio Princeps* (Atlanta, 1997-1999).
van Dijk, T., *Zur Bestimmung Narrativer Strukturen auf der Grundlage von Textgrammatiken* (Hamburg, 1972).
Vivian, A., "Il Lessico Concettuale del Trattato Mishnico Berakhot (MBer)," in Vivian, A., ed., *Biblische und Judaistische Studien. Festschrift Paolo Sacchi (Judentum und Umwelt 29)* (Frankfurt am Main, 1990), pp. 383-534.
Zundel, H., ed., *Midrash Tanhuma.* [Tanhuma, Printed Ed.] (Jerusalem, repr., 1973/1974).

AN AESTHETIC USAGE OF SCRIPTURES IN THE ANCIENT RABBINIC LEGAL CODES

HERBERT W. BASSER

Queen's University

We compare the Mishnah and Tosefta, which both deviate from their subject matters in presenting the laws of Shabbat Chapter 9. The translations are by Jacob Neusner (true to the letter), which I refashioned (credible to the spirit) somewhat to emphasize my particular purpose. Mishnah Shabbat Chapter 8 (end) discusses the minimum amounts of stuffs a person may not carry on the Sabbath:

8:7
A. "Potsherd enough to put between one board and another," the words of R. Judah.
B. R. Meir says, "Enough to scoop up fire."
C. R. Yose says, "Enough to hold a quarter log [of liquid]."
D. Said R. Meir, "Even though there is no proof for the proposition, there is at least a hint for it: And there shall not be found among the pieces of it a sherd to take fire from the earth (Is. 30:14)."
E. Said to him R. Yose, "From that same verse there is proof [for my proposition]: 'Or to scoop up water withal out of the cistern.'"

9:1
A. R. Aqiba said, (1) "From which biblical verse can we support the notion that (*minayin*)[1] an idol conveys ritual impurity to the one who carries it [even without direct touching[?
B. "From that Scripture which states, 'You shall cast them [idols] away like a menstruous thing, you shall say to it, Get thee hence' (Is. 30:22).
C. "Just as the menstruating woman imparts uncleanness to the one who carries her, so an idol imparts uncleanness to the one who carries it."

---

[1] The question presupposes there must be some biblical verse the rabbis used to derive laws that had been stated in the tradition without any source. *Minayin* is a term used to ask from which verse the rabbis derived their information, since the laws defied elucidation in reference to the general legal system.

9:2
- A. (2) "From which biblical verse can we support the notion that a boat is not susceptible to ritual impurity?
- B. "From that Scripture which states, 'The way of a ship in the midst of the sea' (Prov. 30:19).
- C. (3) "From which biblical verse can we support the notion that in a garden bed that is six handbreadths square, five different kinds of seed may be sown, four on the sides and one in the middle?
- D. "From that Scripture which states, 'For as the earth brings forth her bud and as the garden causes seeds sown in it to spring forth' (Is. 61:11).
- E. "Its 'seed' is not said, but its 'seeds.'"

9:3
- A. (4) "From which biblical verse can we support the notion that she who emits semen on the third day [after having had sexual relations] is unclean?
- B. "From that Scripture which states, 'And be ready against the third day, [come not near a woman]' (Exod. 19:15).
- C. (5) "From which biblical verse can we support the notion that they bathe a child on the third day after circumcision, even if this coincides with the Sabbath?
- D. "From that Scripture which states, 'And it came to pass on the third day when they were sore' (Gen. 34:25).
- E. (6) "From which biblical verse can we support the notion that they tie a red thread on the head of the scapegoat [which is sent forth]?
- F. "From that Scripture which states, 'Though your sins be as scarlet, they shall be white as snow' (Is. 1:18)."

9:4
- A. (7) "From which biblical verse can we support the notion that on the Day of Atonement anointing is tantamount to drinking?
- B. "Even though there is no direct proof of the proposition, there is a hint
- C. "From that Scripture which states, 'And it came into his inward parts like water and like oil into his bones' (Ps. 109:18)."

TOSEFTA SHABBAT CHAPTER 9 (ed. Zuckermandel chap. 8).
9:23
- A. (1) "From which biblical verse can we support the notion that one who dyes red on the Sabbath is liable?

B. "From that Scripture which states, 'Ram's skins dyed red' (Exod. 25:5)."
C. What is a wound that one is forbidden to make on the Sabbath? Anything from which blood has flowed out.
D. If the blood was congealed under the skin, even though it cannot flow out, lo, the one who caused this is liable.
E. (2) "From which biblical verse can we support the notion that blood is a drink?
F. "From that Scripture which states, 'And drinks the blood of the slain' (Num. 23:24)."

9:24
A. (3) "From which biblical verse can we support the notion that wine is a drink?
B. "From that Scripture which states, 'And of the blood of the grape you drank wine' (Deut. 32:14)."

9:25
A. (4) "From which biblical verse can we support the notion that honey is a drink?
B. "From that Scripture which states, 'And he made him suck honey out of the rock' (Deut. 32:13).
C. (5) "From which biblical verse can we support the notion that oil is a drink?
D. "From that Scripture which states, 'A feast of fat things, a feast of wine on the lees' (Is. 25:6)."

9:26
A. (6) "From which biblical verse can we support the notion that milk is a drink?
B. "From that Scripture which states, 'So she opened a skin of milk and gave him a drink' (Jdgs. 4:19)."

9:27
A. (7) "From which biblical verse can we support the notion that dew is a drink?
B. "From that Scripture which states, 'He wrung enough dew from the fleece to fill a bowl with water' (Judges 6:38)."
C. (8) "From which biblical verse can we support the notion that the blood of a menstruating woman is a drink
D. "From that Scripture which states, 'Then she shall be clean from the fountain of her blood' (Lev. 12:7).
E. "And further it says, 'On that day there shall be a fountain opened

for the house of David and the inhabitants of Jerusalem to cleanse them from sin and menstrual uncleanness' (Zech. 13:1)."

F. (9) "From which biblical verse can we support the notion that a tear is a drink?

G. "From that Scripture which states, 'You have given them tears to drink in full measure' (Ps. 80:5)."

9:28

A. (10) "From which biblical verse can we support the notion that nasal (Heb.: *af*) liquid that drips from the nose is a drink?

B. "As it is said,' And our afaf gush with water' (Jer. 9:17)."

9:29

A. (11) "From which biblical verse can we support the notion that the arm is equivalent to the hand?

B. "From that Scripture which states, 'And the ropes that were on his arms became as flax that has caught fire, and his bonds melted off his hands' (Jdgs. 15:14)."

9:30

A. (12) "From which biblical verse can we support the notion that one who has been seized by ravenous hunger do they feed fig cake?

B. "From that Scripture which states, 'They found an Egyptian in the open country…and they gave him bread and he ate, they gave him water to drink, and they gave him a piece of a fig cake and two clusters of raisins. And when he had eaten, his spirit revived…' (1 Sam. 30:12)."

I. The Problem

Mishnah Shabbat Chapter 9 is as tedious as the Mishnah gets. This part of the Mishnah is devoted to details of the laws of carrying on the Sabbath. Students of the Mishnah have generally been perplexed by the existence of a prohibition of carrying objects on the Sabbath from private property to public thoroughfares and vice versa (or even just in the public thoroughfare itself). The reason for their frustration stems from the fact that the other categories of forbidden labors on the Sabbath all entail some physical change within an object, but the categories of carrying are *sui generus*. The very act of carrying does not enhance or impair the essential nature of the carried object whatsoever.[2] The person who infringes the carrying laws on the Sabbath is liable to pay for his misdeed only if he carried a certain specified amount of the article in question. The precise determination of these amounts is spelled out in Mishnah Shabbat Chapters 8 and 9. So one is guilty on the Sabbath for taking out "a" amount of wine, "b" amount of rope, "c" amount of leather and so on. And now comes the problem we will address here: at this point, suddenly for no apparent reason, this agenda breaks. In the midst of a well structured pattern of topically arranged rules, the editor of the Mishnah inexplicably inserts a stack of biblical legal interpretations that serve no apparent purpose in the context of Shabbat Chapter 9.

The effect is jarring. These interpretations (each beginning with the Hebrew catchword *minayin*) speak of matters far off the topic at hand and cover a wide range of subject materials with no single manifest theme. It is difficult to see any internal connection between the items in the interpolated materials nor any connection to the theme of the chapter. The effect is that a helter-skelter catalogue of biblical interpretations has been parachuted into remarkably unfamiliar terrain. This confusing interruption of the flow of the Mishnah lasts a full seven units before the topic of the chapters resumes. Biblical interpretations of a legal nature are a rare enough occurrence in the Mishnah, but when they occur they relate to the subject matter at hand. Yet, in the case under discussion, these interpretations cannot be seen to relate to anything pertinent at all, leave alone themselves.

As if this situation were not baffling enough, it is exacerbated when we look at Tosefta Shabbat Chapter 9 (chapter 8 in Zuckermandel's edition). Here we find the exact same phenomenon. As in the Mishnah, the subject matter concerns carrying specific prohibited amounts on the Sabbath. So we are told here that one is guilty for carrying on the Sabbath "x" amount of wine, "y" amount of milk, "z" amount of water, etc., when suddenly a list of legal biblical interpretations interrupts. This extraneous and irrelevant catalogue continues for a full twelve units until the original thread of the chapter is resumed. It can hardly be accidental that in Tosefta Shabbat 9, just as in Mishnah Shabbat 9, we find a totally new catalogue of biblical interpretations that has been parachuted into alien territory.

---

[2] See Tosafot to B. Shab. 2a.

To get an idea of just how bizarre this interference is we should examine the scant role that Scripture plays in the Mishnaic enterprise altogether. For the most part, the Mishnah is not formally involved with scriptural interpretation. Yet, on occasion laws in the Mishnah are cited together with proof texts from Scripture which show how the Mishnaic law was derived. The form of these citations are familiar to the student of rabbinic literature from the compilations of legal interpretations made by the Rabbis. These compilations are called "midrash halakha" and they utilize a limited number of fixed formulas to present their materials These very formulas also appear throughout the Mishnah. Clearly, some are more popular in Mishnah than others. For example, the *"yakhol"* expression which begins with the formal "I might have thought such and such to be the case" ends with the formal "but now that Scripture explicitly states this certain phrase I can no longer think that this would be the case." This *yakhol* expression is found only five times in the Mishnah [excluding *Chapters of the Fathers*]; namely, in Makkot 1, Hulin 8, Kritot 6 (in two places). Interestingly, it is found in Tosefta some ten times; namely, Berachot 1, Rosh Hashannah 2 (twice), Hagigah 2 (twice), Baba Kamma 3, Sanhedrin 14, Arakhin 4 (twice) and Kelim B.M. 6. Yet, and this is significant, nowhere is this formula found in the Tosefta tractates where it occurs in Mishnaic ones. Indeed there are about 350 citations of Scripture (excluding Avot) in halakhic tractates of Mishnah (only 6 books are not cited, Deuteronomy and Isaiah are the most frequent) compared with about 500 in Tosefta and the overlap is not as great as one might suspect the case would be. Only 9 tractates of Mishnah have no explicit biblical citations. The use of the Bible in the Mishnah requires a case by case study.

Biblical citations have been studied by scholars who have attempted to elaborate why the Mishnah cites Scripture where it does

---

[3] I am greatly indebted to Jason Kalman, a doctoral student at McGill University who gave me his paper entitled "Scriptural Citation in the Mishnah—Original Material or Supplementary Addition?" His fine manuscript work allows one to surmise that about 10-20% of the biblical verses in the printed additions of Mishnah are later additions. That means up to 20% of the 500 or more citations might not be original to the Mishnah. Kalman's MA Thesis covers the material in detail: *The Place of the Hebrew Bible in the Mishnah* (McGill, April 1999, supervised by B. Levy). See also, G. Eicher, "Das Alte Testament in der Mischna," in *Bibilische Studien* 11:4 (Breisgau, 1906); J. Neusner, "Innovation through Repetition: The Role of Scripture in the Mishnah's Division of Appointed Times," in *History of*

and why it does not where it does not.³ One of the more interesting citations of Scripture occurs in M. Sheq. 6:6. Here, after restoring the text to its original form,⁴ we can see the rabbis of the Mishnah understood that the High Priests of the First Temple engaged in legal exegesis from the Torah (*midrash*) to decide the rules of the Temple. They found evidence for this assertion in Scripture itself. Somewhat strange is the *midrash* in M. B.M. 2:5, which parses Deut, 22:3 but the citation of the verse has fallen out of the text, while a related verse (Deut, 22:2) is cited two *mishnayot* further (M. B.M. 2:7). In this article we will not discuss the use of Scripture in Mishnah as a phenomenon, although such a comprehensive study still needs to be done. We concern ourselves with a single formula of *midrash* used very rarely in Mishnah. This form is prevalent in the *midreshei halakhah*. For convenience's sake, we shall call this form *minayin*. That is, the form advises, "From which biblical verse (*minayin*) can we support the notion that...is the case? From that scripture which states '...!'" The Tosefta has three times as many citations of this type as does the Mishnah.

We should stress that if we ignore the citations from the text of Mishnah Shabbat 9, then we are left with only two real citations of this form in all of the Mishnah. About half the citations of this formula in the Tosefta occur in Shabbat Chapter 9 (Zuckermandel, chap. 8). These amount to twelve *derashot* in the Tosefta—a number that we shall see in a moment is not haphazard. In the Mishnah, three quarters occur in chap. 9, amounting to seven *derashot* (again a very consciously chosen number), yet not one citation in chapter 9 of the Mishnah matches anything in chapter 9 of the Tosefta. The paucity of these references in the Mishnah and Tosefta in general leads one to believe that some principle is at work to account for the abundance of these materials in Mishnah Shabbat Chapter 9.

In Mishnah Shabbat 9 we can point out that the role of Scriptural exegesis is extraordinary. Except for one unit in the list of *midrashim*, the contents of which are repeated many chapters away from Shabbat 9, none of the seven *minayin derashot* in this *mishnah*

Religions 21 (1981), pp. 48-76.; D.S. Zlotnick, *The Iron Pillar—Mishnah* (New York, 1988); S. Rosenblatt, *The Interpretation of the Bible in the Mishnah* (Baltimore, 1935); and E.Z. Melamed, *Hayahas ben Midreshe Halakha LaMishna velaTosefta* (Jerusalem, 1966). The most extensive study is by Peter Acker Pettit, who devoted his unpublished 1993 Ph.D Thesis at Claremont Graduate School to a study of every Mishnaic citation of Scripture (*Shene'emar: The Place of Scripture Citation in Mishnah*).

⁴ See H. Albeck, ed., *Shisha Sidrei Mishnah* (Tel Aviv, 1959), vol. 2, p. 463.

have to do with materials in Mishnah Shabbat 9 at all.

As for the twelve interpretations in Tosefta Shabbat 9, only the first has anything to do with Sabbath laws. The mention of wine, milk, and blood[5] in the Toseftan *minayin* statements have to do with the question of what is considered a liquid that renders certain food stuffs susceptible to contract ritual impurity (if a contaminating substance contacts the foodstuff). These laws have nothing to with the Sabbath. But it may be the terms "wine," "blood," and "milk" determined somewhat which collection of *minayin* statements to cite, since these terms also occurred earlier in Tosefta Chapter 9, albeit in a wholly different context. So there may be some slight reason that if a list has to be brought, it should be this list and not another. Likewise, the beginning of the *minayin* section in the Mishnah follows a single creative interpretation of a biblical verse from Is. 30, used to illustrate the amount of a shard that is subject to the laws of carrying. This interpretation is not of the *minayin* form. It is here that the "minayin" list intrudes. The first of the *minayin midrashim* cites Is. 30. Is this just coincidence, or might it also explain that if a list of *minayin midrashim* should be cited here in the Mishnah, the list beginning with a citation from Is. 30 would be appropriate? But what reason could there be for citing such lists in the fist place?

To appreciate how purposeful the placement of the list must be, we note that *minayin* statements are all bunched up in Mishnah/ Tosefta Shabbat Chapter 9, but otherwise there are only a handful of occurrences of this form of midrash scattered in a few places in other tractates. On the other hand, some of these interpretations of biblical verses found in Mishnah Shabbat 9 actually occur elsewhere in the Mishnah as proof texts for various minority positions. In these cases, they are assigned to rabbis thought to have held these positions. Most surprisingly, in their fuller contexts elsewhere in the Mishnah, the verse interpretations lack the *minayin* catchword and framework, although they are word for word the same otherwise. However, the particular *minayin* statements of Tosefta Shabbat 9 are not mentioned elsewhere either in the Tosefta or Mishnah. This is

---

[5] See T. Ber. 4:3. Eliezer permits wine to be used for washing hands prior to meals, just as one uses water for that purpose. Professor Ranon Katzoff of Bar-Ilan University in private correspondence to me indicated that Roman literature, referring to the (spoiled) Jews, claims they wash their hands with wine; here, according to him, is one more proof that Roman Jews followed traditions in line with those of Eliezer.

so even if the laws hinted at in these verses are found transmitted throughout the Mishnah and Tosefta[6] in the tractates and places that deal with their specific topics. The English reader can refer to the notes in Danby's translation or the bracketed references in Neusner's translation for a list of the places in the Mishnah that are the primary locations to communicate these laws.[7] The traditional commentaries, like the procedure in the Talmuds, either copy what they have said elsewhere to explain these statements or refer the reader to the place in which these materials are dealt with in their legal contexts.

Clearly, the placement of *derashot* in Tosefta and Mishnah Shabbat 9 was not meant to disclose information about sundry laws mentioned elsewhere in the literature but for some other purpose. Therefore, it must be significant that so many *derashot* do occur, one after another, specifically in a spot discussing minimum amounts of various materials that one is forbidden to carry on Sabbath from one domain to another. The Mishnah and Tosefta are finely worked documents, and there has to be some explanation for the editors' violating the integrity of their highly organized program in this particular spot. Somehow, we fathom it would be nice if the problem of the unique occurrence of intruding lists in the Mishnah at hand and the question of why carrying constitutes a "Sabbath work" could resolve each other.

II. Defining the Issues

a) Minayin *Midrash*

A *minayin* midrash is a very specific type of exegesis that bolsters known laws that are incongruous with the over-all legal system. It occasionally happens that objects, spaces, or time frames that have characteristics that logically ought to subject them to one category of law are in fact subjected to a very unusual category of law. The rabbis developed *minayin* midrash to support these claims. This type of midrash proved popular and was often used to uphold the integrity of their legislation. It was also used in non-legal contexts to

---

[6] See Y. Abromsky, *Tosefta Hazzan Yehezkel* (Seder Moed, Shabbat) (Tel Aviv, n.d.), pp. 40-41, in notes.

[7] H. Danby, tran., The *Mishnah* (London, 1933), p. 108, nn. 3, 6, 9, 13, 14, 15, 16.

explain strange claims made by rabbinic authorities who offered only limited proof for their assertions. The basis of this type of midrash lies in Rabbinic appreciation of scripture. The rabbis perceive the effect of a correspondence between reality, law, and scriptural literary images. An examination of the homiletic usage of *minayin* midrash reveals that typically it claims the details of a given religious norm proclaim in and of themselves a breaking through to new facts. These facts re-create the real world. Scripture warrants its own universe of discourse to be operative in the natural world in which halakhah is practiced. Scripture may disrupt natural patterns and introduce its own categories that are halakhic realities. To invoke the language of mathematics, we note that *minayin* midrashim give us a sophisticated view of transformational halakhic geometries superimposed on the natural world and its conventions of discourse. Here is a paradigmatic example (B. Shab. 119a):

> Said R. Hamnuna, "To everyone who prays on the eve of the Sabbath and says '[It was evening and it was morning—Friday] *and they* [the heavens and the earth] *were finished* (Gen. 2:1),' the Scriptures account it as if he has become a partner in the creation of the world. This accords with the verse, '*and they were finished*.' This is so since the text may also be voweled to mean, '*and they* [God and the righteous] *finished...*'."

The context of the passage implies that an individual might presumably be exempt from reciting the verses beginning with "and they were finished" (Gen. 2:1) in his prayers on the eve of the Sabbath. This biblical tribute is testimony to God's act of finishing creation at the end of the sixth day. According to established frameworks, such witnessing by reciting the appropriate verses is properly reserved for public testimony. But even the person who prays alone at that very moment when creation was finished is permitted, indeed encouraged, to offer this testimony of God's final act of creation. This statement of law is justified by another tradition that is now correlated with the law. One who says such words on the eve of the Sabbath is not only permitted to say these words but it is observed that in acting so, he becomes God's partner in creating the world. By reciting in his prayers the statement "And they were finished" at the moment (late Friday) when God had finished creating heaven and earth he partakes of this creative moment and not only re-enacts creation but shares in it. And so Scripture recognizes this moment and allows the very words to be read as: they—God and the righteous—finished the heavens and the earth and all their contents. And they do this every week at the end of the sixth day of creation. Yet the question remains: speech being merely conceptual, how can mere speech of mortals create the universe? Enter the *minayin* midrash to transform the boundaries of human creativity:

> R. Eleazar said, "From which biblical verse (*minayin*) can we support the notion that speech is like action? From that which states 'with the word of the Lord the heavens were created' (Ps. 33:6)."

Reciting the "word" of the Lord, i.e., reciting Holy Scriptures' description of fashioning heaven and earth, talking about the creation of the heavens in the proper moment in the proper context, is tantamount to physically creating the heavens. *Minayin* midrash is at work here. Again we get dual readings in a biblical verse. The verse is able to mean, in its transfigured reading, that through God's speech the world was created, but moreover by humans' reciting God's words on the very day, in the very hour when God did, the heavens and earth can be created anew. Thus dual readings of Scripture in Ps. 33:6 here confirms the dual readings of Scripture in Gen. 2:1. A law of liturgy finds its justification in a biblical verse (Gen. 2:1) and that verse is later brought into further play with other verses (Ps. 33:6) to make extravagant claims. The observant Jew can do extraordinary things in the natural world because of his engagement in the law of the nonmaterial and spiritual realm.

Minayin midrash provides creative interpretations of biblical verses that transform objects or activities from one conceptual sphere to another. In the above example, the consonantal text *VYKhLU* is revoweled from *VaYaKhuLU* ("and they were finished") to *VaYiKhLU* ("and they finished"). The midrash of this genre provides a mechanism to transform objects or activities from one boundary to another. So in our example, divine activity of creation moves from God's sole domain into human domain, thus crossing the most fundamental boundary of monotheistic religions. The move is not as radical as the Christian incarnation of God in human form, but it is daringly radical for Jewish sensitivities. The rabbis read a biblical verse to show that scripture itself allows for the transformation of an item from its natural category into a new and unexpected category. In this way the rabbis justified applying sets of rules to items that appeared to be ineligible to receive these applications.

Did Eleazar actually mean his words to have the import the

Talmud ascribes to them? What else might he have meant? We cannot know for certain. But we do know the process of the Talmud that brought disparate Rabbinic sayings to focus upon a single theme in order to create a coherent structure. This is the genius of the rabbis. They blend statements of rabbis who artfully blended scriptures to reflect upon a rather prosaic law. In this highly creative enterprise, the rabbis transform the observer of the law into a kind of god. What artist, in any medium, has ever done as much? The talmudic editors give us magnificent structures from the building blocks at their disposal. This is the function of *minayin* midrash

b) *How Others Have Explained the Intrusion of the* Minayin *Lists*

Mishnah Shabbat Chapters 8 and 9 are really one long chapter, the point of the division between them being merely to isolate a group of creative interpretations of biblical verses at the head of a chapter rather than allow the creative biblical interpretations to break up a chapter, as indeed they really do. Likewise the Tosefta's creative interpretations of biblical verses interfere with the flow of the narrative around its single theme of carrying on the Sabbath. Therefore, the traditional commentators could not ignore the oddity of the break in the Mishnah's narrative structure to incorporate these scriptural interpretations. Obadiah Bertenuro (in his commentary to M. Shab. 9:1) attempts to approach the question from two angles. He notes that chapter 8 ends with biblical verses found in Is. 30, and he notes that the list of *minayin* verses also begins with an interpretation of Is. 30. This is insufficient to explain the inclusion of seven obtuse *midrashim* that have no business in Shabbat Chapter 9. If anything, it may explain why the Mishnah before the list of scriptural interpretations is placed where it is. The first unit of the *midrashim* begins with an interpretation of Is. 30 (*"sherd"*), so the *Tanna* (who fashioned this Mishnah) arranged to put the Mishnaic notice concerning the size of an earthenware fragment that may not be carried into a public domain on the Sabbath immediately before the first *minayin midrash*.

Bertenuro also notes that all these creative interpretations of biblical verses are poetic explanations rather than real proofs and therefore form a cohesive unit. Furthermore he accepts Rashi's claim that the collection of creative interpretations of biblical verses is cited for the sake of the one mention of the Sabbath that occurs late in the list. Thus, the whole collection is cited for the sake of the one mention of a Sabbath law (washing a baby in warmed water even if the third day after the circumcision falls on a Sabbath). Ch. Albeck (*Shishah Sidrei Mishnah* Sh. 9) and Israel Lipshutz (*Tifferet Yisrael* chap. 9) go no further and just reiterate Bertenuro's comment.

At a lost to explain the appearance of the *minayin derashot* in the Tosefta in the same spot as in the Mishnah, David Pardo says that apparently the editor of the Tosefta wanted to parallel the Mishnah and so included such a list. Why did the Mishnah do it? He relies on the explanation of Bertenuro and Rashi.

While the attempt to grapple with the problem is admirable and perceptive, none of the above observations is strong enough to account for the placement of materials in both the Tosefta and Mishnah. It is highly unlikely that a group of materials is cited just for the one mention of a law (M. Shab. 9:3) that, although relating to the subject of the tractate, is off topic of its chapter and anyway repeated in a discussion of its own topic ten chapters away (M. Shab. 19:3). We are still left to wonder why these seemingly extraneous materials are interjected will-nilly into a discussion of laws concerning minimum amounts of materials that are forbidden to be carried out of the house into a public domain on the Sabbath (and vice versa)?

III. The Solution

We note that the *minayin midrashim* both in the Mishnah and Tosefta are conscious interpolations. If they are removed, the subject matter they previously separated flows seamlessly. Now, most of the time we find material that appears to be interpolated we discover it is not an interpolation at all. Rather it is a conscious footnote bracketed into the text, shedding light on the material at hand by addressing small side issues. That observation will hold true in the present case as well of Mishnah/Tosefta Shabbat 9. Hence we should not speak of "interpolation" but of "designated note" that provides useful information." Interpolation" is usually a method for introducing "foot-notes."[8]

---

[8] Consider this example from Sifre Ha'azinu:
    A. In the Eschatological Age every grain of wheat will be like two kidneys of a big ox, weighing four Sephorian liters.
    B. And if this surprises you then consider the case of the turnip heads, for

The rabbis saw they had the right to determine the weights and measures operative in divine law and give them meaning. They only recognized a finite number of measurements they held to be divinely sanctioned standards but that they had the authority to apply these whenever they saw fit. In their *minayin* midrash, they noted that Scripture could engage in transformational language and likewise they assumed they had authority not only to interpret such Scriptures but to engage in transformational exercises themselves.

The laws of carrying on the Sabbath are unique in rabbinic Sabbath legislation. Unlike other Sabbath prohibitions, they require no change in the substance of an object, only change in its location. That the rabbis then attached various minimum amounts to be carried, for whatever reasons, to make one liable for the death penalty or sacrifices (depending on circumstances) might make one very uneasy about the cogency of the legislation. How does it happen that some very strange carrying law concerning some very negligible amounts renders one liable to the severest penalties possible? There is something unnerving in these lists of minimum amounts one may or may not carry.

It is therefore fitting that, just at this juncture, the rabbis provide a footnote. They interrupt the subject matter to offer a bracketed explanation of carrying laws. Let us consider the first item in the Mishnaic collection of *minayin* midrashim:

> it once happened that one weighed thirty Sephorian liters. And it happened that a fox made a nest in the head of a turnip. It once happened there was a mustard stock with three twigs and one of them fell off and they covered a whole potter's hut with it. They struck it and they found in it nine *kabim* of mustard.
>
> R. Simeon bar Halafta reported: A cabbage stalk was in the middle of my house, and I could go up and down on it like a ladder....
>
> C. You will not be wearied by treading or harvesting the grape but you will bring it in a wagon and stand it in a corner and it will constantly renew the supply that you may drink from it as from a jug.
>
> A/C forms a single unit, introduced in A by "In the Eschatological Age," and its theme is found in the Second Apocalypse of Baruch 29:5-8 (post 70 C.E.) but may well be prior to it. B interrupts this unit. Such apparent interruptions are not uncommon in the Talmuds and Midrashim. These "diversions" signify "notes," and manuscript comparisons show us they are rarely scribal interpolations. The point of B is to show us an unaffected expectation of prosperity, since such abundance is even evident, although rare, in the present era. The examples at B are not wheat or wine but cabbages and turnips and mustards and hence are secondary notes to the main discourse's visions of future abundance.

> R. Aqiba said, "From which biblical verse can we support the notion that an idol conveys ritual impurity to the one who carries it (even without direct touching)? From that Scripture which states, 'You shall cast them [idols] away like a menstruous thing, you shall say to it, Get thee hence (Is. 30:22).' Just as the menstruating woman imparts uncleanness to the one who carries her, so an idol imparts uncleanness to the one who carries it."

The law transforms the category of idol into the category of menstruant. This law of contracting impurity through carrying is based on a unique law in the rules of purity. The very act of carrying can be an act of transformation in which one's physical person becomes blended with another object (idol or person). By carrying an object or person, one effects substantive legal changes in oneself. The laws of the menstruant illustrate the principle of transformation as applied to carrying. The carrier blends with the carried and absorbs her status even without any direct contact. In sum, the *minayin* interpretation of biblical verses can place an idol in the category of menstruant because Scripture uses language in connection with one that it uses in connection with the other. And the laws of carrying menstruants shows the power of carrying something to have the ability to cause a change in status in the carrier. Thus *minayin* treatments of Scripture are an instrument of legal transformation from one category into another.

The second example in the *minayin* list shows the opposite effect to carrying a menstruant; water carrying a ship makes the ship part of its domain and impervious to ritual defilement in defiance of expected rules of purity.

> From which biblical verse can we support the notion that a boat is not susceptible to ritual impurity? From that verse which states, "The way of a ship in the midst of the sea" (Prov. 30:19).

Since the ship is carried by the water, it takes on the character of the water, and in cases in which it should contract impurity it does not. It is treated like a body of water that is impervious to defilement according the laws of ritual purity. The midrash authorizes this reading of the law. It is the precise opposite of the law of carrying an idol. The idol should be exempted from the laws of purity; but by dint of scriptural associations made by the rabbis, it is transformed into another halakhic category, subject to Rabbinic laws of purity. On the other hand, the boat, although subject to the laws of purity is placed in a new halakhic category where it is outside of the laws of purity.

In the Tosefta, the situation is similar. The first passage relates to the issue at hand, which explains why the list has been situated in this particular spot (although it does not explain why the list existed in the first place).

> From which biblical verse can we support the notion that one who dyes red on the Sabbath is liable? From that Scripture which states, "Ram's skins dyed red" (Exod. 25:5).

> What is a wound that one is forbidden to make on the Sabbath? Anything from which blood has flowed out. If the blood was congealed under the skin, even though it cannot flow out, lo, the one who caused this is liable.

Now it so happens that the allusion here is to the interesting observation that the rabbis did not consider the ram skins to have been necessarily dyed red. An act of work done in the desert tabernacle is deemed to be prohibited labor on the Sabbath. There is a definitive opinion in the Yerushalmi that in the tabernacle they beat the rams and then killed them. The skins remained reddened from having been beaten, and so the prohibition of dying and causing a wound are identical even if no blood comes out. Since the Torah deems the beating identical with dying, it turns out that the Sabbath prohibition of dying will apply to causing wounds. The proof is that Scripture refers to the results of the flaying as "dyed red." Scriptural language becomes the instrument of the transformation of wounded flesh into a dyed material.

The point is that although the Torah intimates that the ram skins were dyed red, in fact this was not the case at all—the congealing of the blood produced a legal concept of dying, that is, of transformation, whereas in fact nothing material had been affected at all, only the blood had moved from one place in the body another. And so in carrying, an object is carried from one place to another, and this affects a legal state, so that, if one repeats this action on the Sabbath, it is tantamount to dying. The one who causes internal bleeding in an animal wittingly is liable to the severest of biblical punishments, although, in effect, he has not caused any real change except for the blood to move from one place to another in the animal.[9] Likewise we have a group of *minayin* statements that show

---

[9] See Y. Shab. 7:2. One might be liable to penalties for the Sabbath infraction

certain thick fluids are identified by scriptural language and considered as watery liquids enabling foodstuffs to be fit to contract ritual impurity.

What is the relationship between these exegetical passages and the laws of carrying? Literary or conceptual associations have the power to effect transformations in legal imperatives. In fact, none of the laws mentioned in these passages actually are dependent on the scriptural proofs. The proofs, rather, are provided as evidence for certain positions as against others. The point appears throughout the Mishnah and Tosefta, but the rabbis reserved a perfect spot for it, in the middle of discussions of laws of carrying, in which, although no substantive change is made, an action anyway is prohibited on the Sabbath. The rabbis selected certain behaviors to determine the amounts subject to Sabbath carrying laws. The knowledge that people act a certain way and generally bother with certain quantities of substances but not others is as powerful an association as a scriptural proof. So the amounts stated by the rabbis that are associated with what one *might* carry such an object for become the foundation for laws involving severe penalties.

The knowledge that people act a certain way and generally bother with certain quantities of substances but not other amounts is as powerful an association as a scriptural proof. What better place to put this notice than in the middle of certain laws that themselves concern transferring objects to another domain where these transfers have important repercussions.

There is also one other curious feature. The list of seven *minayin* midrashim in the Mishnah follows after 6/7 numbered halakhot dealing with carrying (chapter 8 has seven numbered *mishnayot*,[10] the last one indicating the ensuing exegeses),[11] while the list of twelve *minayin* passages in the Tosefta follows after eleven numbered *halakhot* (the first one begins 9:13 or 8:13 in Zuckermandel). It is as if the *minayin* passages are a note to draw our attention to the materials

---

called "taking life" in cases of wounding where blood comes out even if no actual death resulted, simply because "blood" = "life" so that "loss of blood" = "loss of life." The rhetoric produces equations that redefine "loss of life." Apparently the Yerushalmi would render T. Shab. 9: Which wound is forbidden on the Sabbath (under the rubric of "taking life")? Any wound from which blood comes out; but, if the blood only collects under the skin and is not able to come out, then the one who caused this is guilty (of "dying").

[10] M. 8:3 is so tiny it really does not deserve to be numbered separately.

[11] The subject matter is already anticipated in the final passage of chap. 7.

in which they are embedded and to induce us to think of the transformational properties of Rabbinic laws. This observation enhances, although it does not prove, our conclusion that Shabbat/Tosefta Chapter 9 was selected as the proper place for the implied notice of the legal power of transformational thinking because the chapter deals with the laws of transporting items on the Sabbath. In simple terms: to carry is to transfer an object from one domain to another. The halakhah imputes meaning to transferring substances and thereby to transforming their legal states. Other transformations are illustrated in the opening laws of the *minayin* lists. Thus the appropriateness of placing these lists among carrying laws is highlighted. The purposeful moving of an object from location A to B is not a trivial act at all; it is a major foundational principle behind the construction of the Rabbinic legal system. Linking these lists of biblical associations with the Sabbath laws creates the picture that the Sabbath laws of carrying are indeed meaningful. The examination of movement, both abstract and physical, which allows concepts to be associated or differentiated, is the basis of Rabbinic creativity.

Our observation corroborates the notion, put eloquently in a number of books by Jacob Neusner, that the rabbis, besides being masters of philosophic thinking, were poets and artists in the medium of their culture: scripture and Rabbinic law.

PART THREE

THE MISHNAH IN SOCIAL CONTEXT

MASTER AND PARENT: COMPARATIVE ASPECTS OF A DUAL LOYALTY
(MISHNAH BABA MEZIAH 2:11 AND MARK 3:31-35)

GERALD J. BLIDSTEIN

Ben-Gurion University of the Negev

1

I focus here on the way (or ways) in which Talmudic culture negotiated the dual loyalty obliging sons and students vis-a-vis parents, on the one hand, and masters, on the other. Though the major focus is on Judaism, I begin by presenting some Gospel stories that also relate to this issue. The dramatic Gospel materials provide an effective backdrop for the more nuanced Rabbinic norms. Naturally, I am well aware of the difference in literary genres represented and the different sort of readings each invites. Narrative is one thing; casuistic normative literature, quite another. Nonetheless, each provides a stimulating, suggestive, foil to the other—especially if we assume that both the drafter of norms and the author of narrative have fairly free hands in choosing their topics and examples.[1]

The most significant Gospel story from my perspective is found in Mark 3:31-35:[2]

---

[1] I first broached the topic discussed in this article in my book, *Honor Thy Father and Mother: Filial Responsibility in Jewish Law and Ethics* (New York, 1975), pp. 137ff. My (Hebrew) paper in *Te'udah* 13 (1996) presents a more detailed philological analysis of the Talmudic sources than is required for my discussion below, which integrates other materials and perspectives not found in that paper.

[2] The most detailed and rounded discussion of this and related texts is S.C. Barton, *Discipleship and Family in Mark and Matthew* (Cambridge, 1992), esp. pp. 68-86. Interestingly, Barton devotes considerable attention to Jewish materials (pp. 23-47), but this is limited to the apocryphal literature, DSS, Josephus, and Philo; Rabbinic materials are not discussed. It is possible, of course, that Barton limits his inquiry to demonstrably inter-testamental materials, but one imagines that Tannaitic sources of the second century would be relevant to the Palestinian situation of Jesus' time as well. See now as well P. Ahearne-Kroll, "'Who Are My Mother and Father'," in *Journal of Religion* 81, 1 (2001), pp. 1-25. A survey of scholarship on the topic as a whole is found in C. Osiek, "The Family in Early Christianity," in *The Catholic Biblical Quarterly* 58 (1996), pp. 1-24. The terms cited from Barton, below, are on pp. 217, 221, 222.

> There came then his brethren and his mother and standing without, sent unto him, calling him. And the multitude sat about him, and they said unto him, "Behold thy mother and thy brethren without seek for thee." And he answered them, saying, "Who is my mother or my brethren? For whosoever shall do the will of God, the same is my brother, and my sister, and mother."

Jesus elsewhere pits loyalty to himself against loyalty to family and household. His famous reply, "Let the dead bury their dead but go thou and preach the Kingdom of God," was made to a man who wished to bury his father before beginning the life of discipleship.[3] This is but one example. On the one hand, Jesus is not portrayed as "insensitive to the requirements of the fourth commandment....nor as lacking in sensitivity to family suffering" (Carolyn Osiek); on the other hand, S. Barton characterizes Jesus' teaching on family in terms of "devaluation," " strong relativization," "subordination."

But let us return to the narrative in Mark (which, significantly, is found in Luke in a less extreme version, indicating, some say, discomfort with its unsettling message). The story makes two basic points. First, it tells of the devaluation of the concrete claims of family, whom Jesus refuses to see. Second, it provides the ideological basis of this rejection: familial attachment is transmuted, as disciples become brethren, and biological ties are reconstituted in spiritual terms.

This Markan instance should be sufficient background for the Rabbinic materials. M. B.M. 2:11 reads:

> His own lost property and that of his father, his own takes priority; his own and that of his teacher, his own takes priority.
>
> That of his father and that of his teacher, his teacher's takes priority. For his father did [but] bring him into this world, but his teacher who taught him wisdom brings him into the world to come; but if his father was also a sage, his father has first place.
>
> If his father and his teacher each bore a burden, he must first relieve his teacher and afterwards relieve his father. If his father and teacher

---

[3] Matt. 8:21-2 = Luke 9:59-60. M. Hengel's discussion of the filial ethos in early Christianity is largely based on this episode; see his *Nachfolge u. Charisma* (Berlin, 1968) (= *The Charismatic Leader and His Followers* [Edinburg, 1981]). In my paper in *Te'udah* 13, I argue that Christian reading of Elisha's call to prophecy (I Kgs. 19:19-21) , as over against Jewish exegesis of that episode, is heavily colored by this and other gospel materials.

were each taken captive, he must first ransom his teacher and afterward ransom his father....

As with the case of the Christian materials, here too we focus on two points: the norm, on the one hand, and its ideological infrastructure, on the other. In the three given instances—and note the ascending order, from property loss to personal discomfort to a life-threatening situation—the master, to whom the son is to (first?) devote his attentions, is given priority over the parent. It would seem that master completely supercedes parent in the Mishnah. He is preferred over the parent in situations ranging from matters of slight significance to life-threatening ones, which is what captivity could imply in the ancient world. The Mishnah also spells out the ideological basis for this preference: the parent bestowed physical existence alone on his offspring, while the master bestowed (and continues to bestow, in some texts) spiritual being. This gives the master clear advantage as to the son's loyalty and obligation.

The basic issue raised by parallel Tannaitic materials and the Talmuds relates to the identity of the teacher to whom one assigns priority. Judah restricts favored status to a teacher from whom one "has derived the greater part of his knowledge;" but Yose says it is true even for a teacher who has "enlightened his eyes in a single Mishnah only." For Judah, then, a father cedes his priority only to the one central master of his son's life. But for Yose, virtually every teacher is granted that status—extreme doctrine indeed![4] It is possible to mount a critical textual analysis that detaches Yose from the topic of our Mishnah—namely the question of loyalty to parent as over against loyalty to master—and thereby minimize the radical implications of his statement. But Toseftan material makes that option unlikely.[5]

A second point to be noted is that other Tannaitic sources make explicit that the teaching that endows a master/teacher with priority over all is the teaching of Rabbinic texts—not Bible or philosophy, and certainly not the teaching of a manual trade. Only the type of teaching and materials that characterize the Rabbinic es-

---

[4] Students have pointed out to me that by allowing anyone who teaches you even "a single Mishnah" to be accounted your master, Yose enables many fathers to qualify as well. This is an arresting point, but I don't think it accurately describes Yose's intention.

[5] For a text-critical analysis of these sources, see my paper in *Te'udah* 13, cited above.

tate are valorized. This agenda remains even where ideology falters, as in the Mishnaic assertion that "if his father was also a sage, his father takes first place." The father may not be the son's master, and thus may in fact have "brought him" into "this world" alone; but his status as a sage is automatically added to his parental status to give him priority.

Significantly, the Mishnaic formula assumes that the parent has contributed nothing to the cultural/spiritual growth of the child. This is certainly a harsh and extreme stance, one that contrasts with the role of the parent as teacher of the national history and ethos on Passover eve, for example, when "the son asks his father;" or the general Talmudic assumption that all fathers "teach their sons Torah," thereby earning their everlasting awe.[6] It also ignores the no less common teaching of moral virtues and the inculcation of religious piety, teaching at which the home may excel. The Mishnah takes into account the teaching of the Talmudic tradition alone, and by that criterion decides the superiority of master over parent.

Yet this sweeping reading overlooks the fact that the priority of master is located in a specific context, the context of conflicting concrete needs. The Mishnah poses the dilemma: what ought the son do when both parent and master require his help, as when they are both taken captive. It does not articulate a broad pattern of parental devaluation independent of such need.[7] Of course, the concrete character of these Mishnaic situations reflects the concrete nature of the halakhic project as a whole, the type of problem it considers; thus, this chapter of the Mishnah deals with the return of lost objects. Furthermore, the basic agenda of filial responsibility as a whole is fundamentally concerned with concrete parental need. All these characteristics predispose our text to giving the specific kind of example it does.

Thus, there is an interpretative crux to be faced here. Do we read the Mishnah as teaching the overall priority of master vis-a-vis parent,

---

[6] M. Pes. 10:4; B. Qid. 31a (top).

[7] Interestingly, the latter two cases (relieving the parent/master who is laboring under a load; redemption from captivity), give the master priority but assume the parent will be relieved/redeemed as well, if later. What if the disciple/son can help only parent or master? This dilemma was posed to Meir, who, according to Rabbinic legend, was given the possibility of bringing either his father or his master—the heretic rabbi Elisha b. Abuyyah—into the world to come. Different midrashic narratives relate different solutions to this quandary: see *Teudah* 13, pp. 32-33.

even the devaluation of the parental estate with all that can imply independent of the issue of need? Perhaps the concrete instances given by the Mishnah embody an overall ethos that extends beyond the question of need. That is to say: is the cited pericope an ideological text or a normative one? I would urge that both normative and ideological components are present, but that the implied priority is to be actualized only when an actual conflict forces the issue. For there is no escaping the fact that the Mishnah does restrict the priority given the master to situations of conflict over the satisfaction of concrete need. Where no conflict exists, the parent is to be served and saved.[8]

Of course, we must not minimize the radical implications of the Mishnaic norm for a religion that lists "Honor thy father and mother" as the only positive social imperative in its Ten Commandments. Nor can we engage in special pleading. The major point of the Rabbinic materials we have discussed is, clearly, the lowering of parental status as compared with that of the master, whatever qualifications we have attached to that ranking.

The message of the aggadic rationale appended to this passage certainly goes beyond its legal concretizations. "For his father did [but] bring him into this world, but his master who teaches him wisdom brings him into the world to come." That rationale is similarly straightforward yet nuanced. The master's priority seems absolute, on the one hand; it is he who links the son with a higher reality. Parenthood of the spiritual kind is affirmed; indeed it is ranked higher than that of the mere biological sort. Yet the father's status is not denied, either. On the contrary, it remains as firm as the fact that his son is physically alive. True, this fact is of secondary importance when confronted with the son's spiritual being—and that is the basic point of the Mishnah—but it is not denied. Nor is the filial obligation of son to parent denied; it will be trumped only when in conflict with the more significant obligation of son to master. We are once again faced with the question of interpretation; now, a generalized ideological statement is balanced by a limited normative expression. The balance of the Mishnah is, then, crucial to its understanding.

---

[8] The three norms in question—returning a lost object, easing the burden, and removal from captivity—are not specific requirements of filial piety (or duties of a disciple to his master) but are required towards all.

Furthermore, though the master's priority is affirmed, fatherhood itself is not transmuted into a metaphor for spiritual parenthood. The fatherhood of master does not destroy the integrity—verbal or real—of biological fatherhood. The fatherhood of parent and master are, rather, pitted against each other and ranked. One is not absorbed by the other. Both have "brought" the person "into" a "world," though these "worlds" are themselves of unequal worth, a fact that affects the importance of the two progenitors. Interestingly, the master's priority is established through the metaphor of physical birth ("brought him into"), a phenomenon to which we shall later return.

The idea of spiritual fatherhood as applied to the teaching master is indeed found in Tannaitic literature, as we might expect (Sifre Deut. Piska 34 [trans. Hammer, p. 64]).

> "(And thou shalt teach them diligently) unto thy children" (Deut. 6:7):
> This refers to your disciples, for you find that disciples are always referred to as children, as in the verse: "And the sons of the prophets that were at Bethel came forth to Elisha" (2 Kgs. 2:3)—were they the children of the prophets? Were they not the disciples? Hence we learn that disciples are called children. Similarly you find that Hezekiah, king of Judah, who taught the entire Torah to Israel, called them his sons, as it is said, "My sons be not now negligent" (2 Chron. 22:11).
> Just as sons are called disciples, so the teacher is called father, as it is said, "My father, my father, the chariots of Israel and the horsemen thereof..." (2 Kgs. 2:12).

Before attempting to define the parameters of the spiritual filiation here announced, let us note the elegance of the midrashic construct. In the version before us, two prooftexts are offered to justify the proposition that "disciples are called children." The second deals, in fact, with a putative master in Torah, who called those he taught "my sons." The first prooftext calls on the prophetic experience, claiming that disciples of the prophets were also called their "sons." In using this prooftext, the midrash implies the familiar trope in which the Rabbinic master inherits the role and status of the prophetic one. And in some manuscripts,[9] a third prooftext precedes the first two, one that refers Deut. 14:1: "You are children to God your Lord"—the people of Israel are not God's "children" in the

---

[9] See the apparatus in Finkelstein's critical edition of Sifre.

literal sense; rather, spiritual filiation is meant. Thus, the midrash moves from the ultimate spiritual filiation, to God, to a mediate form, the prophet, to the form it in fact attaches to its interpretation of Deut. 6:7, that of discipleship to the master of torah. The master, who is directly described in the third prooftext, has absorbed the status implied in the first two.

Here, then, is an explicit statement of discipleship as spiritual filiation.[10] But let us be precise, once again. With one exemption, the rabbis never claim that biological fathers and sons are now denied those names, which have been emptied of all content other than the spiritual. Disciples are referred to as children, but not all children are disciples. Rather, the midrash expands the usage of the familial terms so as to encompass the spiritual relationship. At the same time, we cannot overlook the more radical application of this midrash to Deut. 6:7, that single exemption to which I referred. Here, in the midrashic perspective, the Deuteronomic "You shall teach them...to your children" is no longer addressed to the father teaching his children but rather to the master teaching his disciples—and, apparently, exclusively so. The spiritual meaning is not added to the biological one—it does displace it.

Yet let us not go too far beyond the Deuteronomic (and midrashic) context. "Children" become disciples, exclusively, only in the context of teaching, thus legitimatizing and indeed valorizing the educational mission of the Rabbinic movement. No one would think of reading "Honor thy father and thy mother" in a way that excludes biological parents. (Indeed Talmudic culture retains other normative areas that are restricted to the biological parent: one mourns parents, for example, to a degree that the mourning for masters does not begin to approach.)[11] Indeed, the midrash does not treat of the issue of priorities at all; it does not confront the needs and/or claims of the parent with the conflicting needs/claims of the master, as does the Mishnah we have been considering. It does not

---

[10] It is possible that even the rendering of *bene ha-nevi'im* as "children of the prophets," and thus disciples, is itself midrashic. See Brown, Driver, Briggs, *Lexicon of the Old Testament*, p. 121, par. 7a. On the other hand, there is no reason to assume that the rabbis were aware of this lexical possibility.

[11] See *Honor*, pp. 147-151. C. Hezser, *The Social Structure of the Rabbinic Movement in Palestine* (Tubingen 1997), pp. 344-345, argues for the virtual equality of mourning for parent and mourning for master, but her materials all deal with the rending of garments, which may be a special case, and not with the overall ritual. See my *Honor* pp. 148 and 221, n. 41.

say anything about the status or privileges of the master at all.

The closest we come to a broad devaluation of biological parenthood is, indeed, the Mishnah passage we are discussing. But, as we have seen, its norms are carefully restricted to conflicts arising in situations of concrete need. They are derived, moreover, not from a midrash that reads "father" metaphorically, eliminating the parent in effect, but from a comparison of biological and spiritual reality—a comparison that preserves both realities much as it ranks them.

Indeed, the fact that the controlling logic of the Mishnah is halakhic, rather than doctrinal or existential, ought give one further pause. Hardly spineless, the complexity of halakhah, its varied vertebrae (so to speak), makes for additional flexibility. All of which is by way of introduction to the Toseftan version of our rule (T. Hor. 2:5 [ed. Zukermandel, p.476]):

> If he, his father, and his master, are held captive—he takes priority over his master, and his master takes priority over his father. His mother takes priority over all.

Here, the issue of need forces the halakhic hand. A woman in captivity is considered to be at far greater risk than any man, and hence ransoming one's mother takes precedence over the need of even one's master.

2

The preference of master over parent embodies a phenomenon common to ideological movements over time, both religious and secular.[12] In a broad sense, this phenomenon is simply an aspect of maturation, as the growing child reaches beyond immediate family for guidance, value, and relationship. Ideological movements cultivate (and manipulate) such development in a radical and totalizing way. Immediate practical implications emerge, as the neophyte's energies and loyalties are diverted to the new calling (note Hassidism and Zionism, for example, in the Jewish sphere); but these practical implications flow directly from the principled re-structuring of

---

[12] Hezser (n. 8 above, pp. 343-346), refers to Peter Brown's discussion of spiritual fatherhood as a "common feature of late antiquity" as background for the Rabbinic disciple's "affiliation and loyalty" to his master.

values and priorities. The ideological home replaces the biological one, as it connects the believer with a higher truth than the physical or natural. Spirit displaces matter. "The new form of grouping is characterized by the concept of relationship or spiritual fatherhood and spiritual brotherhood....it is a definite break with the past and with the ties of nature. Membership in the group may require radical change in social...relationships. Ties of family and kinship...are at least temporarily relaxed or severed" (J. Wach).[13]

Yet, if our analysis of the Rabbinic materials is accurate, they do not fully fit Wach's description. There is no "definite break with the past and the ties of nature," no "radical change in social relationship;" even the idea of "spiritual fatherhood" is nuanced. On balance, then, we do not seem to be dealing with a "new form of grouping." A quick survey of comments interpreting the Christian phenomenon may aid in our quest after the sociological meaning of the Rabbinic one.

As S.C. Barton points out, the demands made of the disciple of Jesus, the "invitation to a new and transcendent allegiance," relativized all other ties. This is heightened all the more by the exceptional charismatic quality of the new leader.[14] Furthermore, the "counter-cultural aspect" of early Christianity dovetails with the "intra-familial hostility" it generated and indeed encouraged as the necessary price of its success: "...children shall rise up against their parents, and put them to death" (Matt. 10:21). Put more prosaically, the individual who converts must, necessarily, be willing to reject and indeed betray his family—subjecting it to severe stress. A more novel statement of this last point is found in John Gager's application of Victor Turner's work to Christian millenarianism. Gager argues—specifically referring to the Gospel materials—that rejection of biological family is part of the rejection of all manifes-

---

[13] J. Wach, *The Sociology of Religion* (Chicago, 1944), pp. 110, 134-135. This should be balanced with the observation of R. Nisbet, *The Quest of Community* (Oxford, 1953), p. 287, n. 3, and others, that "the overwhelming majority of communal or sacred areas of society reflect the transfer...of kinship symbols and nomenclature to non-kinship spheres....Kinship has ever been the archetype of man's communal aspirations." E. Kedourie (*Nationalism*, 3rd ed. [London, 1966], pp. 48-49) notes how this phenomenon functions in " current political rhetoric," citing a contemporary use of the gospel story in Coptic nationalistic oratory!

[14] Note how this phenomenon, ultimately rooted in Micah 7, is evaluated in precisely opposite terms in M. Sot. 9:14, reflecting the Rabbinic affirmation of family stability.

tations of social structure and status, which characterizes, in turn, liminal reality as a whole.[15]

Some of these observations may be useful in understanding the Rabbinic phenomena under scrutiny. It is difficult to deny that the priority assigned the master is an aspect of the overall enhancement of the status of the Rabbinic estate. From the point of view of the rabbis, the commitment to Torah and especially to Oral Torah that was their ideological linchpin required a parallel commitment to Torah's representatives—namely themselves. The sociologist will probably be less interested in the theoretical, justificatory aspect of this re-structuring, than in the social status and power which it generates.

Yet while our major point concerns the significant status now attached to the person of the master, the over-all picture also differs from the Christian one. There is little across-the-board devaluation of family ties, as we have seen, and the rabbis did not exploit the more radical potential of the doctrine of spiritual fatherhood. The family is not devalued, and filial responsibility remains strong. The Rabbinic posture probably has many causes. Certainly, the Rabbinic movement could not claim any figure who demanded the kind of loyalty that Jesus did, a historical fact that of course is no accident. Nor did it build on the charismatic person of any single figure. More significant, Rabbinic Judaism was not counter-cultural, but related positively to its society; it did not rebel against society but attempted to work within its structures, both serving them and deriving support from them. This reality may even be reflected in discussion of our very topic.

Thus, note M. Ker. 6:7: "So, too, in the study of law, if the son gained much wisdom before his teacher, his teacher comes ever before his father, since both he and his father are bound to honor the teacher."

In essence, this parallels the Mishnah-passage with which I opened. There are, of course, interesting differences. The major point for our discussion, though, is the picture of social integration it offers. The priority of the master is not socially disruptive, and it does not come at the price of a break in familial structure or loyalty. Rather,

---

[15] J. Gager, *Kingdom and Community* (Englewood Cliffs, 1975), pp. 32-37. My colleague, Prof. Haviva Pedayah, has applied these categories to the study of the attitude towards family in early Hassidism. See her (Hebrew) paper in M. Ben-Sasson, ed., *Dat VeKalkalah* (Jerusalem, 1995), pp. 345-347.

father and son both accept the fact of the master's priority, a priority that virtually grows now out of the integrated family itself. Naturally, it is possible to read this material differently from a purely normative point of view, but I think its narrative reality cannot be ignored either.

A different, phenomenological way into our problem is offered by Gabriel Jacobovici.[16] Jacobovici points out that Jesus "repudiates his own family in favor of the larger family of God" precisely because Christianity is to become a universal religion. This repudiation of family is of one piece, he asserts, with John the Baptist's saying that "God is able of these stones to raise up children unto Abraham," and Paul's saying that "they are not all Israel which are of Israel...the children of the promise are counted for the seed." And so, "When Jesus says 'no man cometh unto the Father, but by me,' he says something that goes counter to everything in the Hebrew scriptures, as of course he means to do."

For the Jew, though, Jacobowici continues, the commitment to and of God is through the physical Abraham, who is the Jew's biological grand-parent. "God loved Abraham and Isaac and Jacob and so He loves their children." Family, at times extended, is the vehicle through which religious and cultural identity is bestowed and the link to transcendence is forged. There will of course be social implications: "One can always walk out of a community of faith, but one cannot walk out of a family." There will also be, Jacobovici argues, psychological and theological implications. Certainly, Jacobovici does not grapple with the universalistic aspects of Judaism, specifically with the presence of the *ger*, the proselyte, the man or woman who is Abraham's child because Abraham is the spiritual "father of many nations." Nonetheless, Jacobovici captures an essential moment, the moment of "that Passover injunction: 'And it shall come to pass, when your children say unto you, "What mean ye by...."'".

---

[16] G. Josipovici, *The Book of God* (New Haven, 1988), pp. 146-148. From a different methodological perspective, see, too, D. Schwartz, *Studies in the Jewish Background of Christianity* (Tubingen, 1992), pp. 1-26, esp. p. 4. This thematic recurs in studies of different topics; see, e.g., S. Talmon, *The World of Qumran From Within* (Jerusalem, 1988), pp. 242-243. Interestingly, the medieval Jewish polemicist was highly critical of Jesus' attitude towards his family; see S. Krauss, "Un fragment polemique de la gueniza," in *REJ* 61 (1912), pp. 69, 71. For a different understanding of these materials, see D. Lasker and S. Stroumsa, ed., *The Polemic of Nestor the Priest*, I (Jerusalem, 1996), sec. 106 and Commentary (pp. 72, 157).

From this perspective, the refusal to read the parent out is an aspect of Judaic literalism, an insistence on reading the Bible in the non-allegoric mode that preserves its physical meaning, a zeal for halakhah, if you will. For the medieval halakhist, it meant the rejection of a reading that held the patriarchs to be form and the matriarchs to be matter. Earlier (and later) it meant retaining the basic reading of physical, as over against spiritual, parenthood. A more sociological perspective would find it all spun out of the basic allegiance to a people. Yet whichever the cart and whichever the horse, tensions may emerge. Within a system that values study above all, there will be an uneasy truce between master and parent. Symptomatically, Jacobovici says that "the injunction to remember and recount...is in the end much more important than the injunctions to study, learn, and interpret." But this is far from so within the Rabbinic world and the culture it fathered, however accurately it may reflect the Biblical ethos and much of Jewish history.

Thus, sometimes, teacher will in fact be called "father;" and it will be taught that the master—and not the parent—brings you "into the world to come." But, as we have seen, that very assertion is controlled—by the rabbis themselves!—so that it finds concrete expression in a very narrow range of circumstances, however deeply it may resonate ideologically. This contrast between ideological resonance and practical application is also a typical Rabbinic technique, but one that is beyond the scope of this paper.

GENERAL INDEX

Aggadah, intersection with Halakhah, 200–208
Agriculture (Zera'im)
  Bikkurim, 83–86
  central importance of, 41–45
  Demai, 50–53
  Hallah, 77–80
  Kilaim, 53–58
  Maaser Sheni, 73–77
  Maaserot, 69–73
  Orlah, 80–83
  Peah, 45–50
  Shebiit, 58–62
  Terumot, 63–68
  topical origins, 86–87
  topics discussed, 22, 27
  Ushan period's views, 44–45, 48–49, 52, 55–57, 66–68, 71–72, 75–76, 79, 82–83, 84–85, 88–89
  Yavnean period's views, 44, 47–48, 51–52, 54–55, 58–60, 64–68, 69–71, 75, 78, 81–82, 84, 87–88
  see also under offerings; tithes/tithing
Albeck, Chanoch, on M. composition, 169
Amoraim, and M., 192
Antoninus Pius, 162–163
Apocopation, 10, 13, 129
Appointed Times (Mo'ed), topics discussed, 22–23
Aristotelian logic, 103, 110

Baba Batra, 33–34
Bar Kokhba revolt, 7, 41, 88, 105
Barton, S.C., on discipleship, 255n2, 263
Bavli, coverage of M., 94
Bikkurim, 83–86
Books, ancient
  composition process, 173–182
  publication and circulation, 182–187

Christianity, 263, 265
Classification logic, in M., 103–111, 112, 115, 117

Code of Justinian, 149, 153, 161
Courts, Roman, 150–151
Courtyards, status of, 71–72
Creation, perfection of, 138–139

Damages (civil law), topics discussed, 24
Dead Sea Scrolls, 4
Demai, 33, 50–53
Desanctification. *see* sanctification
Didius Iulianus, 156
Discipleship, 255–266
Diverse Kinds, 53–58

Eder, Walter, on legal codification, 189, 190
Edictum perpetuum, 153–155, 158–160
Eduyyot, 9
Eliezer, 66
Epstein, Jacob N., on M. composition, 168–169
Essenes, and purity, 27

Fabrics, in clothing, 56, 57
Familial loyalty, 255–266
Fatherhood, spiritual, 258–262
Fontes iuris Romani antejustiniani, 159
Fruit trees, produce of, 80–83

Gager, John, on familial loyalty, 263–264
Gamaliel, 26
Gentiles, and offerings, 48
Gittin, 34
Gleanings, 48–49
Gospels
  discipleship and family loyalties in, 255–256
  M. in relation to, 134–148

Hadrian, 149–150, 152, 153, 155, 162
Halakhah, intersection with Aggadah, 200–208
Hallah, 77–80
Halvini, David Weiss, on M. redaction, 169
Hanukkah, 204–205
Harlow, Jules, 11226n17
Hebrew Scriptures, indifference to, 4

Holiness
  nature of, 73–74, 76–77, 88–89, 104–105
  and order, 61–62
Holy Things (Qodoshim), topics discussed, 23, 27, 33
Houtman, Alberdina, on M. composition, 170

Indexes, lack of in ancient sources, 174n42
Intentionality
  behavior vs., 88
  classification and, 53–58
  classification of trees, 82–83
  and culpability, 66–68
  offering-requirements and, 63–73
  and Sabbatical Year, 59–61
Israel
  social interrelationships of, 15
  see also Land of Israel
Ius respondendi, 151

Jaffee, Martin, on tithing and intentionality, 70
Jesus, 141, 143–144, 255–256, 264
Jews, status of, 37
Joshua, 66
Judah, 85
Judah ha-Nasi, 168, 169–170, 188–189, 190
Judaism, Rabbinic. see Rabbinic Judaism
Judaism, world-view expressed in M., 21–27

Kalman, Jason, on Scriptural references in M., 240n3
Kelim, 34
Ketubot, 34
Kilaim, 53–58, 59, 61

Land of Israel
  M.'s world-view of, 22–23, 87–88
  Roman ascendancy in, 41
Language, patterns of, 8–21
  grammatical order and balance, 17–20
  memorization as purpose, 13
  tense structure, 16–17
Lapin, Hayim, on composition of M., 171
Leavening, 77–80
Legal codification, 123–124, 189
Lieberman, Saul, on oral ekdosis of M., 131, 172

Logic, 31
Loyalty, 255–266

Maaser Sheni, 73–77
Maaserot, 69–73
Marcus Aurelius, 162–163
Mark, 255–256
Meals, tithing and, 69–73
Midrashim, homiletic
  Amoraic vs. Tannaic sources in, 205–208
  halakhic analysis in, 200–208
  interrelationship of M. and, 213–219
  M. citation practices in, 219–224
  M. quotations recontextualized in, 196–200, 209–212
  M. version cited, 224–230
  pattern of citations in, 195
  textual boundaries in, 198–199, 208–212
Minayin midrash, 241, 242, 243–252
Miqvaot, 34
Mishnah
  accessibility of, 130–131
  audience, 3–4, 191–192
  authorship, 3–6, 6–7, 12, 104, 111, 190–191
  composites in, 125–127
  composition of, 168–181
  cultic matters in, 7
  discipleship and familial loyalty in, 256–266
  divisions, 9, 22–24
  institutional foundations, 123–124
  language patterns of, 8–21, 128–130
  as law code, 121–134, 192
  logical classification in, 103–111
  mnemonic system of, 172–173
  nature and purpose of text, 3–6, 18–19
  oral ekdosis of, 131, 172, 179–181
  origins, 3–6, 124–130, 136–140
  publication of, 182–187
  purpose, 133, 187–192
  redaction of, 168–182
  in relation to Gospels, 134–148
  rhetorical cogency of, 130–131
  Scripture and, 28–35, 118–119, 238–252
  Sifra critiques classification logic of, 103, 111–120

systemic thought and importance, 35–37
topical programs of tractates, 9–10, 127–128, 132–133
world-view of, 21–27, 138–139
Money, second-tithe, 73–77

Nasi, 123–124
Negaim, 33
Neusner, Jacob, on composition of M., 172–173
Neutralization, 82–83
Niddah, 33
Note-taking, ancient practices of, 174–178

Offerings
dough offering, 77–80
heave-offering, 48, 63–68
poor offering, 45–49
separation and payment of, 69–73
see also tithes/tithing
Ohalot, 34
Orality, in tradition, 180–181, 182–184
Orlah, 80–83

Papyrus, 177
Parah, 33
Parenthood, devaluation of biological, 258–262
Peah, 45–50
Pentateuch, 104, 110–111
Perception, and culpability, 55–56, 67, 77–78
Permanence, and language, 16–17
Pesikta Rabbati
citation of M. in, 196n8, 197–199, 204–205, 208–212
history of text, 217
Pharisees, 26–27
Pliny the Elder, 175
Plutarch, 178
Poor offering, 45–49
Praetor's edict. see edictum perpetuum
Priestly caste, 25–26
Produce
first fruits, 83–86
fourth-year, 74
of fruit trees, 80–83
heave-offering, 63–68
mixtures, 81, 82
sale of, 71

Prophecy, 35
Purities (Tohorot), topics discussed, 23–24

Rabbinic Judaism
development of, after Temple, 89–90, 189–190, 192
discipleship and familial loyalty in, 264–266
Pharisees and, 53
Reichman, Ronen, on sources of M., 170
Remission of debts, 58, 59
Roman legal codification
history of, 149–164
and M., 121–134, 189
Rome, war against (132-135), 7, 41, 88, 105

Sabbath, activity on, compared among religious traditions, 143–148
Sabbatical Year, 44–45, 58–62
Sacredness within secular, 20–21
Salvius Iulianus, 150, 152, 153, 155–159
Sanctification, 7, 22, 105
focus on, in M., 43–44
of heave-offering, 63–68, 72
holiness and order, 61–62
of second tithe, 73–77
Sanders, E.P., on Judaism, 140
Sanhedrin, 106–110
Scribal profession, 25–26
Scripture, Hebrew
agricultural references in, 43nn4–5
intersection with M. in midrash, 213–219
minayin midrash, 239–252
relationship with M., 28–35, 118–119, 134–135
Separation of species, 53–58
Septimus Severus, 164
Shabbat, 144–148, 239, 241, 246
Shebiit, 58–62
Sifra
critiques classification logic of M., 103, 111–120
date of composition, 119
material from, in M., 170
structure of, 31, 119–120
Simeon b. Gamaliel, 26
Simeon Bar Kokhba, 6
Small, J.P., on note-taking, 177–178

Tamid, 33
Taxonomy, in M., 103–111, 112, 115, 117

Temple
  destruction as central question of M., 41–42, 104–105, 106
  prohibited, 7
Terumot, 63–68, 72, 73
Text linguistics, 209–210, 218
Theodosian Code, 149, 153, 161
Tithes/tithing
  different from poor offerings, 48–49
  discussed in Scripture, 43nn4–5
  responsibility for, 50–53
  second-tithe, 73–77
  separation and payment of, 69–73
  see also offerings
Tohorot, 33
Torah, M. as part of, 29–35
Tosefta
  arrangement and order of discourse, 94–95
  contrastive presentation to M., 11–12
  discipleship and familial loyalty in, 262
  example of relationship to M., 96–102
  as first Talmud, 93
  material similarities to M., 170–171
  minayin midrash in, 239, 240, 241, 242–243, 250–252
  origin of, 186
  relationship with M., 91–93, 102
  types of material in, 93–94
Tractactes of M., formulary patterns within, 9–11
Tradition, 31–32, 110–111
Transactions, 25
Trans-Jordan, 84
Trustworthiness, 50–53
Twelve Tables, 184–185, 189

Uqsin, 33
Ushan period, views on Agriculture, 44–45, 48–49, 52, 55–57, 66–68, 71–72, 75–76, 79, 82–83, 84–85, 88–89
Utopia, 35

Will, Man's. *see* intentionality
Wills, 161–162
Women (Nashim), topics discussed, 24

"*Yakhol*," 240
Yavnean period, views on Agriculture, 44, 47–48, 51–52, 54–55, 58–60, 64–68, 69–71, 75, 78, 81–82, 84, 87–88
Yerushalmi, coverage of M., 94, 192
Yohanan the High Priest, 74

Zabim, 33

HANDBOOK OF ORIENTAL STUDIES
(HANDBUCH DER ORIENTALISTIK)

Section I: NEAR AND MIDDLE EAST
Abt. I: DER NAHE UND MITTLERE OSTEN

ISSN 0169-9423

Band 32
Muraoka, T. and Porten, B. *A Grammar of Egyptian Aramaic*. 1998. ISBN 90 04 10499 2
Band 33
Gessel, B.H.L. van. *Onomasticon of the Hittite Pantheon*. 1998.
ISBN *Set (2 parts)* 90 04 10809 2
Band 34
Klengel, H. *Geschichte des hethitischen Reiches* 1998. ISBN 90 04 10201 9
Band 35
Hachlili, R. *Ancient Jewish Art and Archaeology in the Diaspora* 1998. ISBN 90 04 10878 5
Band 36
Westendorf, W. *Handbuch der altägyptischen Medizin*. 1999.
ISBN *Set (2 Bände)* 90 04 10319 8
Band 37
Civil, M. *Mesopotamian Lexicography*. 1999. ISBN 90 04 11007 0
Band 38
Siegelová, J. and Souček, V. *Systematische Bibliographie der Hethitologie*. 1999.
ISBN *Set (3 Bände)* 90 04 11205 7
Band 39
Watson, W.G.E. and Wyatt, N. *Handbook of Ugaritic Studies*. 1999.
ISBN 90 04 10988 9
Band 40
Neusner, J. *Judaism in Late Antiquity, III,1*. 1999. ISBN 90 04 11186 7
Band 41
Neusner, J. *Judaism in Late Antiquity, III,2*. 1999. ISBN 90 04 11282 0
Band 42
Drijvers, H.J.W. and Healey, J.F. *The Old Syriac Inscriptions of Edessa and Osrhoene*. 1999.
ISBN 90 04 11284 7
Band 43
Daiber, H. *Bibliography of Philosophical Thought in Islam*. 2 Volumes.
ISBN *Set (2 Volumes)* 90 04 11347 9
Volume I. Alphabetical List of Publications 1999. ISBN 90 04 09648 5
Volume II. Index of Names, Terms and Topics. 1999. ISBN 90 04 11348 7
Band 44
Hunger, H. and Pingree, D. *Astral Sciences in Mesopotamia*. 1999. ISBN 90 04 10127 6
Band 45
Neusner, J. *The Mishnah*. Religious Perspectives 1999. ISBN 90 04 11492 0
Band 46
Neusner, J. *The Mishnah*. Social Perspectives 1999. ISBN 90 04 11491 2
Band 47
Khan, G. *A Grammar of Neo-Aramaic*. 1999. ISBN 90 04 11510 2
Band 48
Takács, G. *Etymological Dictionary of Egyptian*. Vol. 1. 1999. ISBN 90 04 11538 2
Takács, G. *Etymological Dictionary of Egyptian*. Vol. 2. 2001. ISBN 90 04 12121 8
Band 49
Avery-Peck, A.J. and Neusner, J. *Judaism in Late Antiquity IV*. 2000. ISBN 90 04 11262 6
Band 50
Tal, A. *A Dictionary of Samaritan Aramaic*. (2 Volumes) 2000. ISBN 90 04 11858 6 (dl. 1)
ISBN 90 04 11859 4 (dl. 2) ISBN 90 04 11645 1 (set)
Band 51
Holes, C. *Dialect, Culture, and Society in Eastern Arabia*. Vol. 1 : Glossary 2001.
ISBN 90 04 10763 0

Band 52
Jong, R.E. de. *A Grammar of the Bedouin Dialects of the Northern Sinai Littoral.* Bridging the Linguistic Gap between the Eastern and Western Arab World. 2000. ISBN 90 04 11868 3

Band 53
Avery-Peck, A.J. and Neusner, J. *Judaism in Late Antiquity III,3.* Where we stand: Issues and Debates in Ancient Judaism. 2000. ISBN 90 04 11892 6

Band 54
Krahmalkov, Ch. R. *A Phoenician-Punic Grammar.* 2001. ISBN 90 04 11771 7

Band 55
Avery-Peck, A.J. and Neusner, J. *Judaism in Late Antiquity III,4.* Where we stand: Issues and Debates in Ancient Judaism.. *The Special Problem of the Synagogue.* 2001. ISBN 90 04 12000 9.

Band 56
Avery-Peck, A.J., Neusner, J., and Chilton, B. *Judaism in Late Antiquity V,1.* The Judaism of Qumran: A Systemic Reading of the Dead Sea Scrolls. *Theory of Israel.* 2001. ISBN 90 04 12001 7

Band 57
Avery-Peck, A.J., Neusner, J., and Chilton, B. *Judaism in Late Antiquity V,2.* The Judaism of Qumran: A Systemic Reading of the Dead Sea Scrolls. *World View, Comparing Judaisms.* 2001. ISBN 90 04 12003 3

Band 58
Gacek, A. *The Arabic manuscript tradition.* A Glossary of Technical Terms and Bibliography. 2001. ISBN 90 04 12061 0

Band 60
Marzolph, U. *Narrative illustration in Persian lithographed books.* 2001. ISBN 90 04 12100 5

Band 61
Zammit, M.R. *A Comparative Lexical Study of Qur'ānic Arabic.* 2002. ISBN 90 04 11801 2

Band 62
Grossmann, P. *Christliche Architektur in Ägypten.* 2002. ISBN 90 04 12128 5

Band 63
Weipert, R. *Classical Arabic Philology and Poetry.* A Bibliographical Handbook of Important Editions from 1960 to 2000. 2002 ISBN 90 04 12342 3

Band 64
Collins, B.J. *A History of the Animal World in the Ancient Near East.* 2002. ISBN 90 09 12126 9

Band 65
Avery-Peck, A.J. and Neusner, J. *The Mishnah in Contemporary Perspective.* Part I. 2002. ISBN 90 09 12515 9